BURNING RUBBER

CHARLES JENNINGS

BURNING RUBBER

THE EXTRAORDINARY STORY OF FORMULA ONE

Quercus

First published in Great Britain in 2010 by
Quercus
21 Bloomsbury Square
London
WC1A 2NS

A CIP catalogue record for this book is available
from the British Library

ISBN 978 1 84916 092 6

10 9 8 7 6 5 4 3 2 1

Typeset by Ellipsis Books Ltd, Glasgow
Printed and bound in Great Britain by Clays Ltd, St Ives plc

For Susie

CONTENTS

The Age of Men
1894–1958

1 Pre-history   3
2 The New Formula   13
3 Fangio I: The Return of the Germans   21
4 Fangio II: 1956 and the Nightmare of the Prancing Horse   33
5 Fangio III: The Last Win   41

The Age of Brits
1959–76

6 Hawthorn, Moss and the British Revenge   49
7 They Went Back to Front   59
8 1962; Moss, Hill, Brabham: So Very Anglo-Saxon   65
9 Jim Clark, Colin Chapman and Selling Your Soul   79
10 The Tracks   91
11 The Spanish Grand Prix, Jarama, 12 May 1968   99
12 That Little Scotsman: Stewart and the Problem of Death   107
13 Hair, Hotpants and the First Brazilian   121
14 All the World Races Formula One –
   but the Cars Are Made in Surrey. Or Thereabouts   129
15 James Hunt: Last True Brit   131

CONTENTS

The Age of Brains
1977–93

16 Turbos, Side-skirts and Active Suspension:
   Technology Triumphant 149
17 Whatever Happened to the Americans? 161
18 Jones, Piquet and Prost: Two Gorillas and a Professor 171
19 Frank Williams – the Team Boss as Ruthless CEO? 183
20 May, 1982: Gilles Villeneuve, Ferrari, Another End 191
21 The Boredom, Paranoia and Outright Madness
   That Is McLaren, Prost and Senna 205
22 What Strange Names Are These? Part I 221
23 Mansell – You Always Hurt The Ones
   Who Support You Most 227

The Modern Age
1994–2009

24 The End of the Affair: Senna's Death 239
25 The Curse of the Son 247
26 The Global Sport 257
27 Schumacher, Senna and the Art of Taking No Prisoners 259
28 Ecclestone, Mosley and the Rise of the Technocrats 273
29 What Strange Names Are These? Part II 279
30 The Beat Goes On 287
31 And On 295

Appendix I: Grand Prix Championships 303
Appendix II: Top Twenty-six Grand Prix Drivers by Races Won 315

Bibliography 317
Index 321

THE AGE OF MEN
1894-1958

1

PRE-HISTORY

We are back at the dawn of time, the dawn of motor racing: the nineteenth century to be specific. This is an age when motor cars are built like baronial coaches, when drivers dress like arctic explorers, and when racetracks are nothing more than the common highway: loose mixtures of mud, light aggregate, boulders, manure and splintered timber. And whether you are in the vehicle or out of it, fear stalks the land.

Fear, or bewilderment. The motor car at the turn of the last century was so new, so outlandish, that no one much knew what to do with it under normal conditions, let alone in competition. Indeed, the very idea of getting a late-Victorian horseless carriage to last more than 20 miles without a break-down of some sort required a leap of faith of, effectively, religious intensity. We are talking about belt-drive transmission, hot-tube ignition, solid rubber tyres, tiller steering. But the new breed of motorist tried, anyway.

And where there were motor cars, there were motor races. Although Gottlieb Daimler and Karl Benz had first perfected the concept of the petrol-engined automobile in Germany, it was the French who really took it to their hearts. Renault,

Panhard et Levassor and Peugeot all started car production within a few years of the first workable Daimlers and Benzes. And the very first formally organised motoring contest was a French affair: the Paris–Rouen Trial of 1894, offering a prize of 5,000 francs to the driver of whichever vehicle performed best over the 78 miles separating the two cities.

Straightforward in principle, the race was actually won by an enormous De Dion steam tractor, fuelled by a stoker, steered by a driver and drawing its passengers behind it in a separately articulated carriage like a railway train. This was absolutely not what the organisers had in mind. They wanted one of the go-ahead new internal combustion engines to win. So – demonstrating the kind of shameless expediency motor racing's governing bodies were proudly to exercise on many subsequent occasions – they promptly demoted the De Dion and awarded joint first prize to a proper, petrol-engined Peugeot, which had managed an average speed of 11.5 mph, and a Panhard.

Steam cars aside, this set the trend. For the next few years, motor races were all city-to-city, along unmade roads, in conditions of appalling danger and discomfort, generally starting in Paris, and watched by tens of thousands of hysterical spectators – these separated from the hurtling motor cars by nothing more than dust and thin air. They did Paris – Amsterdam; Paris–Berlin; Paris–Vienna. And, by 1903, most of the world was ready for the big one: a sprint from Paris to Madrid, boasting a field of more than 270 cars (and motorcycles) of wildly varying capabilities, several of which could reach 100 mph on the open road, and many of which weighed as much as a gun carriage.

Unsurprisingly, the French Government wanted to ban it. It was too long, they said, too dangerous, and there was no crowd control for the expected *two million* spectators along the route. They were absolutely right. At the end of the first day, two drivers, one riding mechanic and five spectators had been killed, while scores more were seriously injured. The race exacted a heavy toll in shattered limbs and wrecked vehicles. The event was abruptly stopped at Bordeaux, and those cars that could still be moved (only half of the original field) were towed off in shame by teams of horses. It was named 'The Race of Death'. Marcel Renault, brother of the founder of the car company, was one of the fatalities. Clearly, a better way had to be found.

It first appeared in 1907, at Brooklands in Surrey. A rich car nut called Hugh Locke King built the world's first dedicated racetrack, bankrupting himself in the process, but nonetheless establishing the concept of an enclosed, off-road circuit, where paying punters could enjoy an afternoon's sport in reasonable comfort and safety. The fact that Brooklands – a kind of Home Counties Indianapolis, monstrously simple, with banked turns linked by a couple of head-down straights – would become outclassed and outdated almost as soon as it opened was neither here nor there. The real Indianapolis Speedway came soon after, in 1909, and was a huge hit. Le Mans – public roads, closed off for the duration of the race – was next to establish itself, followed, in the 1920s, by Monza, the Nürburgring and Monaco. The landscape was evolving.

As were the cars. Before anyone knew it, proper, modern, (racing) cars were starting to appear. If the Great War achieved anything at all, it was to speed up the development of light, efficient, power units – all those aero engines which came into being and which would go on to influence automotive engine design in peace time. And the sports cars of the 1920s and 1930s testified to this: Bugattis, Alfa Romeos, Sunbeams, Fiats, and, later on, the authentically terrifying Mercedes and

Auto Unions, all used the grammar and vocabulary by which we now understand the idea of the motor car. Unlike the pre-First World War horseless carriages, these machines were light, compact, low, and had a wheel at each corner. Their engines used clever, modern alloys and higher compression ratios. Camshafts multiplied, and lubrication systems got more efficient. Even their brakes worked, sometimes.

In fact, it was round about now that it started to become axiomatic that the only real competition cars were to be found in Continental Europe. Bentleys were all well and good for the Le Mans 24-hour Grand Prix d'Endurance, where their massive indestructability garnered them five wins. But for anything shorter, quicker and more sinuous than Le Mans, you really needed a machine from France or Italy, with their engineering strength-in-depth and their twisty, challenging racetracks on which to learn real lessons about performance motor cars. When the first Championship series was organised (for constructors, only) in 1925, it consisted of four races (one at Indianopolis) and was won by Alfa Romeo. The next two years, it was Bugatti which took the honours. Henry Segrave bucked the trend by becoming the first Brit to win a Grand Prix in a British car in 1923, in a Sunbeam which was really a copy of a racing Fiat. Depressingly enough, this remained the only Grand Prix win by a British driver in a British car until well after the Second World War.

But what was a Grand Prix, anyway? The first motoring event to carry the name *Grand Prix* was almost certainly the Grand Prix de Pau, dating back to 1901. The French, then enjoying their near-monopoly of public motor racing, gave the world the term, and it stuck. For some years after that, there was only one Grand Prix, and that was the Le Mans Grand Prix d'Endurance; but in time, Grands Prix spread across the Atlantic (to Savannah, Ga.) and over the Alps, to Italy. After which, they cropped up everywhere and anywhere. The biggest and most demanding races in the calendar also acquired the title *Grandes Épreuves* – the greatest tests of man and machine that human ingenuity could devise. And who co-ordinated all this activity? Initially, it was the Association Internationale des Automobile Clubs Reconnus, or AIACR, whose sporting committee regulated motor racing at Grand Prix (and other) levels, as well as imposing strict regulations concerning weight and engine size, in a responsible, Gallic, effort to bring order to this new world of competition.

The problem was that, without the active consent of the car manufacturers, there was no order. Sports car makers came and went, lost interest in competition, ran out of cash, suddenly emerged with something new, but proscribed. Race organisers couldn't get a decent field together if they stuck to the rulebook. So, in 1928 a new, semi-spontaneous *Formule Libre* effectively threw out any restrictions or regulations concerning the cars, and, for a few years, a free-for-all reigned. Bugatti Type 35s thrashed hectically away with Alfa Romeo 8Cs, Talbots, Maserati Tipo 26s, $1^1/_2$-litre Delages, 8-litre Mercedes SSKs, in the blood and dust of Italy, Germany and France – to say nothing of such holiday destinations as Algeria, Libya and Tunisia, before the FIA – the Federation Internationale de l'Automobile, as the AIACR was now known – got a grip. After all, if the sport was to be taken at all seriously, it had at least to *look* like a sport: with rules, regulations and a sense of like being pitted against like. So a new Formula came in, in 1934, limiting the weight of the car (minus driver, tyres and fuel) to 750 kg but with no limit on engine capacity.

On paper, this made perfect sense. It would maintain some

consistency; it would tame outright speeds; it would guar-
antee closer racing and more impressive fields. And, like so
many bright ideas from the FIA, it was immediately used for
an end quite different from that imagined by its originators.

The now-Nazi-sponsored Auto Union and Mercedes
concerns had seen it all coming. By the mid-1930s, they were
splitting an annual Government grant of around half a million
Reichmarks between them, and were about to spend millions
more on making some of the most devastating weapons of
competition ever seen. And if this has a properly modern,
phosphorescent glow about it, well, it should. The Germans
took a Formula which was meant to keep speeds down and
ensure a level playing field and instead worked around it to
make cars so light, powerful and technologically mind-
blowing that it would be another thirty years before anything
so potent was seen again.

So, while the splendid mid-1930s Alfa Romeo P3 could
turn out around 250 bhp and reach over 140 mph, Mercedes'
cars – at the height of the madness – were running on an
appalling mixture of methyl alcohol and nitro-benzol, turned
out nearly 600 bhp, and could reach *200 mph*. They were
also using ultralight alloys for the bodywork and were physically as full of holes as a string vest, in order to come in
under the magic 750 kg weight limit: 'adding lightness', as
the technicians put it, reaching for their drill bits and taking
another chunk out of the rear suspension links. In 1937,
Hermann Lang won a non-Championship race at the Avus
racetrack, near Berlin, at an *average* speed of over 160 mph,
clinging like one of the damned to the wheel of a Mercedes
W125.

What kind of supermen – other than Lang – drove these
things? There was the great Rudolf Carraciola (one leg shorter

than the other as the result of an accident; his wife killed by an avalanche, for God's sake, while he was convalescing); the nerveless and doomed Bernd Rosemeyer, one of a handful of people who could control the rear-engined Auto Unions; the hedonistic Achille Varzi; Jean-Pierre Wimille, who later joined the French Resistance; and Tazio Nuvolari.

And it's the name *Nuvolari* which still stops the traffic. Anyone racing in the 1930s was, by definition, both fearless and harder than steel. Quite apart from the German team drivers, there were many others – Giuseppe Campari, Louis Chiron, Philippe Étancelin, to name but three – who were heroes, without question, in their Alfas, Maseratis and Bugattis. But the slightly built Nuvolari was not only brave, successful, terribly fast, and instantly recognisable, with his odd, lean, goblinish appearance, as if he just been cured in a tannery: he was indomitable – epically so.

Enzo Ferrari knew Nuvolari well, and spent some time riding round a succession of corners with him in the 1930s. He noticed with a mixture of horror and deep admiration that, whenever a bend presented itself, 'Tazio did not lift his foot from the accelerator,' and that, in fact, he kept it 'flat on the floor.' The point being that Nuvolari was physically incapable of slowing down; and regarded corners merely as opportunities to explore new horizons in tyre adhesion, or to run empirical tests on the physics of his car's suspension.

Compounding this was the fact that pain was meaningless to him. He drove in one Grand Prix with his leg in plaster. He drove in another with several broken ribs. As time went by, he coughed so hard in the cockpit (his lungs racked by years of exhaust fumes and terrible weather) that he spat blood. Nothing ever stopped him, except the physical disintegration of the car. Ferdinand Porsche called him 'the greatest driver of the past, the present, and the future'. He was known as the Flying Mantuan, and his racing mascot was a tortoise.

And, in July 1935, he beat both Mercedes and Auto Union at the Nürburgring, driving a by now hopelessly outdated Scuderia Ferrari Alfa Romeo P3 *and* following a botched pit stop. Giving away around 70 bhp to the German cars and performing in front of a predictably nationalistic crowd of 300,000, he nonetheless started from the front row of the grid, forced his way between Rosemeyer (Auto Union) and Carraciola (Mercedes) at around the halfway mark, and then came in for fuel, anticipating a useful scrap in the second part of the race. At this point, the fuel delivery pump in the Alfa pits broke down. Instead of the fuel coming out fast, under pressure, it had to be decanted by hand, from churns, the mechanics straining and cursing. It took over two minutes.

By the time Nuvolari came out again, he was down in sixth place, with the Germans long gone. So the red mist came down. He did the first ever lap round the 'Ring in under eleven minutes. Then he started to close in on the new leader, Manfred von Brauchitsch – driving a Mercedes – chewing twenty seconds a lap out of his lead. It was a drive bordering on the maniacal; but Mercedes were pointedly relaxed about the whole thing. After all, at the start of the last lap, von Brauchitsch was well over half a minute ahead, with enough fuel to get him round and no suggestion of mechanical problems with his W25. But Nuvolari wasn't just driving out of his skin: he was using low cunning, too, having made sure to put harder-wearing tyres on the Alfa than von Brauchitsch had put on his Mercedes, thus providing himself with an essential margin of destructibility as he thrashed the Alfa round the track.

Von Brauchitsch was now able to see the Alfa in the

distance, absurd but unshakeable, like something out of a cartoon, but he kept his foot down, hanging on for the final minutes of the race. Yes, he was known with derisive indulgence as *die Pechvogel – the Unlucky Bird* – thanks to his capacity for losing races that he ought to have won, but this one was as near as dammit in the bag, it was his for the taking. Then he watched in horror as his rear tyres, shredded by hard racing, German engine power, a softer compound, and Nuvolari's remorseless pressure, simply fell to pieces, leaving him in tears, rolling along on his wheel rims at 40 mph and letting Nuvolari through to what has been called *The Greatest Victory Of All Time.*

The crowd were baffled and astonished. 'At first there was deathly silence,' according to *MotorSport*, 'and then the innate sportsmanship [*sic*] of the Germans triumphed over their astonishment. Nuvolari was given a wonderful reception.' Adolf Hitler was in the crowd, however, and Korpsführer Adolf Hunnlein, representing the Third Reich, tore up his speech and refused to have anything to do with Nuvolari's victory appearance on the rostrum. Someone dug out a shabby old Italian flag and hung it up. There was no Italian national anthem to play, until Nuvolari pointed out that he always carried with him a gramophone record of the 'Marcia Reale' and that they were welcome to put it on. Which they did.

Afterwards, of course, the Auto Unions and Mercedes reasserted themselves. In the years leading up to the Second World War, the Germans ruthlessly swapped titles – Auto Union taking the Championship in '36, Mercedes in '37 and '38 – not only fixing new standards of team efficiency, engineering thoroughness and collective will to win, but also putting on a display at the British GP at Donington Park in 1937 that appalled and mesmerised everyone who saw it.

It was the first time the Germans had been seen in England.

Racing against a field of diminutive ERAs (English Racing Automobiles) and a few forlorn Maseratis, the Mercedes and Auto Union teams tore the place apart – not least when they fired up their engines, like fighter pilots, only seconds before the start, and revealed to the great British public that the Mercedes supercharged straight-8s *alone* were louder than the rest of the field put together. It was a declaration of naked intent. And while Nuvolari's magisterial Nürburgring drive of 1935 was a piece of pure, timeless, sporting theatre, the Mercedes and Auto Union teams of the late 1930s were something else. They were the shape of things to come.

2

THE NEW FORMULA

How soon after a global cataclysm such as the Second World War is it acceptable to start motor racing again? Less than a year, turns out to be the answer. There was indeed a season in 1946, won by Raymond Sommer in a Maserati, with pre-war figures such as Ascari, Chiron, Wimille all seeing some quite lively action, driving an assortment of scrounged and reconstituted pre-war machines – Alfas and Maseratis, mostly. The Germans, quite apart from being financially devastated, were banned on account of their Nazi past. The British were still digging themselves out of the rubble, although a few ERAs flew the flag. The French drove some Talbots and the odd Delage.

Inevitably things were makeshift, but some fun was had, nevertheless, over the next few years. Monaco and Reims got a fair bit of use; Jean-Pierre Wimille thrashed a field of thirty entrants at Spa-Francorchamps in 1947; 'Toulo' de Graffenried (a Swiss national) won the British Grand Prix at Silverstone in 1949, later making a turn as a stunt double for Kirk Douglas; there were rationing and endless shortages of material and parts; there was an element of survivors' guilt, just as there had been in the 1920s.

And then the modern world arrived at the beginning of 1950. It was in that year that the FIA properly reconstituted Grand Prix motor racing, putting the world's differences to one side by means of wholesome competitive track competition. Why was the 1950 season heralded as a new dawn? Because it was the moment when the new Formula One came into being – the great-granddaddy of today's Formula, the structure supporting and controlling motor racing at the highest level. And in 1950 the rules boiled down, essentially, to this: a car could have a normally aspirated engine of up to 4,500 cc; or a supercharged one of 1,500 cc; and there was no weight limit. At the same time, Formula Two emerged – a cheaper, aspirational Formula, for 2,000-cc unsupercharged and 500-cc supercharged cars. There was order, and there were rules.

There was also a fairly skimpy calendar of six European Grands Prix – British, Monaco, Swiss, Belgian, French and Italian – contested by a mish-mash of thirteen teams with around thirty drivers willing to take part, the whole thing bulked out by another sixteen entirely optional non-Championship races to keep everyone's hand in. These oddball events (the British Empire Trophy; the Grand Prix de Paris; the Gran Premio de Penya Rhin) happened at places like Albi, Goodwood, Pescara, Bari, and even Jersey, an island barely large enough to have motor traffic of any sort. Not that they were all to be sneered at. Some (especially those sponsored by a newspaper) offered good prize money; many of them drew the top drivers, however out-of-the-way they might have been. There were sixteen non-Championship events in 1950; over thirty by 1952.

The usual suspects turned up, whether Championship contenders or not. There were Alfa Romeo (who would have taken the 1950 Constructors' Championship had there been one), along with Maserati, the new-look Ferrari team, plus, inevitably, a few limping Talbots and a couple of wonky ERAs. Nino Farina (who took the 1950 Drivers' Championship), plus rising stars Juan Manuel Fangio and Alberto Ascari, were the headline acts, assisted by stalwart triers such as Maurice Trintignant and Reg Parnell. Everything went about as well as it could, given the fact that much of Europe still lay in ruins, and that the Nuremberg Trials had only just finished.

The only real oddity came, perhaps unsurprisingly, from the British – in the form of British Racing Motors (BRM), whose arrival on the scene now appears so bizarre as to be almost dream-like in its strangeness. Other British-based constructors – McLaren, Williams, Lotus – would, years later, get into the habit of picking off titles like ripe cherries. But BRM, the first of the true Brit constructors, went about things the hard way, almost as an article of faith. For them, it was all about pain and humiliation.

The team was actually started by pre-war racer Raymond Mays, who, in the 1930s, had headed the ERA racing *équipe* and had even competed in the 1935 German Grand Prix, along with Tazio Nuvolari. Mays was keen on teams with three-letter names – and, allegedly, women's clothing. It was said that he often raced in a spot of eye-liner, while relaxing at home in something fetching in polka dots. The motoring press habitually referred to him as 'immaculately dressed' and 'elegant'. His mother was a formidable presence around the place, once seen disinfecting a saloon car with *FLIT* after Peter Berthon's wife had just got out of it – Berthon being Mays' long-term business partner and, possibly, more than that. According to one authority, 'Some did suspect that he was conducting an affair with Mays himself,' a situation which led to much barely stifled hilarity among the team mechanics.

Lifestyle orientation notwithstanding, Mays was seething at the routine domination of Grand Prix racing by foreign teams. ERA had done its best with the modest resources at hand, but the fact remained that it was the Italians and Germans who had enjoyed two generations of near-supremacy at the highest level of competition. Now it was time to put an end to those terrible decades of British underachievement. BRM was formed in 1945 and quickly became a national prestige project, attracting the involvement of 100 engineering companies, as well as an eleven-man main committee, a production committee, a finance committee and a publicity committee. Rolls-Royce were commissioned to design a new kind of two-stage supercharger for a fabulous engine to be built under the new Formula: a 1,500-cc supercharged V16 of staggering complexity, whose pistons were the size of eggcups, which (in theory) revved up to 12,000 rpm and which (in theory) produced 600 bhp – just like the monstrous pre-war Mercedes W125, but with one-third the engine capacity.

Well, the rival Ferrari 125 and the Maserati 4CLT both had similarly exquisite supercharged V12s, and both had achieved some racing success, so the BRM scheme was perhaps not as deranged as it might at first seem. It merely required the single-minded addition of a third as many cylinders *again* as the Italians had managed, into an engine of the same capacity. In everyone's imagination it would then be equivalent to putting a Canberra bomber in a field full of old Lancasters, especially once the thing was let out onto the track and pitted against the Ferraris, Masers and, best of all, thunderous old Alfa Romeo 158s (which had been around, in one form or another, since 1938). Even Alfred Neubauer, the feared pre-war Mercedes team leader, came to the factory and called the car 'one of the finest designs I have ever seen'.

It was actually being built in a big shed round the back of Raymond Mays' home in Lincolnshire, previously a billet for the Parachute Regiment and so cold in winter that the draughtsmen had to wear special aviators' gloves to keep their fingers moving.

Things came together incredibly slowly. Simply making the components within the required tolerances was bad enough: 'It nearly drove us all mad with frustration,' said Mays. Then, when the car was driven on the track, it shredded its tyres on account of the power churning out of the V16; it badly burned its drivers, thanks to a misplaced exhaust; it sprayed them with hot oil; it broke down.

Worse: it had been five years in the making, and now the British public wanted to see the damn thing perform. The 1950 British Grand Prix, the very start of the new Formula One, the first great race of the post-war era, was the launchpad. It took place at Silverstone, an old bomber airfield tarted up with some stands and a few prefab pits. The big names – Fangio, Louis Chiron, Farina, Philippe Étancelin – were all there. George VI and Queen Elizabeth turned up. The BRM was nursed out of its transporter. What happened? The car was so far from being ready that the mechanics 'couldn't even get it to run on all cylinders'. Tens of thousands of spectators saw the BRM totter onto the track, give a brief demonstration run with Mays at the wheel and go home. Amazingly, they cheered and applauded, leaving Farina to win the actual race in an Alfa. That was in May.

By August, the Daily Express International Trophy loomed, and the car now had to do something that at least resembled racing, not merely because the *Daily Express* had produced an hysterical sixty-two-page booklet about what it thrillingly called 'the £150,000 car'. The International Trophy didn't count towards either the Drivers' or Constructors' championships; but it was a proper race, well attended and offering better prize money than the British Grand Prix. Two BRMs were entered, but only one made it onto the grid – and at the back, having missed practice due to technical problems. Raymond Sommer, the well-worn French ace who had been hired for the event, sat in the lime-green car, watched the flag fall, dropped the clutch. The BRM skipped forward five inches, like a fat man being jabbed with a stick, and stopped. The driveshafts had broken.

This time, boos and jeers broke out. People tossed pennies into the cockpit. 'Blooming Rotten Motor', said the *News Chronicle*, simultaneously capitalising both on the *Express*'s over-investment in the project and the British love of self-flagellation. A week later, Nino Farina won the World Championship for Alfa Romeo. The old order carried on, as before.

'None of us has lost faith in the car in any way,' wrote Mays, not long after. Destiny had different ideas. Two BRMs struggled through the British GP of 1951. One actually scored a couple of points. Then the FIA changed the rules of the new Formula (not least because Alfa Romeo had dropped out of competition), deciding that the fans would see larger fields (fields of any size, indeed) if the races were run according to Formula Two rules – that is, with cars powered by unsupercharged 2-litre engines. A world entirely filled with cars running to F2 specifications in both the F1 and F2 Championships came into being; while the BRM became ineligible, overnight. And, in 1952, poor Raymond Mays, deliciously turned out as ever, found that Sir Alfred Owen, his principal backer, had finally lost patience with him and taken control of the organisation. The fact that Maserati were similarly stuffed by this rule change (Ferrari, as it turned out, had that season, and the next, almost to themselves) made no difference to the hapless Mays' fate. And no one in their right mind would have predicted that the Brits, fifteen years later, would have become *the* pre-eminent car designers and builders.

It was a terrible, spectacular dream, and, dream-like, the single most lasting thing about the V16 BRM is its most ephemeral characteristic – its sound: a furiously resonant, bowel-loosening howl, a noise so frightful in 1950 that it physically intimidated other drivers, and which has been lovingly preserved in archive recordings by GP fans ever since.

3

FANGIO I:
THE RETURN OF THE GERMANS

When Alfred Neubauer called in on Raymond Mays, back at the start of the 1950s, the new-look, rebuilt Mercedes team was still a dull rumour, a nervous anticipation of the pre-war years. Mays was flattered by the association, but not necessarily scared by it.

By 1954, however, BRM were still nowhere, whereas everyone knew what Mercedes were capable of: which was just about anything. In the space of a few years they had got to the point where they had exceptional Grand Prix cars; they had some of the best drivers – if not *the* best – in the world; they had money behind them (although not limitless – Mercedes were still getting back on their feet, after the war); they had organisation; and they had a team manager whose name, even today, inspires a kind of nervous awe. They were properly contemporary: and Neubauer was their man.

He had made his reputation in the 1930s, corralling the likes of Von Brauchitsch, Carraciola, Fagioli, making sure that everything was just the way they wanted. He yelled ('a bull-like bellow', apparently) at people who got in the way, muscled his outsized form around the track and the pits or sometimes just stood there, immobile and huge in a tent-like raincoat, a collection of stopwatches slung round his neck. To the outside world, he was a predictable German bully; to the drivers, he was 'like a mother hen with her chicks', even taking it upon himself to stand out on the grid at zero hour and reassuringly perform his own version of the official starting signal 'by counting down the last seconds – 5-4-3-2-1-OFF – on the fingers and thumb of his right hand'.

Control, order and organisation were everything. And yet he was relatively sparing in his use of team orders. If a driver had got a job with the Mercedes team, then he was, axiomatically, good enough to race, and should be left to make his own decisions. Once a Mercedes driver – whichever driver – had secured a sufficient (i.e. one-minute) lead, his teammates were not to challenge him unless instructed specifically to do so. The exception was when there was a special title at stake, and more complex orders might apply. Then there would be much use of Neubauer's famous red and black flag, held sternly at differing heights to tell a driver to slow down/speed up/stay put.

The rest of his time was spent drawing up hugely complex season schedules (Mercedes were racing sports cars as well as Formula One) and eating a tremendous amount of food (breakfast alone being a strenuous mix of rye bread, Bologna sausage, tea and Jamaica rum). He had a genius for the job, and when Mercedes returned to racing, he was effectively unchanged from twenty years earlier, except for several additional centimetres around his vast waistline.

The post-war cars? The W196s were, naturally, powerful ($2^1/_2$-litre straight-8s, fuel-injected, plus fancy valve gear), reliable, beautifully made and very low. They looked intensely modern then; still look it now. The team proceeded to add extra ferocity by filling these cars up with an explosive charge of benzol, methyl alcohol, high-octane petrol, acetone and nitro-benzine – a fuel so disgusting that anyone who breathed the fumes for long enough got double vision, nausea and a blinding headache.

They also ran a mobile workshop from track to track – a Mercedes-Benz lorry, kitted out with welding gear, precision drills, grinding equipment. They built a special high-speed car transporter, which could whisk a GP car across Europe at speeds of over 100 mph. They had, eventually, over 270 people directly involved with the racing team, obeying the orders of Alfred Neubauer and engineering director Rudi Uhlenhaut. And as principal driver, they employed the Argentian Juan Manuel Fangio, who was about to take two World Championships, back to back, and who thought he was in Heaven.

Through the long lens of history, it now all seems like a foregone conclusion: Fangio + Mercedes + Alfred Neubauer = Grand Prix supremacy. But how, actually, had Fangio got to this point? And how did he become the unquestionably dominant Grand Prix driver of the 1950s – and, in the end, one of the very greatest drivers of all time?

On the face of it, he didn't look like much. Described at the time as 'an extremely quiet chap, short, thickset, extremely powerful, balding, beefy', he also spoke 'with a surprisingly high, small voice'. His nickname was *El Chueco* – 'The Knock-kneed One'. He was forty years old in 1951, which, even by the standards of the day (Farina and Chiron were older) was getting on a bit. He had learned his trade before the war, driving a succession of terrifying, stripped-out Chevvy two-doors in immensely long and gruelling South American road races – rallies, effectively, on unmade tracks and mountain passes. Stirling Moss claimed that you had to be 'mad' even to get into one of Fangio's home-built specials, one of these 100 mph dustbins, let alone drive it. But he did, was Argentine National Champion in '40 and '41, and got national funding to take him across to Europe in 1949.

He duly made his mark, winning five non-Grandes Épreuves in fine style. But when the Alfa Romeo team offered him a contract for 1950, Fangio, the reticent backwoodsman, was at a loss. 'The trouble is,' they said, 'we don't know how much money you want.' Neither did Fangio. He signed the contract, left the payment section blank, handed it back to Alfa and said, 'Fill it in however you like. You put in the noughts.'

He loved the team, and the team loved him. At first, he had to play second fiddle to Nino Farina, both driving fairly mature, but extremely competitive, supercharged Alfetta 158s. Farina – exponent of the stylish straight-arm driving style, lounging back in the cockpit, rather than sitting conventionally hunched and straining over the wheel as if trying to snap it off the steering column – won three Championship races. Fangio won another three; but Farina took the title in 1950, much to Fangio's irritation.

The next year, though, he asserted himself and became champion for the first time. Farina's best driving years had been squandered during the Second World War, and the field was open to Fangio, all of five years younger. He won the Swiss, French and Spanish Grands Prix, finishing each one nearly a minute ahead of the second-placed driver. Tony Rudd, of the BRM team, reckoned that Alfa Romeo in the early 1950s, were 'quite Teutonic, actually, no Italian excitement – they were calm and efficient', which suited the Argentinian down to the ground. More so, in fact, than BRM and their crazed device: when he tried out the V16 in some non-Championship races, all he did was complain about the impossibility of controlling its power ('You had to keep it over 7,000 rpm all the time, and like a lot of gear-changing') and the autodestructiveness which resulted ('You could strip the tyres in the course of a single lap').

The problem was that in '52 Alfa dropped out of Grand Prix racing. Fangio, driveless, twiddled his thumbs for half the season, then made his big mistake. At the start of September, Maserati unexpectedly agreed to loan him a car for the Italian GP at Monza. Desperate to race in a proper Grande Épreuve (he was, after all, in danger of finishing the season having scored *no points at all*), Fangio found himself having to travel from London to Italy across a fog-bound Europe, in twenty-four hours, in order to get to the track. Having made it as far as Clermont-Ferrand in the middle of France (and in the middle of the night), he got up before 7 a.m. on the day of the race, frenziedly drove a borrowed saloon car all the way across the Alps and northern Italy and finally arrived at Monza at 2 p.m. This gave him just time to shower, change into his racing clothes (yellow top, old blue trousers, no fancy overalls for him) and be racing by 2.30.

By 3 p.m., he was in intensive care, having wrecked the car – the result of exhaustion, traversing Europe in a day – and having very nearly killed himself. He suffered multiple injuries, not least of which was a broken neck. The only good news, so far as he was concerned, was that, from the start of 1952 on, drivers had to wear hard crash helmets as opposed to the old-fashioned linen (or silk) hair protectors of pre-war times. 'Before it became compulsory,' Fangio noted, drily, 'we used to say that people only wore helmets because they were scared.' It was the crash helmet which stopped his head being opened up like a hard-boiled egg.

The rest of the season went by with Fangio sitting about with a cast round his neck, wondering who his real friends were. From then on, he could only turn from one side or the other by moving his entire torso, like a ventriloquist's dummy. The crippling headaches which used to beset him had mysteriously gone; but everything else was looking bad. Ageing, squeaky, crocked-up, and managing only second-best in 1953 with Maserati – a single GP win, back at Monza – the Old Man looked to be in fairly terminal shape. But then he snatched his second World Championship in 1954 – and everything started off again.

It was a champion's ruthlessness at work. Fangio started '54 in a Maserati; but the moment Neubauer offered him a drive with Mercedes, he took it. However lovely the 1954 Maserati 250Fs were, they were awfully new, and not entirely dependable. Fangio's first allegiance was unquestionably to himself, and the prospect of a weapons-grade Mercedes W196 was too good to pass up.

It wasn't just the car that was good. Fangio was still a truly great driver: adaptable, intelligent, very precise, capable of incredible turns of speed. Stirling Moss, his team-mate at Mercedes, liked to say that 'The best classroom of all time . . . was the spot about two car-lengths behind Juan Manuel Fangio. I learned more there than anywhere else.' Peter Collins, a rising star in the second half of the 1950s, similarly claimed that Fangio could 'size up a circuit and its hazards with almost slide-rule accuracy'.

He was also deeply and meaningfully unsentimental, driving for four teams (Alfa, Maserati, Mercedes and Ferrari) in the space of eight years. He used his authority on and off the track (old enough to be father to some of the other drivers, and he knew it) to get what he wanted. Poor young

Collins got stuffed by Fangio's autocratic needs in 1956, at Monaco, when he was ordered to hand over his Ferrari to the Maestro, who had broken his own car; and then committed self-immolation in the same year by *volunteering* his car at Monza, thus depriving himself of a win and a possible Championship, ceding the title to Fangio. 'I was astounded when he handed over his car,' Fangio later said, disingenuously, 'but I did not stop to argue.' He even temporarily thieved Moss's then-girlfriend, Sally Weston, at some point in 1955, eliciting only the mildest response from the super-competitive Moss: 'Rather him, I suppose, than anyone else.'

How much of his success was down to this kind of sheer exertion of willpower over nicer people, such as Collins or Stirling Moss (Enzo Ferrari, a comparably sized ego in sunglasses, couldn't stand Fangio and 'that inscrutable expression marked by the shadow of an indefinable squinting smile')? How much of it was down to the fact that – in the days when Grands Prix routinely lasted the best part of three hours – Fangio, battle-hardened by 1,000-km slogs across the Pampas, twenty years earlier, could simply keep his stamina and concentration longer than anyone else? (Froilán Gonzales, another hard-nut 1950s Argentinian – *The Pampas Bull* to his fans, *Fat Head* to his colleagues – was huge and similarly tough, but nowhere near as consistently quick.) How much was down to Fangio's legendary 'Little Pills' – which wicked tongues claimed were full of cocaine, while the more respectful reckoned were made from that native Argentinian booster, Yerba Maté? How much of it was simply down to the fact that he didn't spread himself around in rallying and sports car racing as much as some drivers, but kept his main energies for single-seaters, which he knew he was best at driving?

Fangio helped the enigma along by being almost exces-

sively polite, affable, reserved. His reminiscences are passionately anodyne. Of his first GP win, for example, at Barcelona
in 1950: 'When I left the pits I was still in the lead, and
won.' After one successful season, 'Once back in my garage,
with my hands covered in grease and oil, I felt relieved . . .
I had risked letting the glory go to my head, but I was still
really myself.' Even being kidnapped by Cuban rebels in 1958
– by Castro's July 26th Movement, in fact – was a bit of a
thrill, but not too much. He spent a well-mannered two days
with his captors, was released, then went on to appear on
US television, the best bit of which was the fee generated by
his new, additional, celebrity: 'They were going to pay me a
thousand dollars for a ten-minute appearance on *The Ed
Sullivan Show* – along with Jack Dempsey.'

His private life was, on the surface, just as undemonstra-
tive, side-affairs notwithstanding. He may have had a fling
with Evita Perón (yes), but for twenty fairly monogamous
years he lived with 'Beba' Espinosa, a buxom, raven-tressed
divorcee (her ex had been a potato farmer), with whom he
had an illegitimate son. 'In my life,' he said, 'I had beside
me a very strong woman.' But when things got awkward, he
walked away from her just as he walked away from Alfa
Romeo and Ferrari: 'She said if I didn't like being with her
I could leave. So I left.' There you go. The only things which
wholly engaged his passions were being in a racing car and
winning. And it was the mid-1950s, the Mercedes years, that
represented an ideal state for him. He won six of the nine
Championship races of 1954 (four for the German team),
then took four out of the seven races for 1955.

Moss likewise reckoned that Mercedes were about as good
as a team could possibly get. Indeed, he never quite recovered from an early dream-like encounter with a Mercedes
mechanic who came up to him where he had just stopped

his car in the infield of a test track, in the middle of nowhere, and held out a bowl of hot water, a bar of soap and a small towel, just so that Moss could wash away the grime and brake dust. The mechanic even politely clicked his heels at the same time. Similarly, when he expressed a preference for a three-spoke steering wheel instead of the standard four-spoke, the next day, soundlessly and as if by magic, a three-spoke wheel had been fitted to his car.

This was also the period when Moss dedicated himself to haring round in Fangio's wheeltracks, getting a free education from the Old Man. One observer commented, 'So closely did he track Fangio that from some angles, the Stuttgart team appeared to have entered an eight-wheeler.' Otherwise known as 'The Train', this nose-to-tail Mercedes combo caused Neubauer endless heartburn. Quite apart from the fact that Moss collected stones and bits of track flung up by Fangio's rear wheels, what if Fangio made a mistake and took them both off the track? 'Juan Manuel simply did not make mistakes,' was Moss's answer. And again: 'No one who ever sat in a racing car made fewer mistakes than Fangio.'

Quite often, Fangio and Moss were the only two drivers on the same lap, yoked together by the brilliance of their driving and the supercompetence of their cars, while Gonzales and Hawthorn in the Ferrari Tipo 625s ploughed on, some-where else on the track, getting lucky once in a while. Oh, and Maserati and Connaught (another early green shoot in the British flowering) similarly cobbled together some wins in the non-Championship races.

Otherwise, the world simply bowed before the might of the Germans, and the genius of Fangio. At the German GP in '54, he finished a minute and a half ahead of the joint second-place drivers – Gonzales and Hawthorn, indeed, who had taken over Gonzales' car halfway through the race. At

Monza, the same year, he was a whole lap ahead of Hawthorn by the end. At the Argentine GP, 1955, Fangio was again a minute and a half ahead of the second placer, Gonzales. At the British GP, that year, Mercedes managed a 1-2-3-4, coming in *three laps* ahead of Hawthorn, in fifth.

How long would it have gone on like this? It was claimed that in 1954, no fewer than 4,000 applicants wrote in to Mercedes, asking for a place in the team. The *équipe* was glazed with the impossible sheen of victory: everyone wanted to be part of it. And as long as the parent company wanted to bankroll Neubauer and Uhlenhaut, it seemed that they could have gone on indefinitely.

Except for Le Mans, June 1955.

Mercedes was, of course, a two-headed monster at this time, with interests in both Grand Prix and Sport Car racing. Its sports cars had already won at Le Mans (in 1952), at the Nürburgring, the Mille Miglia, the Carrera Panamericana, the Targa Florio, and would duly take the Constructors' Championship in 1955. Sports cars – the legendary 300 SLR – were more than just trophy-winners, they were good commercial publicity, feeding straight back into the road-going Mercedes sports models.

For Le Mans '55, the German team were fielding the well-worn Pierre Levegh and Fangio himself, as well as Moss and Karl Kling, with their eyes on a big showdown with Jaguar, Aston Martin, Ferrari and Maserati. And it was there that Levegh's 300 SLR clipped Lance Macklin's Healey, going past the pits. Levegh was driving hard at the time. His car took off, hurled itself into the crowd, exploded. More than eighty people were killed: the worst accident in motor-racing history. The French, German and Spanish Grands Prix were called off; the Swiss banned motor racing outright. At the end of the season, Mercedes called a halt to their racing programme. All the titles were won; but the price was too high.

Thus, for 1955, Fangio took the Argentine, Belgian, Dutch and Italian Grands Prix, plus the Drivers' Championship, and then found himself wandering into Ferrari's embrace. Moss won the British GP at Aintree and went, in a roundabout way, to Maserati. Mercedes' Silver Arrows were mothballed. It was a terrible way to end.

But the legacy was this: in those two seasons, Mercedes had shown what a modern Grand Prix team could look like: well resourced, highly motivated, thorough, disciplined, properly structured, boasting two stellar drivers, and wholly intimidating. Just as in the late 1930s, they had turned out to be a glimpse of the future.

4

FANGIO II:
1956 AND THE NIGHTMARE
OF THE PRANCING HORSE

Ah, but Ferrari. How did Fangio ever win the '56 Championship, given the truly terrible relationship between him and the Ferrari team? How, for that matter, did Ferrari get to be in a position where Fangio wanted to drive for them?

In Formula One, everything heads back, sooner or later, to the figure of Enzo Ferrari, a figure out of Grand Opera; or a John Grisham novel; or the Middle Ages. Ferrari was scary: not only was he never seen without his Mafia Don sunglasses, he gave the impression that he might even wear them in bed, just to intimidate the dark. Indeed, the image of the seigneurial Enzo, bulky, unsmiling, hyper-moody, capaciously suited, is still so familiar – to say nothing of the ubiquitous Prancing Horse trademark that he filched off an Italian Air Force ace in the 1920s – that it's hard to believe that there was a time before Ferrari existed.

In fact, just as with Fangio, it took him a while to *become* Ferrari. Before the war, he ran Alfa Romeo's racing team – as Scuderia Ferrari – engineering components for them and acquiring a useful knowledge of car design. He managed to carry on his engineering business during the war, then, in 1947, produced the first proper Ferrari – the 125S, a V12 sports-racing car of considerable pace and flair. The pattern was set. He would make and sell sports cars for the general public, and plough the profits back into the racing team, establishing a tidy synergy which neither Alfa Romeo nor Maserati (to say nothing of Lotus) could ever quite match. Indeed, this balancing of pure racing with commercial enterprise is a properly impressive achievement. Jaguar and Mercedes, far larger concerns, went racing in the 1950s, like Ford in the 1960s, mainly so that they could sell more of their day-to-day production cars; it was Ferrari who really managed to keep the connection between track and showroom alive.

So, in 1948, Nuvolari, who knew Ferrari from way back, drove a 166S – both a racer and, differently fettled, a customer sports car – in the Mille Miglia, building a savage lead over the rest of the field, even as the Ferrari disintegrated around him. At one point, the driver's seat collapsed, and he commandeered a bag of oranges to sit on. The suspension gave way, the mudguards and bonnet fell off. At last, the thing simply ground to a halt. 'We'll do it again, next year,' Ferrari said. But while Ferrari's career was just getting going – the Mille being great publicity, despite the chaos – Nuvolari's was all but finished. They never did race together again.

What did Ferrari care? He was off, now. In 1949, a 166M won Le Mans; Froilán Gonzales gave the team its first GP win at the British GP of 1951; in 1952 and 1953, the fairly frantic Alberto Ascari won back-to-back Formula One World Championships in a Ferrari at the same time as the team was gearing up to win two more back-to-back titles in the World Sportscar Championship.

Enzo's role in all this? More inspirational than strictly mechanical. According to the great engineer Aurelio Lampredi, 'Ferrari is a man who instils enthusiasm in those around him, but he is no technician.' Then again, he didn't even bother to instil enthusiasm if he didn't particularly feel like it. In 1951, Ferrari indicated to a very young Stirling Moss that he wanted him to drive for the team, the following season. It was still early days, but both Ferrari and Moss were names to conjure with. Stirling went all the way to the circuit at Bari, in southern Italy, where the meeting had been set up, only to be told (by a mechanic, even) that the car was earmarked for Piero Taruffi and that Stirling was surplus to requirements. 'I did not forget,' seethed Moss, 'and I would not forgive.' When Luigi Villoresi (whose brother had been killed in a Ferrari) won the Modena GP in '52, 'Ferrari actually said *thank you*.' Villoresi then added, grimly, 'That didn't happen very often.' Ferrari and his Scuderia sailed implacably on.

And then, suddenly, by the mid-1950s, the team was in a slump. The Formula had been tweaked again – from the makeshift Formula Two-style 2-litre regs to a new $2^1/_2$-litre-unsupercharged formulation. Firstly, this caught Ferrari on the hop with their four-cylinder Tipo 625, which just wouldn't perform properly; secondly, Mercedes-Benz had arrived. Having been comfortably in charge, Ferrari now were lucky to pick up three more GP wins, two in '54 (at Silverstone and Pedralbes, in Spain), the third in '55, at Monaco. Scuderia Ferrari was now marked by what one motor-racing historian has called 'the atmosphere of barely suppressed paranoia and the fear of taking responsibility that tended to envelop the team in times of failure'. The *Commendatore* went into a sulk, threatening to give up racing entirely. The cars remained unsatisfactory. In 1955, Ascari died at the wheel of a 750, testing it at Monza. The only way forward was to take over the remnants of the short-lived Lancia F1 team, fit the cars with Ferrari engines and acquire the problematic Fangio.

Luckily for Ferrari, Fangio himself was feeling the pinch. The Perón Government had just fallen in Argentina – and with it, patronage for the Old Man. His business interests were compromised, and his personal finances were being investigated by the incoming military regime. Mercedes had dropped out. He needed a drive as badly as Ferrari needed him to drive for them. The car Ferrari offered him was actually the rather interesting Lancia-Ferrari D50, which had quite a lot going for it, including pannier side fuel tanks for better weight distribution and an offset engine to help keep the height down; it also had some things going against it, among them an unhealthy and vicious tendency for the back end to overtake the front on corners.

The biggest problem, however, was the complete, intense, and mutual antipathy which existed between Ferrari and Fangio. The year 1956 got off to a tricky start when Ferrari refused – as was his habit – to name a number one driver in the team. This disgusted Fangio. However good his fun-loving teammates Peter Collins, Luigi Musso and Eugenio Castellotti might have been, they were not world champions, nor was any of them likely to become champion in the next twelve months. Still less was this an echo of the Mercedes' team rules concerning basic race tactics and equality among drivers. There, Fangio was always the presumptive number one, and it worked very nicely for him. Ferrari, on the other hand, simply liked to see his drivers slug it out.

The first race of the season was in January, at Buenos Aires, Fangio's home patch. Disaster loomed when his fuel pump packed up halfway through. Fangio promptly commandeered Musso's car, got back in the race, and was gifted a win when the leading Maseratis broke down. Moss then took Monaco, in a Maserati 250F – even after Fangio had pulled rank again by taking over Collins' car – while Collins took a quiet revenge on Fangio by winning the next two European races. This was categorically how Fangio did not want things.

He won at Silverstone and the Nürburgring, all right, but by now, the season was turning into a marathon of accusations and counter-accusations with the Ferrari team, which dragged on even after Fangio had left in disgust for Maserati. His agent, Marcello Giambertone, complained – among other things – that Ferrari had sabotaged Fangio's Mille Miglia car, drilling holes in the bodywork to let the rain *in* rather than *out*; and that Ferrari specifically tried to stop Collins from volunteering his car at Monza – a gesture on Collins' part which had turned out to be futile, anyway, given that Moss not only won the race (the last of the season) but also set fastest lap.

Even the Italians would start to get unhappy – less at the way Fangio was being treated, more at the rate of attrition experienced by the rest of Ferrari's drivers. There was Alberto Ascari; there were Eugenio Castelloti and Luigi Musso – both team-mates with Fangio; and there was Fon de Portago, the loveable Portuguese nobleman: all killed between the years 1955 and 1958, all in Ferraris. And it wasn't just the fact that they were dead, it was Ferrari's perceived indifference to the deaths which really hurt: the well-respected *Osservatore Romana* going as far as to call Ferrari 'a modern Saturn', a Saturn who, although a thoroughly progressive captain of industry, 'continues to devour his own sons'. The *Commendatore* himself did nothing to alter this view and, two decades later, would still be coolly advising his team, 'Every time a driver takes off, we write him off in our book. When he comes back, it's a bonus.'

Besides, he was now producing the road cars that would make him both a household name and a kind of Pole Star for the next two generations of spotty boys and yearning men. From being an expedient sideline, street-legal Ferraris were now essential to the whole Ferrari plan. The 250 was Ferrari's first volume-production model (insofar as volume could be done in such fantastically small quantities) followed by the fabulous 410 Superamerica of 1955. Depending on the bodywork (as often as not, a minor work of art by Pinin Farina) and the level of appointments inside (radios! Upholstered seats!), these cars offered a kind of driving experience – to say nothing of kerbside presence – which even Maserati had trouble matching. Zsa Zsa Gabor got one; as did William Holden, Roger Vadim, Roberto Rossellini: that kind of person. Ferrari was getting to be big, in other words, bigger than anyone who could possibly ever work for him, bigger than anyone who might bear a grievance against him – a figure of talismanic glamour, whose stunning road cars were legitimised by the Grand Prix cars; which were, in turn, funded by the road cars.

And soon enough, Peter Collins, quick, impossibly handsome and charming, an Englishman who spoke Italian, a surrogate son to Enzo himself (whose own son, Dino, had died by degrees from muscular dystrophy), was killed, in a Ferrari 246. He delivered two Grand Prix wins in 1956, a third in '58, at Silverstone. And then, at the Nürburgring, August 1958, he was chasing Tony Brooks' Vanwall when his car shot off the track, throwing him into a tree. He died of head injuries, a few hours later. He was twenty-six years old.

Did Ferrari mourn? Later, he would say of Collins, 'He was a fine driver and a fine man – a true gentleman.' But at the time he gave every impression of being ruthlessly unconcerned. Why? Not least because Collins had just betrayed

Ferrari – and all the time and energy he had invested – by marrying a pretty young actress called Louise Cordier. Ferrari's jealously bitter assessment of the lovely bride? 'She was the type of girl you find in the pits.' Girls were fine (Ferrari enjoyed hearing about his drivers' womanisings), but wives were both a distraction and a threat to his overweening centrality. From the moment that Collins married, he became a lesser person. Only Ferrari and his vaulting ambition truly mattered.

It was with all this in the air that Fangio took the '56 Championship with three wins, two second places and four fastest laps (each of which scored an extra point) to his acolyte Moss's two wins and one second place. The atmosphere was heavy with wounded *amour-propre*. Ferrari's summation was that 'Fangio was a really great driver, but afflicted by a persecution mania. I was not the only one against whom he entertained all kinds of suspicions.' Worse yet, *'Fangio did not remain loyal to any marque.'* Fangio, very earnestly, told Stirling Moss: 'By all means drive the cars, but never, ever, sign for Ferrari.'

The thing was, though, that Ferrari was the greatest survivor of them all, the only survivor. Alfa Romeo had dropped out of Formula One. Maserati were looking sickly. If you wanted to drive Italian, pretty soon there would only be one team to choose from.

5

FANGIO III:
THE LAST WIN

The Nürburgring, some way south of Cologne and set in the
Eifel Mountains, was originally built in the 1920s: a four-
teen-mile-long circuit with over 170 corners, and so sprawling
that a driver might start his race in bright sunshine only to
find, on the far side of the circuit, that, instead of it being
a pleasant summer's day, it was actually pitch dark and pouring
with rain. It came to be known as *The Green Hell*, and only
a handful of drivers ever really mastered it, before it was
finally taken out of the Formula One calendar in the 1980s.
It had terrifyingly fast stretches; stomach-turning gradients
of one in six; a banked section known as the *Karussell*; humps
in the track that made cars take off; numerous blind spots;
a tremendous number of pine trees to smash into; a ruined
castle in the middle; and the probability that, if you did
wreck your car or yourself, it would be a long time before
anyone found you. Drivers respected it, feared it, loathed it.
By the second half of the 1950s, it had already claimed the
lives of eleven competitors, including the first death under
the new Formula One regime – that of Onofre Marimón,
Fangio's compatriot, in 1954. With its terrible length and

complexity, it was more dangerous even than Monza. It was the greatest leveller of men and machines in Europe.

So when Fangio took his last (and possibly greatest) race win, at the Nürburgring in August 1957, all the elements were in place for a Nuvolari-style moment of definition. He was really old by then – forty-six – against a field full of men half his age. He was known as the Old Fox, the Old Man, the Maestro, but still kept his counsel, talking only when he had to, in his high, quiet, hoarse voice. And he had shuffled back to the financially wheezy Maserati *équipe* for the endgame, in a much-developed 250F, the car in which he had started his '54 Championship year.

If Alfa Romeo had been Teutonic, then Maserati were, by all accounts, authentically, chaotically Italian. The three-year-old 250F, with its unsupercharged straight-6, its conventional (but sweet-handling) chassis, and its classic good looks, was in many ways the definitive post-war front-engined machine. But the Lancia-Ferrari 801s driven in '57 by Peter Collins and Mike Hawthorn, although equally mature, were more powerful, and had much younger men to drive them. And Vanwall, the new British hope, driven by Moss and significantly tweaked by that rising young engineer Colin Chapman, was making real, worrying, progress.

Fangio could see his rivals creeping up on him as the season progressed. After a comfortable start in Argentina and Monaco, he found a pack of Ferraris after him at the French GP (Luigi Musso taking fastest lap), while at the British GP at Aintree, an increasingly fired-up Moss took Vanwall's first Championship win, with Musso's Ferrari second, Hawthorn third, and Fangio out of the race with a blown engine. He was well placed in the Championship, all right; but there was a clear trend emerging, as the race calendar moved on to Germany.

Then again, there was the Nürburgring. Fangio himself claimed, back in 1951, that 'It's impossible to get to know it all in a short time . . . It is difficult to keep fourteen miles in your head, so for that reason I tried to blot from my mind all the slow parts. What you had to keep in mind were the fast bits . . .' Since then, he'd won there twice and had got a much clearer conception of it. And, in August 1957, he felt, despite his own age and the increasing venerability of the Maserati, moderately confident. As motoring journalist Rodney Walkerley put it, watching him in practice, 'Fangio erupted from the bridge with a blast of sound which was like an explosion, his foot hard down after a quick lift 200 yards earlier, and took the curve with the car in a full slide, fighting the wheel all the way, and was gone – so much faster to the eye than anyone else that it made even Mike Hawthorn look slow.'

Which turned out to be the case for the first half of the race. When he came in for a routine pit stop on lap twelve, he was well in the lead, thirty seconds ahead of Collins and Hawthorn, who were travelling more or less as a matched pair in their Ferraris, a couple of miles behind. Moss and Brooks, in the Vanwalls, were not having good races, and seemed out of contention. It was looking promising. But the pit stop turned into a disaster – just as happened to Nuvolari in 1935. The mechanics, rigid with nerves, bungled everything. The tyre changes went to pieces. Fangio waited and waited. By the time he left the pits, he was fifty-one seconds *behind* the two Ferraris.

So, like Nuvolari before him, he went into a kind of controlled madness. 'I began,' he later explained, as if anyone would believe him, 'to take nearly all the bends in a higher gear than I normally would have done.' This put him – the man who liked to win 'as slowly as possible' – at the absolute outer edge of control. It also meant that he shattered the lap record over and over again, bringing it down to nine minutes. seventeen seconds. on lap twenty, with two laps to go and only a couple of seconds left to make up before he reached Collins and Hawthorn.

The two Ferrari drivers, meanwhile, were not entirely abreast of developments and had decided to carve the race up between them. Collins drew alongside Hawthorn on the straight, 'Put his thumb up, then pointed to me with one finger and then back to himself with two. He wanted me to win and was prepared to come second himself, which I thought was a very sporting gesture,' as Hawthorn subsequently confessed. A couple of minutes later and Fangio had not only chewed up both Collins and Hawthorn, but made a point of getting away from Hawthorn before reaching the straight again, 'Because there he might have taken advantage of my slipstream and passed me.'

The Ferrari mechanics, according to Walkerley, 'gesticulated and tore the air, they fell on their knees to their drivers', while in the Maserati pits team manager Nello Ugolini merely 'smiled at his watch'. Fangio won by three seconds. Hawthorn and Collins, bless them, 'were ecstatic, as if they had been the winners. They never stopped congratulating me and shaking me by the hand. They were both very good lads.' Pictures after the final flag show a shattered Fangio being born aloft by his team and being embraced by the two young Brits: both of whom wear the gleeful, incredulous expression of someone who has seen something astounding, a performance of scarcely plausible brilliance.

'I believe on that day I finally managed to master it,' Fangio said, forgivingly, of the 'Ring. He then went and took his fifth and last World Championship. Moss, his protégé, cleaned up in the last two races for Vanwall, Fangio humbly coming second both times. At the end of '58, he retired from the sport, alive, in reasonable health, and went to live a life of quietly virtuous industry as a national hero in Argentina, leaving the rest of the world to argue whether he was, or was not, the greatest Grand Prix driver of all time.

No, he never showed his versatility by winning Le Mans, or the Mille Miglia, or Indianapolis. And the Formula One seasons in which he raced were infinitely shorter than today's – between seven and eight mostly European Grandes Épreuves, spread out between May and September. And the fields could be of pretty variable quality. But the fact remains that with twenty-four wins out of fifty-one starts, Fangio's winning *percentage* is unlikely ever to be beaten. And there will always be the Nürburgring, 5 August 1957.

THE AGE OF BRITS
1959-76

6

HAWTHORN, MOSS AND THE BRITISH REVENGE

January 1959, and new world champion, Mike Hawthorn, was being fêted at the National Sporting Clubs Dinner, in the presence of such luminaries as Henry Cooper, Joe Davis, Donald Campbell and Tony Brooks. Charles Forte presided and presented the guest of honour with a fine cocktail cabinet, stuffed with liquor. In his acceptance speech, Mike hoped that some of the assembled company would come round in the not-too-distant future and help him empty it. A couple of days later – 22 January 1959 – and Hawthorn was dead, in his own heavily modified Jaguar saloon, having got into an asinine road race with Rob Walker's Mercedes on the Guildford by-pass, where he lost control and smashed the car into a tree. He was twenty-nine years old. 'Motor racing's Gay Cavalier' had been champion for all of three months.

It was a wretched end to a curiously tangled, disjointed twelve months. Yes, Hawthorn had become the first Brit to win the Drivers' Championship. Yes, he was the tall, dashing, fun-loving daredevil that schoolboys worshipped: six feet two inches in height, brick-chinned, as blond as Marilyn Monroe and so very English that he raced in white trousers, a green *blouson* and a spotty bow tie. 'If I can't drive a green car,' he said, in 1953, having taken the Ferrari seat, 'at least I can wear a green jacket.' And yes, he was the frontman for a sudden British efflorescence in the Grand Prix world.

After all, the 1958 season was Fangio's last. He had retired after the French Grand Prix in July, following an indifferent spell with the outdated Maserati 250F. Suddenly, after years of watching *El Chueco* relentlessly adding to his silverware collection, spectators of Formula One found that the field was wide open.

And who was making the running? Well, an inspection of the top five places at the end of the 1958 Drivers' Championship reveals, in ascending order: Peter Collins, Roy Salvadori, Tony Brooks, Stirling Moss and, at the top, Mike Hawthorn himself. This startling roll-call – 100 per cent British – is even more impressive when you consider that, back in 1950, the dawn of the new Formula, there was only one Brit in the whole of the top ten, a solid racer called Peter Whitehead, with old Reg Parnell languishing in eleventh. Stranger yet: three out of the top four car builders in the Constructors' Championship were now also British.

A generation of drivers and constructors had been assiduously training itself up on the DIY specials and club circuits of Great Britain in the decade following the war and was now reaping the rewards. Tony Brooks, 'The Racing Dentist', had scored the first Formula One win by a British driver in a British car, in 1955, in a Connaught. The only pity was that it was at Syracuse, in a non-Championship race. Stirling Moss had already been driving brilliantly alongside (or inches behind) Fangio in the Mercedes team (only a matter of time before he became champion, patently) before getting Vanwall up to speed. Peter Collins was quick and successful, if not entirely dependable, in the V6-engined Ferrari 246. Roy Salvadori, driving a whacky rear-engined Cooper-Climax, had come a very respectable second in the '58 German Grand Prix, behind Brooks.

In a way, it was fortuitous that Hawthorn became champion at all, given the competition that was stacked up behind him; and given the fact that, in his entire racing career, he only ever won three Grands Prix. In the year of his Championship, he won but one race, with Moss taking four, Tony Brooks three. But then, Hawthorn's career was a lot less blithe, sunny and effortless than it appears at first sight.

Consider the presentation drinks cabinet, so cheerfully unveiled by Charles Forte in 1959: there is something unnerving about it, given that, for much of his young life, Mike Hawthorn was shitfaced, about to get shitfaced, or recovering from having just been shitfaced. When stationary, he liked to have a drink – usually beer – in his hand, or at least, not far away. This was despite a chronic kidney disorder which made any trip to the lavatory 'like peeing grit'.

The proximity of a motor race made no difference. The British Grand Prix of 1955 took place at Aintree, a 3-mile circuit built within the confines of the famous Aintree Racecourse, and using the same grandstands. Hawthorn (in a Ferrari 625) started off badly and was soon lurching round the track in such a state that he eventually got out in mid-race and simply gave up the car to team-mate Eugenio Castellotti. 'The weather was fantastic for Aintree,' Hawthorn – who had happily raced at summery Reims and sultry Monza – later assured the press, 'sunny and extremely hot, and I began to feel the effects, so I handed the car over.' Sympathetic voices announced that his kidneys were playing up again. But others reckoned that, so far from being a saintly valetudinarian, he was in fact massively hungover, having had a huge row with his then girlfriend (the styl-ishly-named Moi Kenward) the night before, gone out, got smashed, and then had to face the consequences at the wheel of a racing car.

It happened again, a year later, when Hawthorn was due to race at Monaco for BRM. This was their first appearance with a new machine, the P25 – and a proper green car for Hawthorn to drive. You would have thought he might have treated the event with some reverence. But no. En route to the circuit, he found himself drunk in a brothel, in Paris, with a tall, equally drunk, BRM hand called Neil McNab. According to McNab, boredom set in and, stark naked, the pair of them 'went into some of the other rooms to see if we were missing out on any good crumpet. We'd just lift the bloke off his tart, have a good look at her and drop him back on again.' A minor riot ensued. McNab and Hawthorn escaped and made it to Monte Carlo the next day, where Raymond Mays (now back running the team he had started, on behalf of Sir Alfred Owen) looked at the bleary wreckage that was his principal driver and said, 'My God, Hawthorn – what are we going to do with you?' Not much: the engine turned sour; Hawthorn was a non-starter for the race and went off to recover in the dark.

Left alone in the company of notorious roister-doister 'Drunken' Duncan Hamilton – famed for his Jaguar exploits – Hawthorn was even more volatile. At around 4 a.m., following a party after a race in Portugal, in 1954, Hawthorn and Hamilton 'decided we would change our bedroom furni-ture round', according to Hamilton. They opened their respec-tive bedroom windows. 'Using knotted sheets I lowered all my furniture down to Mike's room; he, in return, helped me pull all his up to mine. A poor drunk on the second floor who chanced to look out of his window as dawn was breaking was convinced he had the DT's when a large armchair went by.'

Fast-forward to 1956, and Hamilton, Hawthorn and fellow drivers were in Sweden, having completed a sports car race (Hawthorn, along with Musso, Castellotti, Portago, Collins – *all* dead within two years) and in need of some after-track stimulation. Working as a team, the six of them stole a crate of whisky from behind the bar. Several hours later, and a plastered Hamilton had set off a fire hose in Hawthorn's bedroom, the hose had run riot, the corridor was flooded, a similarly plastered Hawthorn had grabbed the hose, and squirted a couple (who were having sex) clean out of their bed. Hamilton only managed to turn the thing off by attacking it with a fire axe.

Well, you could get away with that, just about, back in the mid-1950s. But if all this could be glossed as mere youthful alcoholic high spirits (even Hawthorn's dog was called Grogger), there were more intractable problems elsewhere.

There was, for instance, the National Service scandal. By 1954, Hawthorn was eligible for two years in the Armed Services, the duty of every able-bodied young Englishman in those days. He got it deferred, then had to flee to the Continent, where he skulked for fear of being pinched by the Ministry of Defence the moment he returned to England. Questions were asked in Parliament as to why a young man fit enough to race Formula One cars was not able fulfil his basic military obligations. The *Daily Mirror* sneered, 'Why not come home, Mike? There is a reasonable chance you can still go on seeing the world – in a British uniform.' It followed up this cheerless Fleet Street sarcasm with the headline 'CATCH THIS DODGER', causing Mike's father, Leslie, to try and placate the press with breast-beating interviews in which he blamed himself for his son's apparent delinquency. The thing dragged on until October, when Hawthorn had to have a kidney operation, effectively rendering him unfit for National Service once and for all.

This did nothing for his public image. At the same time, his private life was becoming just as unduly complex. Hawthorn (who 'drives in devil-may-care style, his husky frame hunched over in the cramped cockpit', according to *Time* magazine) was so far inclined to take his pleasures where he could that he fathered an illegitimate child. While hiding abroad to avoid the call-up, he had an affair with a delectable Frenchwoman, Jaqueline Delaunay. This yielded a son, Arnaud, in 1954. The child looked like Mike in every particular (apart, as it turned out, from being short and dark) and was clearly his. Hawthorn then spent two years carefully avoiding this boy and all the burdensome responsibilities he incarnated, before Mlle Delaunay cornered him at the French GP in Reims. There, she held up a toddler dressed in diminutive white trousers, green jacket and bow tie – a miniature Mike – before the errant father, who could only give in and, after that, make financial provision for him.

Then, back on the track in 1955, he was centrally involved in the catastrophic Le Mans crash. In the minutes after the disaster, he haggardly insisted to Lance Macklin – the other surviving driver caught in the maelstrom, who had set it off, indeed, by having to avoid Hawthorn's Jaguar – 'I killed all those people. I'm really sorry. I'm certainly never going racing again.' Except that he did, straight away, winning the race for Jaguar, before doing a promotional film the following year, in which a camera was lashed to his D-Type and in which he drove round the track giving a commentary – *while ordinary motorists used the same road*. The track hadn't been closed off, but there was Mike, hurtling past *camionettes* and private cars, announcing, 'I've got to be a little careful today, because there's quite a lot of traffic on the road,' and, 'There's somebody in the way ... cyclists everywhere ... typical French!'

And so on. By the start of the 1958 season, in other words, Hawthorn was a long way removed from the cheeky twenty-one-year-old who drove a Riley Imp at the Brighton Speed Trials of 1950 and made himself One to Watch. He was now a somewhat compromised and chastened Hawthorn – having tangled with illness, controversy, injury, illegitimacy, tragedy and drink-related folly. And he was not helped by the fact that his greatest rival, Stirling Moss, was coming to the top of his form.

Hawthorn, it must be said, didn't care for Moss. So far as he was concerned, Moss was a *player*, a racer who took it seriously, professionally, who went racing as a business; who even had his own manager. Hawthorn, on the other hand, saw himself as a *gentleman* who did it for the love of the sport, a stance which gave him, as he saw it, the moral edge. But there was no doubting who was the better driver.

Moss was, in fact, a perpetual reproach to Hawthorn. Moss had cut his racing teeth on Coopers, like Hawthorn, and by the mid-1950s was one of the very hottest properties in Formula One. Plainly, he was incredibly quick: he could sit on Fangio's tail all day if necessary and never seem to break a sweat – except, in 1955, when he had a mild rush of blood to the head and nipped over the finishing line at the British Grand Prix, half a car's length ahead of the Maestro. He copied Giuseppe Farina's straight-arm driving style, not because it felt better (it didn't, and took a lot of getting used to) but because 'it looked cool' – thereby unnerving his competitors as well as making himself seem special.

And he was astonishingly versatile – he could flog a very

middle-class Sunbeam Talbot to victory in the Alpine Rally, demolish the 1955 Mille Miglia in a Mercedes 300 SLR, or win the Nürburgring 1,000-km three years in succession, twice in an Aston Martin, once in a Maserati Birdcage. He could drive whale-like Jaguar Mk VIIs in saloon car races, or dinky Coopers, just as they were making the break into Formula One. Nuvolari actually spotted Moss's genius as far back as 1949. 'Watch him,' he said, 'he will be one of the great ones.'

To give him his due, Hawthorn was a fine sports and saloon car driver too, and would never have got the hot seat with Ferrari if he hadn't been able to drive. But Moss was consummate. He was trim, fit, super-adaptable, highly profes-sional, not a great boozer (although he was a great skirt-chaser: 'I think the pit's all the better for a bit of crumpet') and he knew the rules backwards – noting that it was perfectly acceptable to play as close to what was permitted as was humanly possible, but that cheating was right out. He was nerveless, too; after a big crash at Monza in 1958, he tumbled out of the wreck of his Maserati and stood there thinking, 'Well, if this is Hell, it's not very hot, or if it's Heaven, why is it so dusty?' Moss was a complete driver, and a completely modern driver.

Having Moss around was altogether imperfect, and Hawthorn, to his lasting discredit, liked to refer to him behind his back as *Moses* – a glancing reference to the fact that Moss's father was Jewish. Added to which, as the season went on, it became clear that, if Hawthorn did take the title, it would be as a percentage player, a steady accumulator of points, rather than as the bow-tied swashbuckler his fans liked to paint him. Moss took two out of the first three races, while Tony Brooks took three out of the next six. Collins won at Silverstone – the race Hawthorn would have liked to have won more than any other – while at the Portuguese Grand

Prix, Moss (gallingly stuffed with useful information about the rules, and acting in purely *gentleman*, rather than *player*, fashion) got Hawthorn's points reinstated following a minor technical infringement: handing him the title, as it would turn out, by a single point.

All of which would have been just about bearable, except for this: Peter Collins had died at the Nürburgring, three weeks earlier, on 3 August. Romolo Tavoni, Ferrari team manager, escorted Hawthorn to the hospital after the race: 'There was Peter, like he was asleep. Mike took one look, turned and went out into the corridor, where he leaned against the wall and slid down to the floor. He just sat there, saying nothing.' Ferrari may have scorned to show emotion at the time, but Hawthorn was now shattered, arriving back at London Airport in floods of tears. After all, Collins was Hawthorn's special *Mon Ami Mate*, his better-looking, more charming alter ego, the person Hawthorn would most like to have been. They partied together. They raced in the same team. Collins had just got married to Louise Cordier, Hawthorn was about to marry the gorgeous Jean Howarth. It was all going to come right. And then Collins was dead.

So Hawthorn steeled himself, picked up some more points – useful second places – collected the title and retired. 'He wishes to get married to a beautiful girl and dedicate himself to his promising business interests,' said Enzo Ferrari in disgust. The Duke of Richmond and Gordon gave Hawthorn a gold medal. Stirling Moss got the OBE. 'I've had eight years of racing,' Hawthorn said at the National Sporting Club's dinner, 'and in eight years I've got to the top. So I decided – now's the time.' He and Duncan Hamilton were going into partnership; he had the Tourist Trophy Garage in Farnham to keep him busy; companies like Shell and Mintex were paying him handsomely to endorse their products; he was going to survive.

And then he caught sight of Rob Walker's Mercedes, a 'Kraut car' and, as such, in need of a trouncing. Hawthorn hit the ton on the Guildford by-pass. And that was the end of Britain's first champion.

7

THEY WENT BACK TO FRONT

Hawthorn's Championship win in '58 was a big deal for the Brits, plainly. One of their chaps had taken the title, however tragic the final chapter had been. But what happened the following year was, arguably, a bigger deal. Tough, swarthy, Aussie Jack Brabham won *his* first title, *in a rear-engined car*. And not just any rear-engined car – a smart little Cooper-Climax, the true descendant of a succession of bonkers rear-engined midget motorbike-powered 500-cc racing cars which Charles and John Cooper produced in a shed in Surbiton.

It was a close thing: Brabham took two wins – Monaco, and the British GP at Aintree – while runner-up Tony Brooks, in a conventionally front-engined Ferrari, won at Reims and the German GP at Avus. It was Brabham's extra podium places that got the job done – especially when you consider that Stirling Moss took two wins (Portugal and Italy) in another Cooper-Climax, with Bruce McLaren nabbing a fifth (United States) at the end of the season for the Surbiton eccentrics. Brabham finished four points ahead of Brooks, however, and the rest is history . . .

Nowadays the only question is, why did it take them so long

to turn the cars round? In the mid-1950s, conversely, the only question was, *how dare they?* Sticking the engine at the back was not only against nature, a perversion once attempted by the evil-handling Auto Unions, but out of the question for serious racing. Maserati's Nello Ugolini could barely contain his dismay at 'those dreadful horrors they are producing in England', while Ferrari simply tried to wish them away. The Italians referred to John Cooper as a *garagista*, which sounded even more contemptuous and threatening than the equivalent French sneer, *garagiste*.

Even in Britain, turning the car back to front provoked unease. The British Vanwall team, started by engineering magnate Tony Vandervell as a response to the bureaucratic flab of BRM, was, like Cooper, a portent of things to come and a pretty good outfit, too. They had Colin Chapman and Frank Costin as designers, won the British GP in '57, came top of the Constructors' table in the same year (adding the Pescara and Monza GPs to the British, all courtesy of Moss). Their cars were intelligent, full of interesting thoughts on brakes, suspension, aerodynamics, and were very nicely put together. But their engines were at the front, and they were correspondingly bulky. Connaught likewise used the conventional front-engined layout. Even Colin Chapman's first GP Lotuses had the engine ahead of the driver.

John Cooper himself, full of native self-deprecation, claimed that moving the engine to the rear was originally a virtue born of necessity: 'When we came to make our first 500-cc racer, it was just a hell of a lot more convenient to have the engine at the back, driving a chain.' It wasn't until they moved up to larger machinery that they realised that the principle held good, empirically. 'We built the bob-tailed sports car in the mid-fifties, with its engine at the rear,' and it was then 'that we really began to think that we might be on to something.' The car was light, balanced, didn't wear out its tyres: 'It just seemed so right.'

And then, in January 1958, Stirling Moss (of course) drove an underpowered Cooper-Climax T43 to victory in the Argentine Grand Prix – while waiting, as it happened, for the Vanwall that he was supposed to drive that season, to be made ready.

The race organisers at first didn't want to let the car start; they thought it was a joke. Quite apart from its dainty proportions, its whacky layout and its heterodox, curvy-tubed chassis, the Cooper was powered by a reinvention of a four-cylinder fire-pump power unit, blagged from Coventry Climax, instead of being propelled by a proper, thoroughbred six-cylinder racing engine. The Climax powerplant was not only a mongrel: it was nearly half a litre smaller than the Ferrari and Maserati engines, gave away as much as 100 bhp, and looked fit only to run a lawnmower. But then, what do you know, Moss drove a non-stop race, letting the little car conserve its tyres and fuel, while the suddenly obese Italians shredded their rubber and charged into the pits for more high-octane gasoline. Moss tiptoed home on canvas covers: one of his paradigm-shifting drives. 'Moss Refutes Pessimists', said *The Times*, sagely. 'Fine Performance In British Car.

It's tempting to see this image of Moss – clever, professional, supercompetent – at the wheel of the Cooper – small, light, intelligent – as *the* moment at which the modern Formula One world arrived. But one shouldn't read too much into it. He himself didn't see the rear-engine revolution coming, that's for sure. The Vanwall was front-engined. And only a few years earlier, he had bought himself (helped out by money from ShellMex–BP) a Maserati 250F for the colossal sum of £5,500. Two things struck him about this purchase: it was the same price as a new Spitfire fighter plane would have been, a decade earlier; and he reckoned he could get a good couple of seasons' use of it. Things changed all the time in Grand Prix racing, but not so fast that you couldn't keep up, provided you had a good (front-engined) car.

Now, though, there was a strange scent of insurrection in the air. Moss won in the Argentine, the first win by a rear-engined car in Formula One. Maurice Trintignant took the next race at Monaco, also in a Cooper-Climax. The next year, Brabham and Moss gave Cooper-Climax the Constructors' Championship, and even Ferrari had to pay attention. The world of Fangio and Farina and Gonzales, real tough guys who sat up and hurled big, brutal cars into four-wheel power-slides, their wrestlers' arms working, banging the gearchange around as if unblocking a drain: all that was suddenly history. Moss lay back in the little Cooper, half-hidden from view, nimbly tweaking it round corners, relishing its balance, never fighting it. It was like a light being turned on: partly because it showed how all Formula One cars were going to be configured from now on; partly because it was Cooper, a small, resourceful, nimble-minded privateer, who had done it.

Because there were really two revolutions. The look and shape of the car was one. The place of origin was the other. Out of the Cooper *garagiste* insurrection came Lotus, based in Hornsey, then Cheshunt, then Hethel; Brabham, originally in Chessington; McLaren, of Woking; even a lightened and rejuvenated BRM, based in Bourne. All of them were small, specialist, nimble operations. All of them were based, quietly and purposefully, in England, where craft skills lingered on in odd places. And they all did well at airfields.

One line of thought argues that those Second World War airfields – Silverstone, Thruxton, Snetterton, Goodwood – which had been commandeered to make racing tracks for all the post-war DIY racers, were key to the whole thing. There was no road racing in the UK to speak of, but there were these *tracks* – flat, with adequately smooth surfaces, useful collections of bends, all easily accessible to the British racing fraternity, all begging to be used, weekend after weekend. At the same time, while the *garagistes* had access to all kinds of bits and pieces of engineering, as well as freebooting engineering talent, what they didn't have was an abundance of engines: 750 cc units scrounged out of old Austin Sevens; JAP motorbike engines coming in at 500 cc; not a lot else. So they had to learn the virtues of making light, agile, reasonably aerodynamic cars that extracted the most out of what power they had, rather than start with a big, powerful engine and work their way back from that. And the airfield circuits, unlike the tough, lumpy road circuits on the Continent (jigsaw puzzles of bumps, ridges, manhole covers, bridges, kerbs), encouraged subtle chassis and braking arrangements, rather than something that would, mainly, be built for punishment. In other words, the *garagistes* were working in something quite like a modern racing environment before the rest of the world had caught up: an advantage they have yet to relinquish.

It meant that, for the foreseeable future, the Age of Italy was going to have to make way for a new, compromised world. The *garagistas* were taking over.

8

1962; MOSS, HILL, BRABHAM: SO VERY ANGLO-SAXON

Stirling Moss was now driving as well as he had ever driven – and yet was quite unable to land that World Championship. In 1958, he lost out by a point to Mike Hawthorn; '59, he came third behind Jack Brabham and Tony Brooks; '60, he came third behind Brabham and Bruce McLaren; '61, he was third again, behind Phil Hill and Wolfgang 'Taffy' von Trips. How did he manage to snatch defeat from the jaws of victory so consistently?

Especially when you consider that in 1961, he managed not one but *two* astonishing drives, one in May at Monaco, one in August at the Nürburgring – drives which have gone down in history, along with Fangio v. the Ferraris, or Nuvolari v. Mercedes, or Stewart at the 'Ring in '68.

What made them so epic? The fact that Moss was driving a hopelessly outdated, underpowered, privateer's Lotus 18/21: and was pitched against the steaming aggression of, not only Ferrari, but also cunning young upstarts Porsche, making their foray into GP racing.

In some ways, it's the sheer *look* of Moss's car at Monaco which has helped to fix the race in the Pantheon of sporting moments. Time, after all, has not been kind to the aesthetics of the Lotus. The outer skin gives the impression of having been shaped around a loose mixture of cornflake packets and shoeboxes. The pantomime Coventry Climax engine is so small and so shrouded by sheet metal as to be invisible. The roll-over bar appears to have been taken from a pram. For 1961 the whole thing was painted in Rob Walker's uninspiring dingy dark blue, with a modest white nose stripe and white 'wobbly web' wheels, the jellyfish-shaped curiosities Lotus used instead of the more normal light alloys. Even by the standards of the day, the overall effect is like a kid's home-made go-kart racer in a field full of, say, Triumph TR3s – especially when seen on the grid, parked up against the sexy red sharknose Ferrari 156s, new for '61 and with *success* written all over them.

First, though, Moss had to start his weekend by rescuing Innes Ireland – the latter one of the great arms 'n' elbows tearaways – when Ireland crashed spectacularly in practice going through the Tunnel just after the Grand Hotel Hairpin. It was a huge mess, and Ireland was sprawled on the ground, bleeding badly, when Moss jumped out of the Lotus to come to his aid, get him a cigarette, generally calm him down. This allowed Innes subsequently to deliver the fabled observation: 'Ah, yes, '61; that was the year when I came out of the fucking Tunnel without the fucking car.'

His charity work done, Moss promptly went on to take pole position.

Come race day, more complications. The weather was unusually hot, so Moss had the side panels taken off the chassis (causing the Lotus, minus half its bodywork, to look even more risibly home-made) and had himself drenched with a bucket of water to keep the heat at bay (declaring in passing that he found himself rather fetching in wet-look).

Then, while sitting in the car, on the grid, waiting to start, he noticed a crack in the chassis tubes. Typical Lotus, light and fragile as a leaf. Whereupon he called over his mechanic, the legendary Alf Francis, who phlegmatically wrapped some wet towels around the tubing and the neighbouring petrol tanks – containing 30 gallons of explosive AvGas – and *welded the car back together there and then with an oxyacetylene torch.* Moss kept fatalistically calm. The car was bodged back into more or less one piece as if it were the most natural thing in the world. The race started.

Richie Ginther took the lead for Ferrari, but, before the race was a quarter done, Moss was in front and drove the rest of the race at a speed which was no more than half a second slower per lap than his pole position time. Thus he not only set joint fastest lap, but also found the monstrous cool to humiliate the other drivers by emphasising his head-back, out-for-a-spin, no-pressure, driving style *and waving at the spectators as he passed.* He was like an electric hare being chased by greyhounds: they could get close, but never close enough to catch. After 200 miles and nearly three hours of unremitting pressure, he won the race, just over three seconds ahead of Ginther. When the American finally came into the pits, he was so shattered by the pursuit that he had to be physically lifted out of his own car. Moss, perched on the ridiculous-looking Lotus 18, got the Champagne. And if you had to choose one race to remember the peerless Moss by, this could be the one.

It was driving of this sort – bravura, dazzling, arrogant – that finally made Enzo Ferrari dissolve with helpless admiration. At the end of '61, he told Moss: 'I need you, tell me what kind of car you want and I will make it for you in six months. Put your ideas on paper for me. If you drive for me, you will tell me on Monday what you did not like about the car on Sunday and by Friday it will have been changed to your taste. If you drive for me, I will have no team, just you and a reserve driver. With Moss, I would need no team.' This was submission enough. But there was more: he was prepared to let the car be entered by Rob Walker – the gentlemanly team manager who had been in charge of Moss's Lotus up to that point – and run in his colours of dark blue and white. Not a bit of Ferrari red anywhere. That's how much it meant.

And if there was any justice in the world, Moss would have driven a Ferrari in '62, and taken the crown. The 156 which gave the American Phil Hill the '61 title had plenty of life left in it. If Ferrari had kept his side of the bargain, Moss would doubtless have made the car even better. It was Moss's best chance. His Formula One career had, up to this point, always described a queasy passage from marque to marque, either ending up in a good car but a subordinate position (Mercedes); or in a good position, but the wrong car (Vanwall, Lotus). Everything could, finally, have been settled with Ferrari.

Then, in April 1962, he smashed up his Lotus in the International Glover Trophy Race at Goodwood, smashed up his career and smashed himself up, very nearly terminally. He suffered terrible leg, arm, chest and head injuries. His personal belief up to that point, with regard to crashing, had generally been that 'I like seat belts in closed cars, but in a racing car I want to be thrown out, or have the choice, mainly because of fire.' This time, there was no fire, but the car had wrapped itself around him liked a crushed cigarette packet. Newspapers reported that, while trapped in the wreckage, he had asked someone to tell his mother that he was 'fine' and that she was not to worry. He was then rushed to hospital, where he spent weeks in a coma.

The recovery was long and dismal. By the following year, he felt well enough to get behind the wheel again. But when he did drive, he felt that something vital had gone, the irreducible edge that he had always had. In 1963, he announced his retirement – typically enough, framing it with reference to his hero, Fangio. Asked if he had any regrets about never winning the Drivers' Championship, instead of answering *yes of course*, he said, 'None at all. Fangio did it five times. If I won it six times, would it make me better than Fangio? I know it wouldn't, because I am not. I would rather go down in history, if am to go down in motor racing history, as being a pretty good driver who never won it, because I don't think you can match Fangio. He is the greatest driver who ever lived.'

Whatever one makes of this, the fact remains that, even today, decades after he last raced in anger, Moss is still being picked as one of the all-time masters of the sport – his greatness somehow endorsed rather than diminished by his failure to take the F1 World Championship. However modern, however career- and business-minded Moss was in his heyday, however many noses he got up, it's not a big, blatant title that characterises him, it is, rather, the artistry of his individual performances, and the sheer daunting fluency with which he raced whatever car he got into, that speak volumes. Sixty-six starts in F1; sixteen wins; sixteen pole positions. The Mille Miglia in 1955. The Alpine Rally in 1953. The 1957 Sebring 12 Hours. The 1958, 1959 and 1960 Nürburgring 1,000 kms . . .

Which raises the question: how do we judge the career of a Formula One driver? To put it another way, what does one make of the extraordinary Graham Hill, a driver who even now raises a smile of recognition, a baffled shrug and the acknowledgement of a life lived slightly larger than normal, and who succeeded as much as anyone could hope to succeed, but who has always suffered from his proximity to more brilliant competitors?

Even Hill's fans would admit that part of the problem was that there were two separate Graham Hills, forced to co-exist within the same body.

First, there was the Graham Hill of popular legend, the sly, humorous party beast, a weird conflation of Sir Henry Segrave and Errol Flynn, who would win at Monaco an astonishing five times, each time attending the formal, glamorous, post-race dinner given by Prince Rainier, before excusing himself and, according to Tony Rudd, wandering, like a sailor on shore leave, down to the Tip Top. This was 'a club on the way down the hill from the Casino, and he would be singing rowing and football songs. It used to be quite a rowdy evening, which went on till dawn.' From Princess Grace to *Eskimo Nell*: Hill's guiding philosophy, in this respect, being 'You've got to have a bit of fun, haven't you?'

And indeed, fun was to be found all over the place. It could mean getting smashed in a night club; or donning a wig and dancing the can-can; or, infamously, as the decade wore on, jumping onto the table at a dinner and hurling himself at a stripper who was performing at the other end of the room.

This last took place at ex-racing driver Cliff Davis' do, as it happened, in a mid-1960s knees-up. 'As I was sitting at the top table,' Hill later wrote, 'and she' – the stripper – 'was at the far end of the room, it meant running along the table to reach her. Well, unfortunately, as I was tripping daintily between the glasses – the dinner was over of course – one of the tables collapsed and I went with it. I fell onto one of the wine glasses, the tulip broke off and the stem went straight into my leg, just below the knee. Fortunately I was in my underpants at the time or else I would have ruined my trousers.' It did ruin his leg, however, and once the blood had been staunched, 'I walked out with my trousers over my arm and hailed a taxi to take me to the Charing Cross Hospital.' 'Hill Hurt At Party' yelped the *Daily Sketch*, without going into the sordid details; also: 'Motor Ace Cuts Leg.'

Did any of this matter? After all, Hill was doing no more than enjoy the traditional racing driver's birthright of partying and crumpet; Hawthorn would have approved.

On the other hand, there were now new, added, dimensions of hedonism and media invasiveness, which changed the mood somewhat. Naturally, Mike Hawthorn and Peter Collins and Stirling Moss had all surrounded themselves with pretty girls at one time or another: but the figure of the Racing Driver was starting to acquire some larger symbolic purchase on the popular imagination. Drivers were becoming jet-setting social animals, rather than filthy toilers in the grime and dust of provincial race tracks. Hill, with his appearances on radio and TV, his newspaper-worthy partying, his international presence, embodied the change. Moss said of Hill at the time: 'He is the archetype of the driver of the future, precise, smooth, knowing. Graham is just as smooth as he looks.' And it was a kind of smoothness that led to more partying, and even prettier girls. As his incredibly long-suffering wife, Bette, observed, 'Many girls threw themselves at him, they were so obvious – but often *very* beautiful.' How relaxed was she about this? Not terribly. She soon got 'sick of listening to these girls telling Graham how absolutely marvellous he was at motor racing – so fantastic and all that.' And yet there was nothing she, nor the other drivers' wives could do. 'We disliked the dolly birds. They were always around.' Hill, on the other hand, took their attentions as due tribute, and if there were no *dolly birds* to dance around him at the end of a race, or at a social function, he would be quite out of sorts.

There was another distinction between past and present. Whereas Collins and Hawthorn partied and raced and crashed through the 1950s and gave little thought to the future, Hill had a gloomier alter ego, sitting uneasily alongside Hill the party beast. This was Hill the joyless, grim-faced grafter, the man with his eye on the prize, the Hill of 1962, who, having joined the monumentally unsuccessful BRM in 1960, went on strike – as team leader – to make sure that the properly professional Tony Rudd was given full technical control, at the same time seeing to it that Raymond Mays (him, indeed) was sidelined. This was the Hill who listened seriously to Sir Alfred Owen (who had let it be known that he was sick of bankrolling a laughing-stock, and that if more success was not forthcoming – after a solitary victory at the Dutch GP in '59 – he would ditch the concern) and put his back into making the team work. This was Hill, not of the Tip Top Club, but of BRM.

What were BRM up to, at this point? The BRM P48 had appeared at the end of the 1950s, a flurried response to the Cooper revolution and predictably unsuccessful. The Formula, meanwhile, had been tampered with yet again, leaving normally aspirated engine capacities at a miserly $1^1/_2$ litres, and creating a new breed of dainty, somewhat compromised machines. But BRM, directed by Rudd and badgered by Hill, produced a potent enough little V8 with dragster-style stack pipes (which tended to break off in the heat of a race) and a neat green chassis for it to go in. It was called the P57 and, what do you know, thanks to the hard work and tenacity with which Hill helped to straighten it and the team out, BRM got their second-ever win in May 1962, at the Dutch GP at Zandvoort.

Bruce McLaren (Cooper-Climax), Jim Clark (Lotus-Climax) and Dan Gurney (Porsche) then took the next four GPs, before Hill surged back at the Nürburgring, followed by Monza, where 'a clear-cut and solid victory for Great Britain brought engineers and mechanics lining the Monza pits to their feet.' Clark took the US Grand Prix at Watkins Glen; and the pummelling season-long fight only ended when Hill won the last race in South Africa, sprinted twelve points clear of Jim Clark in the tables and took his first (and BRM's only) Championship. Fifteen years of breath-taking underachievement were wiped out, and all the 'Intrigue, jealousy and backbiting,' as Raymond Mays tragically characterised BRM's prinicipal features, were, for a time, forgotten.

This was a funny thing. Here, at the close of '62, was Moss, thirty-three years old, the most gifted driver of his day, nursing his injuries, now resigned to never landing the title. And here was Hill, thirty-three years old, solid but not dazzling, a bit of a wild card, in a BRM, up against the brilliant young Jim Clark in an equally brilliant Lotus, taking the Championship with four convincing wins to Clark's three. How had he managed it?

Well, in the years following the war, Hill trained as an engineer, and ever after kept a succession of little black books in which he noted down all aspects of his cars' setups, plus endless items of interest about the tracks he drove on. Having done his background preparations, he then turned into a pit-lane martinet, driving his mechanics mad, checking and rechecking mechanical details, insisting on things being done his way and his way only. ('He could be very, very demanding, very brief and abrupt.') He would go out and practise a single corner twenty times in succession, just to get it right. He liked his cars set up as hard and solid as they could be: no slack, no unnecessary give. Once in his overalls, he was as uptight and pedantic as his Armed Forces appearance suggested. John Surtees diplomatically put it like this: people thought 'Perhaps he was a little wavy in things he did off the track, but generally on the track he was at his steadiest.'

All of which was given an extra sharpness, an extra relief, by the fact that he had Jackie Stewart as team-mate at BRM, followed by Jim Clark as team-mate at Lotus – two of the greatest drivers ever, forever breathing down his neck. There he was, not only wrestling his way to the top of his profession, fighting his own imperfections, but doing it under the noses of two of the most naturally talented drivers of the post-war period. One feels he ought to get a special award for keeping cool in such company: but even allowing for that, his record is one that any driver would be proud to claim, including two World Championships, fourteen wins, thirteen pole positions, ten fastest laps, five Monacos, plus the unequalled triple – Formula One World Champion, winner of the Indianoplis 500, winner of the Le Mans 24 Hours. *No-one else* has managed this, not Moss, Fangio, Clark, Prost, Senna, Schumacher. *And* it beats the achievements of his contemporaries John Surtees, Denny Hulme, Phil Hill – and, by a mile, those of Mike Hawthorn. And he did it without compromising himself. 'He was a team-mate,' said Stewart, with evident affection, 'he was a friend, and absolutely always a gentleman.'

And yet, and yet. What was really going through gentleman Rob Walker's mind when he declared, 'My view of Graham as a driver was that he was definitely not talented. He did it by pure hard work and guts and slog'? Tony Rudd, likewise, argued that 'Graham, on his day, could beat Jimmy [Clark], but he wouldn't have those days very often,' which sounds pretty niggardly, coming from your former team director. 'Graham would have to be provoked to do really well,' Rudd would also say, as if he had a grudge against him. Moss may have called him 'smooth' and 'precise', but it was the *guts and slog* handle which would stick. Even when the great Walter Hayes, Vice President of Ford Europe, lauded Hill, it came out seasoned with reservations: 'Graham Hill was a great driver. Nobody will ever persuade me that he wasn't. I doubt if anybody else had more true grit and determination.' Typically enough, Hill announced after his successful 1966 Indy 500, 'I'm a bit surprised to have won,' thus ruefully pre-empting the jokes at his expense. It was a strange way to be successful.

And why did none of this ever seem to happen to Jack Brabham, Hill's rival and contemporary?

Brabham's record is virtually the same as Hill's, except that he managed to get three Championships out of *his* fourteen Grand Prix wins; and he never won at Indianapolis.

No question, Brabham was not only a redoubtable driver – having learned his trade on the dirt ovals of Australia, where the drivers 'were all lunatics', and the conditions were 'terrific driver training' – but was also a talented engineer, and made himself indispensable to Coopers soon after his arrival in Britain. And in 1966, he became the only driver to take the Championship in a car bearing his own name – a feat unlikely to be equalled. But why is it that diehard race fans are often happier to raise a toast to Sir Jack than Graham Hill?

A crucial, even decisive, factor, was that Brabham was always reticent to the point of taciturnity. This is a sensible way to be, in a sport in which garrulity can draw criticism (see Jackie Stewart) and manly modesty delights (see Fangio, Jim Clark). Once in a while, he would come out with the observation that there was 'No way you could call those 1,500-cc machines Formula One,' or that 'For two seasons, 1966–1967, Repco and Brabham had been on top of the world.' And he would make a dour joke at his own expense at the '66 Dutch GP, appearing on the grid leaning on a walking-stick and wearing a W. G. Grace fake beard, mocking the fact that he had turned forty a few days before. But these were only temporary lapses. The rest of the time he was famously cautious with money, and never anything less than plain-dealing, keep-his-own-counsel Jack Brabham, just as Denny Hulme was only ever a tough, balding racer who took the title – in a Brabham – in 1967.

In other words, Brabham was never a chattering media monkey in the way that Hill was perceived to be. Viewed purely reductively, he did all the right things for a surprisingly long time but still managed to quit driving before he became an embarrassment. He wasn't *Mr Motor Racing*, or the *Sport's Ambassador*, or any of the other soubriquets Hill attracted. Nor did he cavort with strippers, judge the *Miss World* contest (yes) or appear with shameless frequency on TV, being droll and curiously eel-like. Hill, on the other hand, did all these things, was an indefatigable toiler who stayed on far too long, played up the Loveable Card act rather too much and would apparently do anything to be the centre of attention.

And where was his beautiful race for 1962, his Championship year? Where was his Moss at Monaco? Apart from being on the telly, what did he do better than anyone else on the track? Where was the defining victory?

It was just a little bit too showbiz.

9

JIM CLARK, COLIN CHAPMAN AND SELLING YOUR SOUL

By 1963, Cooper was starting to fade on the Grand Prix scene. Brabham had taken back-to-back Championships in '59 and '60, driving Coopers, and had scared the life out of the dotards at Indianapolis in 1961 in a tweaked version of the Cooper T53 F1 car – the first rear-engined car to compete there effectively, running as high as third place, before finishing ninth. But after Cooper came Ferrari with Phil Hill; and after Ferrari came BRM with Graham Hill. And after *that*, it was down to the apotheosis of the *garagiste*, Colin Chapman with his Lotus 18, 21, and then, the delicious Lotus-Climax 25, with which Clark savaged the opposition (BRM, Ferrari, Brabham – making his own cars, now – and Cooper) right through the '63 season.

The tide was turning, again. Cooper may have had the single biggest idea of the modern Formula One age, by putting the engine at the back and making it work. But Chapman more than matched him with the sheer brilliance and fecundity of his innovations. The Big Idea with the Lotus 25? The monocoque chassis. Instead of building a cage-like space-frame, cladding it in metal, cradling the engine at the rear and sticking a driver in the middle, Chapman and chassis genius Mike Costin had devised a stupendously effective all-in-one structure for the 1962 season: discarding the space frame entirely, welding sections of sheet metal together for the sides and tanks, with steel bulkheads front and back to hang the suspension on. It was vastly stiffer than the old spaceframes, much, much lighter, too, and, being generally a neater exploitation of resources, smaller and with a reduced frontal area, therefore good for wind resistance.

If the whole package wasn't quite as earth-shattering as Cooper's original insight (and pre-war, there had been one or two attempts at competition monococque construction; while Lancia's inspirational Lambda touring car dated back to 1922), it ran it pretty close. Allegedly, Cooper took a look at the Lotus-Climax 25 at the Belgium GP at Spa, and asked where the chassis was. He then watched Hill take the '62 title in a conventional spaceframe BRM.

But there were no such difficulties for 1963. Suddenly, we were in the Promised Land. There was Jim Clark, who had seamlessly taken over Moss's title as The Most Gifted Driver in Formula One, driving for the most exciting team in motor racing, in a car which was not only brilliant in design and execution, but which *looked* terrific – sleek, purposeful, free of clutter, like a 1950s jet fighter. Clark won a preposterous seven out of ten Grandes Épreuves in '63, with seven pole positions, and six fastest laps. And there was Chapman, *Il Miglior Fabbro*, at his right hand.

In fact, the dynamic relationship between driver and constructor reached some kind of perfection at this point. One of Clark's mechanics observed that his 'technical ability and feel for what the car was doing were phenomenal. It was uncanny. Unique. He knew when something was wrong. He'd feel a slight vibration in the rear and we'd pull the car about and find nothing. He'd insist something was still amiss and later we'd discover a wheel bearing was going.' But this hyper-awareness was, in turn, predicated on Clark's capacity to penetrate the essence of whatever car Chapman gave him. Not everyone could get the best out of a Lotus. You had to know how to access its tricksy little soul; and Clark could.

And then, just to make it even more special, there was the fact that Clark and Lotus were both so very flaky: both teetering on the brink of disaster, personal and financial, on an almost daily basis, for years.

Jim Clark first. On-track, he drove with the kind of effortless fluency that defied categorisation, whatever the car. Off-track, he was barely able to get dressed in the mornings. He had trouble picking a tie to wear; he couldn't decide where to eat lunch; he chewed his nails to the quick, fretting; he never knew which girl to stick with. His longest-serving girlfriend, Sally Stokes, noted with stoical understatement, 'When he stepped out of the car – that was a sign for this indecisiveness to take over.' Ditto, from Peter Warr, of Team Lotus: 'He could get befuddled through this extraordinary indeciveness.'

Actually, he was even capable of freezing up at the wheel, provided he was away from the racetrack. Despite setting some kind of unofficial speed record from his home in the Scottish Borders to the Team Lotus HQ in Cheshunt, he was repeatedly flummoxed by a particular fork in the road about two-thirds of the way along the route. Either side of this fork was usable, but the imposition of choice so threw him that, more than once, he simply ploughed on into the grass in the middle. Or again, sitting in a rented car at a single-track level crossing in Florida, with Jackie Stewart, Clark stared for minutes at the lone railroad track, stretching for miles in either direction, empty of trains. According to Stewart, 'He glanced at me warily and said, "Well, what do you think?" I thought I must have missed something. So I looked left and right and saw again that there was nothing within miles of us. He was still sitting there in a quandry. "I think it's safe to go, Jim," I said. "OK", he said, and we continued on our way.'

He discovered, once he made it to the big time of Grand Prix racing, that he could get girls with dependable ease; but then got into an ethical tangle with the precepts engendered by his Scottish upbringing. He would sit in his motorhome at the track, while women wandered around outside; all he had to do was 'smile or make a little move, and one would come, and he would take her out for dinner and then she would be his'. But then he'd be struck by the paralysing terror that his clean-living, buttoned-up, Scottish farmer relations would find out about this laxity and give him hell. As the – highly respectable – Sally Stokes, observed, 'If he was being photographed, I was careful to keep out of it. He told me he did not want his parents to get the wrong idea.' Or, as Jackie Stewart put it, 'He was really insecure.'

Nor was he even quite sure whether he liked to race for its own sake – pure and simple, the twenty-eight-year-old Clark haring blithely around one afternoon in April, '64, driving a Lotus 19, followed by an Elan, followed by a Lotus Cortina, all at the same meeting, winning every race he entered – or whether he really wanted the kind of deliciously burdensome wealth a race like Indianapolis brought with it.

In 1963, he went to the Brickyard with Lotus for the first time. There was a sweltering controversy with the ultimate winner, Parnelli Jones, but second-placed Clark not only managed not to get caught up in the fight, but also congratulated himself on how much he had earned, notwithstanding: $56,000 for, as he put it, 'turning left 800 times'. When he won, two years later, the deal was that he got paid $150 for every lap he led. He led for 190 out of the 200 laps. 'It was so funny,' he observed. 'I was like a cash register. I kept going around thinking, click, click, $150, $150.'

It's tempting to see these inner frictions as the product of a childhood spent in the farming communities of the Scottish Borders, with four protective sisters, an upright and doughty mother, education at the smart and socially conservative Loretto School just outside Edinburgh, followed by admission into an adult world of livestock auctions and rural decencies and cups of tea. The only things to disturb these timeless verities would have been occasional, delightfully amateur saloon car escapades with a team known as the Border Reivers. These would in turn generate a burst of disapproval from the family, who regarded such things with deep distaste and wished Jim would give them up. It was an essentially genteel existence, one whose interior values Clark could never quite leave behind, and which became more and more of a contradiction, the more successful and worldly he became.

Did Clark eventually start to believe in his own myth? It was no use asking him, for instance, how he managed to drive the way he did. He wouldn't, or couldn't, say. Some mixture of reflexes, eyesight, supreme balance, fitness (he had forearms like a navvy) and precision accounted for it – but that would have been true for any number of his fellow drivers. All anyone could come up with, was that he possessed something so special that even an unsentimentalist like Denis Jenkinson (who had fearlessly navigated Moss's Merc in the Mille Miglia) could say that Clark racing in the wet was as deft and fastidious as 'a cat on a shelf full of china'. And as time went on, and the head-turning adulation and the money and the fame and the girls all expanded to fill his available space, he changed – evolving from a modest, smiling, tea-drinking, cardigan-wearing Scotsman into a gourmet, a wine connoisseur, used to living abroad more than in Britain, serious, keen to avoid income tax, increasingly conscious of his own worth. His mate Jabby Crombac observed around about this time that Clark 'could be a complete bastard if you stepped upon his toes', and there was no question that with age and celebrity came a gradual extinction of that happy innocence with which he had regarded the world at the end of the 1950s.

How much of this was then down to Colin Chapman? The two cannot be parted, even after death. Find a picture of Jim Clark in his heyday, and the odds are that Chapman will be in the same shot, crouching down beside the car in which Clark sits, explaining a point about the setup; or rapt in conversation somewhere on the pit wall; or, as often as not, with both of them grinning ecstatically after a win, Chapman sometimes riding on the rear suspension as Clark tools round the track, always there, always at Clark's shoulder. For Heaven's sake, Chapman was there at the very start of Clark's racing career: the Border Reivers wanted to acquire a Formula 2 Lotus for Clark to drive, but the sight of a wheel dropping off Graham Hill's similar machine made Clark decide, like so many drivers, that any Lotus was too dubious to risk, and that he would stick to sports cars for the time being. A year later, and after a fundamental revision of opinion, he was signed to Chapman's team.

Which made Chapman what, exactly? Clark's brother-in-arms, one half of the Likely Lads, his soul mate? Or his smiling exploiter, a worldly, even Mephistophelean, genius, who spotted Clark's driving talent, battened on to him and drained him dry?

Chapman was some eight years older than Clark. He grew

up in an immediately post-war London, went to University College to read engineering and did his bit for the economy – while still a teenager – by flogging old cars in Warren Street, before starting to make his own sporting Lotus specials in a lockup in Hornsey.

You had to hand it to him: the boy had flair. It only took a few years before his Mark Eleven sports cars were winning races, while his Mark Thirteen performed magnificently at Le Mans in 1957, winning the Index of Performance. What he didn't do, of course, was move the engine from the front to the back. While Cooper was turning out the 'bob-tailed' mid-engined sports cars of the mid-1950s, Lotus was still doing it the traditional way, engine first, with the 11s and the 13s. However brilliant Chapman was, that one trans-forming insight had not come to him.

Unsurprisingly, he referred to John Cooper as 'that bloody blacksmith'. Cooper – who had great respect for Chapman's ideas, if not his methods – retaliated by calling Lotus 'that crazy lot from Hornsey', and suggesting that every Lotus sold should come with a free welding kit. But it didn't take Chapman long to adapt to the new dispensation and, by 1960, he had his first Grand Prix win with Moss in the Lotus 18: the legendary giant-killing of Monaco. In the same year, Clark, who had already been driving Lotus in junior formulae, got his first F1 drive, still with Lotus, at the Dutch Grand Prix. The connection was made.

It was, in fact, Chapman's great good fortune, as the new king of the *garagistes*, to be active at a time when conditions in Britain were such that clever and inventive and gifted people were happy not to go into large-scale (and increas-ingly moribund) manufacturing industry, but take their chances in the compact and fast-moving world of racing car construction. It was a peculiarly British thing: we couldn't do the big stuff particularly well, but where driving talent met ingenuity plus craft skills, *and* had a seasoning of back-to-the-wall, small-time improvisation about it, we were in our element.

So if Clark was being tipped for greatness by this stage, Chapman, too, was acquiring a reputation; partly for extreme cleverness, partly for excessive daring. *Keep it light* was the guiding belief, but as Keith Duckworth (of the Ford-Cosworth DFV engine) noted, 'Colin was a brilliant conceptual engineer, but he had no idea of limits and fit, the details.' In practice, this led to Stirling Moss having to have his car welded up on the Monaco grid; it led the hapless Innes Ireland to complain bitterly about the failure rates of the Lotuses he had to drive, shortly before being ignominiously sacked as team leader in favour of Clark; it was a Lotus which folded up around Moss in his catastrophic '62 crash. When Jackie Stewart briefly drove a Lotus in a non-Championship Formula One race, one driveshaft snapped in two, while the other buckled irretrievably: 'Jackie decided that Chapman made unsafe cars and never again drove a Lotus.' Or, as Graham Hill would later put it, 'If one of my rear tyres overtakes me, I know I'm in a Lotus.'

The cars were light to the point of frailty; as were Chapman's finances. 'The history of Lotus was littered with scams,' was one way of putting it; and it was a combustible mix, what with Chapman paring down the engineering at the same time as he was shuffling slivers of money from one dark corner of the Lotus empire to another. The Norfolk HQ was suffused with a perpetual atmosphere of mild commercial panic, old racing models being sold off as soon as they looked even slightly dubious, partly to make room at the works, partly to keep the cashflow from breaking down. In some ways, it was an East Anglian version of life among the

Ferraris at Modena, the crucial difference being that Enzo Ferrari had relatively little to do with the actual design of his Grand Prix cars; nor with the racing – other than to impose his idea of team orders on whoever he employed. As a brooding, totemic presence, he wrote his personality everywhere and on everything, but often kept himself at one remove from the action, actually staying away from the track on race day.

Chapman, conversely, was ubiquitous: designing the cars, overseeing their construction, scurrying off to test tracks and race meetings, blagging components, signing dodgy cheques, and all the time hustling Jim Clark – a terminal ditherer wrapped in a world of purposeful chaos – to new and greater achievements.

In this febrile environment, not unnaturally, Chapman took quite a lot of pills, just to stay upright. Ron Hickman, one of Chapman's lieutenants, remarked that 'Colin was completely open about his use of uppers and downers. His use was brought on not only by the incredibly long days he worked, and the broken sleep, but also by his often crossing twenty time zones in a few days. Most of us were more understanding than horrified.' He then turned his pilled-up charms on his workforce, his drivers, his creditors, his sponsors, in order to get exactly what he wanted. He was 'charismatic, which meant that he could get the best out of people right to the time he wore them down. He would drain every last ounce from a person.' He was wired and endlessly competitive even when it came to bread-throwing contests in restaurants. Chapman 'would be the first to start throwing rolls', declaring loudly that Team Lotus were the best roll-throwers in the business, while at the same time making sure 'that you first dipped your bread roll in wine', in order to splatter the opposition a bit more effectively.

There was team-building, there was soggy-bread-roll-throwing, and there was living in each other's pockets, for at least half the year. Team Lotus finances were so tight that not only did the team swap first-class plane tickets (when they got them off organisers or sponsors) for economy class, pocketing the difference, they also shared hotel rooms on a regular basis. At Indianapolis, 1963, Clark and Chapman had one room, twin beds. One night, Clark went on the prowl, got himself a girl, brought his conquest back to that same hotel room. Finding Chapman already in bed, asleep, Clark and the girl had a noisy shower together, before jumping into Clark's (American, king-size) bed. Chapman was now wide awake, grimly pretending to be unconscious. The girl said, 'What about him' – pointing to Chapman – 'won't we wake him up?' To which Clark replied, 'Don't worry about him – the silly bugger never wakes up!' At breakfast the following morning, a red-eyed Chapman groaned to a Lotus co-worker, 'God knows what time I got to sleep.'

That was just how things were. In the days before Formula One discovered big-money sponsorship, quite a few teams obliged their staff and drivers to share digs – getting on well or badly, depending on team politics at any given moment. What was remarkable about Clark and Chapman was that, now matter how much time they spent together, no matter what pressures Chapman put on Clark, no matter what nervous disorientations Clark was suffering from, they rarely fell out. According to Rob Walker, 'Jim was probably the only driver that Chapman was really fond of. I never saw them have a row.'

The upshot was this. Clark absolutely pulverised the opposition in 1963, taking the Drivers' title by twenty-five points from Graham Hill. In '64, ex-biker John Surtees took the title for Ferrari by one point from Hill (with Clark in third place) and became the only man in history to win World Championships on two and four wheels. In 1965, Clark and Lotus came roaring back, winning six out of ten races, and leaving Hill the runner-up again. It looked like a marriage made in Heaven. How long could they keep it going?

10

THE TRACKS

By the mid-1960s, the geography of Formula One was starting to acquire some consistency. The cars came from England; or Italy. The drivers came from all over, but were based in Europe. And the circuits which dominated the Grand Prix season were the hard core of Monaco, Silverstone and Brands Hatch, Nürburgring, Spa-Francorchamps, Monza, Zandvoort.

Which meant that, clearly, the old, improvised, anywhere-there's-room ethos of earlier days was pretty much defunct. Jump back to the 1950s, and any list of Formula One venues would have included: the Oscar Gálvez track in Buenos Aires; Bremgarten, near Bern; Pedralbes, near Barcelona; Pescara, on the east coast of Italy; Boavista, near Oporto; Ain Diab, in Casablanca. And these were just the venues for the Grandes Épreuves. Non-Championship F1 races happened at all kinds of unpredictable locations. Whatever happened to Syracuse? Dundrod? Pau? Bari? Gavea? Aix-les-Bains? Crystal Palace? Albi? Eläintarhanajot? And what on earth were they like when you got there?

Syracuse, for instance, in the south-eastern corner of Sicily, was a $3^1/_2$-mile-long street circuit, shaped a bit like a wedge of cheese, threading its way around what Cicero called 'the greatest Greek city and the most beautiful of them all', a key settlement in Magna Graecia and with a cathedral dating back to the seventh century. The exact opposite of Silverstone, in fact. Tony Brooks made his little piece of motor racing history there in 1955, when he won his non-Championship race in a Connaught. Spectators liked it, because they were right on top of the racing; drivers quite liked it, because, being a street circuit, there was no room for error. As Brooks put it, 'At Syracuse there is none of this business of using a foot of grass, as on an English airfield circuit, and then bobbing back.' Instead of grass and open spaces, there were things made for destroying cars: concrete walls, trees, telegraph poles, picturesque buildings, an awful lot of bumps. The track punished you.

And what went for Syracuse went, in many ways, for the others. On the old road circuit at Albi, in the south of France, the track went sprinting up through the unyielding bricks and stonemasonry of the village of St Antoine, before turning a 320° hairpin at St Juery, going over a level crossing and then launching cars into the air over a vicious hump on the way down to Montplaisir Corner. Pau, in the Pyrenees, was – still is – a street circuit in the Monaco style, many delightful buildings, absolutely nowhere to go if you make a mistake. Gavea, at Rio de Janeiro, was known as 'The Devil's See-saw', or alternatively, 'The Devil's Trampoline', on account of its unspeakable hairpins – five of them together in the space of half a mile. Ain Diab, west of Casablanca, another street circuit, had a fine stretch along the shoreline, was very fast and extremely dangerous, being both quick and cramped. Poor Stuart Lewis-Evans burned to death there in 1958, and they never raced Formula One again. Bremgarten was lined with trees, had an unpredictable surface and unnervingly wonky light conditions; but at least it only menaced drivers for a few years, given that the Swiss banned all motor racing in 1955. Dundrod, in Northern Ireland, was narrow, way up in the hills, and had a surface that was worse than emery paper for wearing out tyres. Pescara (birthplace of Gabriele d'Annunzio) was a kind of Italian Nürburgring, terribly long, terribly dangerous: Moss won there in '57, a non-Championship race, but the place was littered with straw bales, wandering goats and vulnerable spectators. Eläintarhanajot was a mixture of cramped street racing and (like Donington) dense parkland filled with completely hittable trees; it was also in Finland.

So what happened to all these venues? There was no mystery about it: as the cars got faster, so the circuits had to offer more consistent layouts, better surfaces, more space to run off, better protection against hazards. Around this time Stirling Moss said that he *didn't* advocate 'taking out trees, for instance, eliminating things that make for interest', claiming that he and other professional drivers 'like the natural hazards. We'd like to race around Hyde Park or Central Park without any changes at all in the topography. We accept the hazards, as at Monaco, of hitting a building or going over a drop; after all, it's no fun gambling for match-sticks.' But there was risk-taking and risk-taking. Crashing was okay. Dying horribly – in the manner of Lewis-Evans, or Orjan Atteberg, crushed by his own car at Eläintarhanajot – wasn't. The old tracks had to go. Soon, only Monaco would be left of the street circuits, sustained by its ineffable glamour as well as its historic centrality.

Not that this meant that the other, bigger, tracks were very much safer or less capricious. The terrors of the Nürburgring were well known from before the war. But so were those of Spa-Francorchamps, the 'Ring's 9-mile-long junior sibling.

This was on the Belgian side of the border, but not that far from the great German track, and sharing many of its characteristics – including some very fast sections, unpredictably awful weather, extensive hilly scenery and a persistent reek of danger. Many drivers loved (still do) its stupendous challenges. Others thought it was something you were grateful to get through alive. The Masta Kink alone was enough to cause nightmares: a vicious twiddle in the long straight between Malmédy and Stavelot, approached at top speed – 180 mph, say – which forced you to jump to the right, then left, then straight on again, leaving you (you hoped) heading flat out towards the Stavelot hairpin. And this on a track lined with about as many hard objects as you can think of, almost nothing in the way of crash protection, with marshals and safety crew both untrained and strung out at odd distances, plus a good chance of a downpour at some point in the race.

Zandvoort, near Haarlem in Holland, was evidently much less terrifying. But it was a trifle cranky. Home of the Dutch GP, it was a track built on roads once laid down by the invading German Wehrmacht, containing a bend named *Tarzan* and was so close to the sea (separated, in fact, by a long, straight, dune) that sand frequently blew across the track, playfully ruining tyre grip and filling engine intakes with grit. Or there was Watkins Glen, a funky old track in upstate New York, with a corrugated surface and some real he-man bends; where the starting and prize money made the cash on offer at the European tracks look like loose change; where the fall colours lit up the countryside; and where races were started and finished by a man called 'Tex' Hopkins, who chomped a comedy cigar and wore a lavender suit. Or Reims, on-off home to the French GP, a kind of poor man's Le Mans (and similarly old-school, an old open-road circuit), with a fantastically long slipstreamers' straight, shimmering heat, and nothing between you and the open fields on either side, except possibly a hoarding for Total petrol and a Frenchman with a camera . . .

Or, consider Monza. The name alone has to be one of the most potent and evocative words in the whole of motor racing. And with good reason. Like Spa and the Nürburgring, the track has tremendous historical resonance, dating back to well before the Second World War. Unlike Spa and the Nürburgring, Monza is really only about one thing: the lust for sheer speed. If you want to hit 200 mph and more, Monza is the place to do it. And it is also a great place to crash.

The original layout saw twenty-seven spectators and one driver killed in an appalling accident in the 1928 Grand Prix. Three drivers were killed in the 1933 GP. After the war, the circuit was completely rebuilt – still as a temple to speed – only for Alberto Ascari to die there in 1955, and for Taffy von Trips to die in 1961, in a catastrophe at the Curva Parabolica in which fourteen spectators were also killed, after von Trips' Ferrari came into contact with Clark's Lotus. The famous banked curves (as at Brooklands, or Avus) were still there in the mid-1960s, but only in the background: concrete expressions of risk, now shunned by the Formula One drivers. The vast straight, on the other hand, leading out of Parabolica and heading down to the Curva Grande, still meant nothing less than a sweltering drag race followed by a hugely fast right-hand bend. From the opening of the track in 1922, up to 1965, some twenty-five drivers lost their lives, trying to bring Monza to heel. Well into the 1990s, Professor Sid Watkins – Formula One's revered safety Godfather – still found much to detest about the circuit. 'It is *the* place,' he wrote, mordantly, 'I approach with resigned reluctance; it is my personal nightmare of the year.' Monza was, and would remain, a sacred monster.

In other words – and this is the real issue – although the really dodgy, small-time circuits, the idiosyncratic non-Championship tracks of the 1950s, had been edged out as the sport became bigger, the ones that did remain were pretty much the way Fangio, Ascari, Hawthorn knew them from a decade earlier. So it was said of Jim Clark that he 'caressed the Nürburgring into surrender' – when he won there in '65, fifteen seconds ahead of second-place Graham Hill, leading all the way from pole position *and* setting the fastest lap, nearly a minute quicker than Fangio's time in '57: an advertisement of modernity. But Fangio, going back a whole racing generation, would have felt entirely familiar with not only the track that Clark caressed into surrender, but the bleak absence of safety precautions. The view would have been the same for both drivers: pine trees, concrete fence posts, rocks, earth banks, all lining the tarmac for mile after mile, only an occasional under-prepared track marshal to help if things went badly wrong.

It was the same at Monaco, where pre-war-style sandbags were still being tied optimistically around stone bollards to cushion the effects of a shunt, and where there were plenty of those surprisingly hard straw bales to smash into. Even at comfortable old Brands Hatch, the earth banks and steel poles (holding up ads for Girling and Dunlop) were only ever a few feet away from your relatively low-grip tyres. It was a world, according to Jackie Stewart, of 'grass banks that were launch pads, things you went straight into, trees that were unprotected'. It was a world of hazards.

But the cars – hadn't the cars got safer, even if the tracks hadn't? Well, they had, of course, evolved, enormously. Fangio sat up at the wheel of a Ferrari or Maserati, in a gale of dust, engine heat, pulverised brake linings, small stones, the whole lot four-wheel-drifting with the uneasy composure of a power-boat on a lake. When Clark raced, on the other hand, he was in the supine, modern position, only his head getting the worst buffetings, the steering-wheel tiny in comparison with the dustbin-lids Fangio had to use, the gearlever a stub by his hand, his car snipping out the corners. He also, by the second half of the 1960s, had twice as much bhp coming out of the engine as Fangio, plus a combination of chassis and tyres that Fangio would have marvelled at.

And yet the cars of the mid-1960s weren't an awful lot *safer* than the ones of the mid-1950s. Like Fangio, like Moss, like Hawthorn, like all of them, Clark wore no safety belts, had no proper flameproof overalls, was surrounded by raw petrol slapping around in easily ruptured plain steel tanks, could find himself on the wrong end of a catastrophic tyre failure or mechanical collapse at any time. He sat in a mono-coque that was stronger than the old spaceframes, but which was probably going to experience higher-impact speeds in the event of a crash; and which had the same fantastically hard objects hurtling towards it, the same tough old circuits. Things were changing; and yet nothing had changed.

11

THE SPANISH GRAND PRIX, JARAMA, 12 MAY 1968

Why the 1968 Spanish GP? Was it a great race? Did it herald the arrival of a new driving star? Was it a disaster? Or was it just one of those moments which now acts as, not just a snapshot, an encapsulation of where Formula One had got to, but also a harbinger of the way things were going to be: an emblematic event?

It was, first of all, an occasion overhung by tragedy.

On 7 April 1968, Jim Clark was killed, driving a Lotus, in a Formula 2 race at Hockenheim. There are certain observations that routinely come to mind whenever Clark's death is recalled. The most common, among the racing fraternity, is that Clark was indestructible, the one man who could cheat death: if it could happen to him, then everyone felt their mortality that bit more keenly.

The second observation, common among spectators of the sport, is, what was he doing flogging around in a Formula 2 race anyway? He was Formula One World Champion in 1963 and '65; he was well paid; in 1968, he had the best car on the grid and every prospect of winning a third Championship. Why was he at Hockenheim at all?

In answer to this second point – well, there was a lot less job demarcation in the 1960s. Grand Prix drivers took part in all kinds of other events, much as they used to do in the '50s. They appeared at Indianapolis (Clark actually missed Monaco in '65, in order to go and win the Indy 500). They took part in the Tasman Series – an off-season series of races held in Australia and New Zealand. They raced in Formula Two – Hill, Brabham, Clark, Stewart – for money, and because they were contracted to. They raced in sports cars. They raced in the Can-Am series. There weren't so many Grands Prix to get through – twelve in 1968, as opposed to seventeen in 2009 – and they liked to keep busy. That was what they did.

As to the first point. Well, Clark had survived many a spin, many an incident, both racing and in practice, thanks to reflexes and a genius for interpreting situations. But he knew perfectly well that death was all around him and that dealing with it was just part of the job. 'I don't think I am callous,' he said, speaking of track fatalities, 'but I have been blessed with a bad memory for such things.' A day after someone else's death, 'You feel a little better.' Three days later, 'You start packing your bags for another race.' His own demise was the result, almost certainly, of a sudden tyre deflation at around 170 mph, an event which turned him from a driver into a passenger, somersaulting through the air, then smashing into a tree. There was nothing he could have done about it. He knew that it could happen to him, just like it could happen to anyone.

At the time of his death, he had won more Grands Prix and taken more pole positions than any other driver in the sport. He was thirty-two.

Faced with this disaster, Colin Chapman went to pieces. Later, he would say of Formula One: 'I can't say I've ever felt quite the same about it since '68.' At the time, he simply disappeared, not even turning up for the Spanish GP. The rest of the team arrived, but no Chapman. 'Nobody knew where Colin was,' said said Bob Sparshott of Team Lotus. 'It was Graham Hill who pulled the team together.'

But Hill already had plenty on his plate, even before Clark died. For a start, he and the rest of Team Lotus were still getting to grips with the Lotus 49 and its magical new Ford-Cosworth DFV 3-litre engine, which had first appeared a year earlier: powerful, awkward and destined to become the most successful racing engine of all time.

At the Dutch GP in '67, the first competitive outing of the new combination, Hill had taken pole position, a blistering three and a half seconds quicker than the previous year's time. Clark, meanwhile, won the race (after Hill's engine had given up) and set the fastest lap, apparently without even trying. But he was trying, quite hard. When Hill first tested the Lotus 49 Cosworth DFV in early 1967, he announced, cheerfully, 'It's got some poke: not a bad old tool.' But Clark was much less flattering. 'When the power comes in at 6,500 rpm,' he complained, 'it does so with such a bang that the car is almost uncontrollable. You either have power or you haven't.' The car and engine both looked fantastic: but the chassis had its quirks (including a marked tendency to dive under braking); and the engine was clearly intractable.

It was also less than reliable. Lubrication snags let to major failures, and the major failures meant that, however rapid the new Lotus was, the 1967 Championship went to Denny Hulme in an unburstable Brabham-Repco – completing a highly impressive back-to-back with Jack Brabham, who had taken the '66 title. Still. As the engine reliability improved, confidence grew. Clark took the opening race of the '68 calendar, at South Africa, the last Grand Prix he would win.

In the meantime, though, Chapman had taken another giant conceptual leap forward. The Lotus 49s which raced in South Africa were painted a conventional, chaste, British racing green with a yellow Lotus stripe down the middle. The single Team Lotus car which turned up some four months later, in Spain, was epically different in appearance. It had a white lower half, a red upper half, and a gold-painted nose. An escutcheon on each side read 'GOLD LEAF TEAM LOTUS' and in the centre of this was an image of the John Player & Sons iconic cigarette-packet sailor boy: an only slightly camp naval rating in a beard, surrounded by a ship's life ring. The whole effect was as tasteful as a gangster's bracelet and as unexpected as a macaw in a suburban back garden. Gold Leaf Team Lotus, as everyone had to get used to calling them, had clearly sold their soul.

Not that there wasn't already commercial sponsorship in 1968 – there was plenty of it. Tyre companies, petrol and oil companies, spark plug manufacturers, all contributed to the budgets of the Formula One teams – around £50,000 per team, when put together. As a rule, though, any promotional logos were still confined to nothing more than a label sewn onto a driver's overalls, or perhaps a modest sticker on the side of the car. No one thought that the time would come when Grand Prix cars would be tarted up like Indy 500 competitors – with their acne of sponsors' logos, and their primary funding from business envelope manufacturers. No, the graphical palette available to teams at the end of 1967 was pretty much the same as that available in 1957: cars were painted green, red, blue, silver or white. And they could put stripes – white, yellow, or red – on their machines if they liked.

But Chapman and Lotus led the way – albeit in an entirely unpremeditated, spontaneous fashion. As it happened, there was a vague rumour going around the Lotus offices, early in '68, that the John Player Tobacco Company was interested in using motor racing as a new, promotional tool. Inconveniently enough, Esso and BP had just dropped out of F1 sponsorship – each having spent up to £500,000 a year on the sport – so money was definitely on teams' minds. Andrew Ferguson, a Lotus exec, went to the Player's HQ in Nottingham for an exploratory talk. To everyone's astonishment, he emerged two hours later, clutching a deal.

After that, things moved fast. The first major European outing for the new-look fag-packet Lotus 49 was at the Race of Champions, Brands Hatch, in March 1968. Hill was the only Lotus driver who made it to the starting grid and went on to have an uninspired race, retiring with a broken driveshaft. The organisers, on the other hand, were sent into mild hysteria by the lurid object on the racetrack. They made Lotus cover up the Player's sailor boy logo with tape, even *black-flagging* one of the team's two cars during practice for going out with the tape missing. Later on, the sailor boy was replaced by an unexceptionable Union Jack – but, even so, the BBC and ITV sports departments started grumbling that they might not be able to show motor races of any kind if the cars were covered in ads.

The Spanish organisers were similarly queasy about the Gold Leaf sponsorship and likewise had parts of it covered over. But by then, there were bigger things on everyone's mind. There Hill was, driving the sole Team Lotus car, with Clark dead, the grief-stricken Chapman vanished, the team disorientated. Black sticky tape was neither here nor there. From Hill's point of view, about the only good news was that the worryingly fast Jackie Stewart, now driving for Ken Tyrrell and his Matra-Cosworth team, was out of the race with a fractured wrist.

On the other hand, McLaren had just put down their marker for the future by producing their first Grand Prix car, the McLaren-Cosworth M7A. Everyone who saw it agreed that it was an extremely thorough, competent design, very smart-looking (bright orange!), and beautifully built. It also had Bruce McLaren himself to drive it, along with Denny Hulme, the reigning world champion. And it had won at the Race of Champions, a few weeks earlier. McLaren then spoiled the glamorous visual effect of the car somewhat by lumping on a couple of side-pannier fuel tanks, and sawing off the nose to reduce the chance of collisions round the squiggles of the Jarama track, but you knew that they meant business.

Practice worked out badly for Hill. He ended up sixth on the grid, with Chris Amon taking pole for Ferrari, and with both the McLarens ahead of him. But this was one of those times when sheer grit – the thing that Hill possessed more of, probably, than anyone else on the track – was the thing to have.

The race started. Various people took the lead, including Jean-Pierre Beltoise in the Matra-Ford, and Mexican daredevil Pedro Rodriguez in a BRM. One by one, however, they succumbed to mechanical collapse, or, in Rodriguez's case, to accident. Not only did Rodriguez fly off the track after hitting a patch of oil and crash into some safety netting – he then had to watch as a mob of happy spectators 'descended on the car like vultures and . . . stripped off the mirrors, seat, windscreen and nose cowling before the mechanics arrived.'

Hill, meanwhile, didn't hit anything, go off the track, or break down. With admirable calm, he waited out the war of attrition going on around him and when Amon's Ferrari 312 packed up on the fifty-eighth lap, he moved seamlessly into the lead, held on to it and won.

After the race, he was understandably ecstatic. 'I had absolutely no trouble at all – the car went perfectly.' Ever the compulsive note-taker, he calculated that he had changed gear 1,350 times and then admitted, 'We badly needed this win just now.' Lotus badly needed the win, *he* badly needed the win: his last GP victory had been two and half years earlier, at Watkins Glen, and he was now thirty-nine years old. But he had kept his nerve, done what was needed and, indeed, set himself on the way to his second World Championship. 'After practice,' said Bob Sparshott, with sincere admiration, 'Graham took the entire team to dinner at a top restaurant in Madrid. Next day, Graham won the race.'

Maybe Hill never had a clutch of exquisite wins under his belt and the reverence of the racing *cognoscenti*. But for leadership, grace under pressure and, most important, delivering the goods, you'd have to say that the '68 Spanish Grand Prix showed him at his absolute best. In answer to an earlier question: this was, in fact, his beautiful race.

12

THAT LITTLE SCOTSMAN: STEWART AND THE PROBLEM OF DEATH

With Jim Clark gone, there was clearly a vacancy for the position of Best Driver In The World. How surprising was it that the spot should be filled by another Scotsman? Clark grew up in Duns, just west of Berwick-upon-Tweed; Jackie Stewart grew up in Dumbarton, to the north-west of Glasgow, about 100 miles from Clark's home. Like Clark, Stewart's background was respectable Scottish middle-class, with a family who (again, like Clark's) disapproved of motor racing. Stewart, though, suffered from none of Clark's internal schisms. Once he took to motor sport, he moved with typical consistency through sports cars and Formula 3, before (having turned down Lotus for F1 purposes) signing up for BRM, with Graham Hill as team leader and unofficial older brother.

As Stewart's career evolved, Clark – three years older than Stewart – could not help but notice the lively, garrulous young man who was starting to make such an impact. Indeed, at the time of his death, even he was starting to fret at the challenge Stewart represented. 'If I had to say which Scot was the best,' Jack Brabham later mused, 'I would have to say that, although they were both top drivers, Jackie had a better knowledge and feel for the car than Jimmy.' This sounds almost sacrilegious. But Brabham's reasoning was this: 'Jimmy was very reliant on Colin Chapman, and as Jimmy drove when the Lotus was the top car with the works engines from Coventry Climax and Cosworth, that also became an unbeatable combination.' Stewart had some good cars, in other words, but no Mephistophelean genius at his shoulder: for him, it was more a question of working effectively with what he was given.

He picked off his first Championship win at Monza in '65, and ended the year – his rookie season – in third place in the drivers' table. John Surtees had taken the Championship for Ferrari in 1964 – Scuderia Ferrari wouldn't see the title again until the mid-1970s – and Clark won it for Lotus in '65. Nevertheless, Stewart was optimistic about the '66 season. It wasn't so long since Hill had taken the Championship for BRM; the team was in reasonable spirits; they had a neat chassis to work with, and the promise of a new, wonderfully powerful 3-litre H16 engine – all ready for the latest engine capacity about-face in the Formula regulations.

Unfortunately, the H16 turned out to be an echo of the old V16 of 1951. It was an insanely complex solution to a given problem, could not be manufactured to the correct tolerances, and was unreliable and unbelievably heavy. It took six mechanics to lift it, and Stewart was believed to have compared it unfavourably to a ship's anchor. It was also late in development, so the team had to use a bored-out version of the old $1^1/_2$-litre V8 in the interim. In fact, Stewart won at Monaco, Moss-style: the first race of the calendar and another portent of the young Scot's future triumphs. It was, though, very nearly, his last ever win.

The next race was the Belgian GP at Spa. It rained, hard, as hard as it possibly could. Visibility was non-existent. Having qualified his P261 an impressive-enough third on the grid, Stewart took off into the weather and never finished the first lap. At something over 150 mph, he went off the track at the Masta Kink, crashed down a ravine and wrapped the car round the buttress of a stone barn. The steering wheel crushed him in his seat, the fuel tanks ruptured, and he sat in a bath of petrol, waiting for the whole lot to go up in one enormous fireball, frying him where he lay.

His great good fortune was this: Graham Hill lost it at the same spot, collected the spin before he hit anything, ground to a halt at the side of the track, looked around him, 'and as I looked down, I said, bugger me, that looks like Jackie down there, in a car!' Hill at once forgot about trying to get his BRM going again. 'I thought, good God, he doesn't look so good, he looks a bit second-hand! I could see he was in some sort of trouble, so I jumped out of the car, and of course he was trapped.' Stewart was stuck there for twenty-five minutes, while Hill and Bob Bondurant – another BRM driver – 'got me out', as Stewart recalled, 'using spanners from a spectator's toolkit'. There were no marshals, no rescue team, no ambulance service. At last, he was taken to a makeshift medical facility, where he was laid out on a concrete floor, littered with fag ends. An ambulance arrived with a police escort, took him off in the direction of Liège, lost the police escort, and finally lost its way to the hospital. In the end, an agonised Stewart was plucked out of Belgium altogether and flown to England in the air ambulance. Back in London, he recovered from broken ribs, a broken collarbone and fuel burns. No wonder he held Hill in such high regard: the bloke saved his life.

And the race itself? Seven drivers, out of a field of fifteen starters, crashed out on the first lap. Only five finished, with John Surtees taking a brave win in his Ferrari.

Other drivers than Stewart might have allowed themselves to be patched up, thanked the gods for letting them live again and simply gone back to the track. But Stewart has always been a great thinker, as well as doer. There he had been, at Spa, 12 June 1966, lying in a shattered car full of petrol, helplessly waiting for somebody to do something before he joined Harry Schell, Chris Bristow, Alan Stacey, Giulio Cabianca, Taffy von Trips, Ricardo Rodriguez, Gary Hocking and Carel de Beaufort – all of whom had died in Formula One accidents since the start of the decade. Two months later, John Taylor was burned to death in the German Grand Prix at the Nürburgring. The following year, Lorenzo Bandini was burned to death at Monaco. It all affected him, permanently. He brooded on it. 'If this was the best we had,' Stewart said, 'there was something sadly wrong: things wrong with the racetrack, the cars, the medical side, the fire-fighting, and the emergency crews.' Time would not mollify him, and the '66 crash would become a defining event in his life, every bit as much as his first Grand Prix win, or his first Championship.

He also had plenty of time in the following year, 1967, to ponder the meaning of life, given the incredible unreliability of the BRM (or *British Racing Misery* as it was now known) P83: he only managed to finish *two* out of the eleven Grands Prix that season. A bold move to Ken Tyrrell's Matra-Ford hybrid was the only way out for 1968 – which started slightly haphazardly with a 'Mule' version of the car in a snot-green undercoat at South Africa, followed by a serious injury to his wrist in a crash in the Formula Two race at Jarama, which forced him out of both the Spanish GP and Monaco.

His wrist healed, slowly and imperfectly, allowing him to take some points at Spa. By the time he arrived at Zandvoort for the Dutch GP, he was sporting a plastic brace round his forearm, was in great pain and had been told by his doctor on no account to compete. So he went out and won the race, in heavy rain. The next two Grandes Épreuves saw him in the points again and then, at Nürburgring, he had one of *those* drives: a life-defining, career-defining race, in catastrophic conditions of torrential rain and zero visibility, just like Spa in '66. And with his wrist still not properly healed. 'I couldn't see my braking distance marks,' he observed. 'I couldn't see the car in front; it was just a great wall of spray.' Or, to put it another way, the track was so narrow, so bumpy and so twisty, that even on a good day it was impossible to remember what came next, 'but in fog and ceaseless spray you just have no idea at all.' And yet, by virtue of (a) some cunning wet-weather tyres from Dunlop, (b) astonishing natural talent and amazing toughness, he came home first, a shattering *four minutes* ahead of a drenched and disbelieving Graham Hill. The great drivers can master rain; and they could master the Nürburgring. Stewart did both, compellingly.

The contradiction, though, is this: Stewart's nerve and commitment to racing – as seen, first at Zandvoort, then at the Nürburgring, cannot be doubted. He didn't like the conditions he had to race in but he dealt with them as convincingly as any driver could ever hope to. And, like Moss, like Fangio, he lived for the sheer charge of driving, of being able to take it right to the edge – revealing in '68, that 'because it's dangerous, this gives the extra thrill. This is where money doesn't exist.'

Yet the thing people are apt to remember him for is not

so much his genius behind the wheel as his endless crusade to get the tracks rendered even half-safe – as if this somehow diminishes his bravery and daring on the track. At the time, men in rally jackets, who would go to their graves without ever competing in a motor race of any kind, nonetheless felt entitled to disparage Stewart and his safety campaign as if the whole point of the sport was to stand a good chance of dying an unnecessary and painful death. In their world, the ethos of motor racing entailed, not a love of living on the edge, but a deathwish, and any attempts to lower the risk were somehow contrary to the sport's fundamentals. And Stewart was a coward for even daring to raise the issue.

This was further muddled by the historical stridency of the times, in which collectively motivated interest groups were always mouthing off, one way or another, and of which Stewart appeared to be yet another exemplar. Spa, 1969, to take a case in point, saw the Grand Prix Drivers' Association successfully boycott the race: the track was just too dangerous. It was a near-unanimous decision by the drivers, especially significant (according to Stewart) considering the complete immovability of the organisers, 'who would not make any safety concessions at all.' And who boldly went to the authorities on behalf of the GPDA, thus attracting all the opprobrium? Jackie Stewart.

People *outside* the sport understood: 'The only people who have been critical of us,' Stewart noted tartly, 'have often been those closely connected with motor racing.' But within motor sport, there were claims that earlier generations of drivers had indebted themselves to the racing community by facing death, voluntarily: to seek, now, to reduce the probability of dying, was to try to escape that debt, to renege on the sacrifices made in the past, and, at the very least, to prove oneself a sissy. But this gladiatorial pose makes little sense in the modern world, and it made little sense to other Grand Prix drivers at the time. Chris Amon (whose gift to history is to be known as the Unluckiest Driver Ever, having been a shoo-in for several victories for an underperforming Ferrari team, but having always been denied a win at the last minute) took his hat off to Stewart, because his attitude to safety 'was never ambivalent. He worked hard for circuit changes, and he drove hard.'

Stewart cunningly noted, meanwhile, that improving safety measures for drivers improved safety measures for spectators, which improved prospects for promoters. At the 1969 Spanish GP, Hill and Jochen Rindt crashed heavily into some newly erected barriers. Not only did the two drivers get away relatively unscathed, so did the spectators a few feet away (although, let's be clear, one man lost an eye; another got a broken arm through flying debris). But it could have been a lot, lot, worse, and the relative usefulness of a length of Armco allowed Stewart to argue that plenty of places would want to put on motor races so long as they could be promoted as a fairly classy attraction rather than something most people would avoid in droves 'for fear of being mown down by a racing car'.

Safety issues aside, this same '69 Spanish GP was won by Stewart, who had already won at Kyalami, the South African GP, and was thus signalling his clear intention to go for the title. He had come close to taking it in '68; and in '69, he would not be denied. He won six out of the eleven Championship races, and also gave the multicultural Matra-Ford MS80 (French chassis, Ford Cosworth V8, British team under Ken Tyrrell) the distinction of being the first French-built car to win the Constructors' Championship.

Method was everything. The Matra-Fords were meticulously prepared, as was Stewart himself, who was exacting in his own pre-race preparations. Long before the flag fell, he would go into a process of self-hypnosis, thinking of himself as a gradually deflating (but not completely collapsing) rubber ball, getting magisterially calmer until all emotion had drained away, imagining the man with the starting flag raising it, lowering it, and Stewart himself driving away in a state of Zen tranquillity. Come the race itself, he would find himself tackling the first, chaotic, corner 'with no more excitement or drama than I would if it were the fiftieth lap of the race.' Naturally enough, he deeply admired Fangio, for his strategic cunning, his impeccable driving technique, and his charismatic self-possession. You could always tell when Fangio was around, according to Stewart, 'because he gets more attention than Graham and Jochen and Ickx and everyone else put together', which was entirely as it should be, 'because Fangio is the Grand Master of our business and everyone in Motor Racing knows it.' Mental clarity, a stable environment and the measured approach were always desirables in Stewart's world.

Which made Jochen Rindt's death, in 1970, all the more insupportable. It wasn't just that Rindt died, or that Stewart and Rindt were colleagues in the mad world of motor racing – such that Stewart paid Rindt the compliment of calling him 'as good a racing driver as I ever raced against during my career', while at the same time acknowledging the Austrian's tendency to get his car radically sideways much of the time. They were also mates; they were close neighbours in Switzerland; their kids played together; glamorous Nina Rindt and glamorous Helen Stewart made a compelling duo in the pits. Rindt was, in short, part of Stewart's mental and emotional furniture.

He was also a wizard at Formula Two, but was taking some

time to make his mark in Formula One. He had done his apprenticeship with the fading Cooper team, drawing this comment from Ron Dennis (yes, *the* Ron Dennis), who had been his mechanic at the time: 'He was arrogant and didn't really treat people properly. Especially the mechanics.' He then spent a year at Brabham, where designer Ron Tauranac, by way of contrast, claimed that 'We really got on famously.' Money was tight, so 'We used to share a room together for much of the year. He was a good bloke.'

Both opinions were valid. Rindt was quick, and he knew it; he was, indeed, arrogant; he held grudges against people and was pathologically keen to freeze out anyone who had crossed him. He was also droll, good company, and, if you kept on the right side of him (if you were Jackie Stewart, say), he was a stalwart friend. He was ambitious, too, and famously remarked that he was so desperate to win the World Championship that he would even consider leaving the amiable Brabham team (with their relatively sturdy, but not superfast, spaceframed cars) and sign up for the unnerving potentialities of Lotus.

Which he did, full of misgivings, for the 1969 season.

It didn't take long for Rindt and Colin Chapman to start bickering. Rindt had been with Lotus barely six months before he felt compelled to write to Chapman, complaining about the fragility of the cars he was being asked to drive. Having noted that in three years with Cooper and then Brabham, he had had all of two crashes, he went on to observe that, in less than a year with Lotus, he had already had three shunts. 'Your cars are so quick,' he said, 'that we would still be competitive with a few extra pounds to make the weakest parts stronger.' In desperation, he added, 'Please give my suggestions some thought. I can only drive a car in which I have some confidence and I feel the point of no confidence is quite near.' The only effect this had was to get on Chapman's nerves. He would later ask, rhetorically, 'What am I going to do with this bloke? He has lightning reflexes, is bloody quick, but keeps telling me how to design my cars.'

To add to the friction, Rindt took a while to achieve his first GP win, slogging through the majority of 1969 without even getting onto the podium. Denis Jenkinson, by now the doyen of motoring correspondents, particularly loathed Rindt and declared that the day Rindt won a Grand Prix, he, Jenkinson, would shave off his trademark hedge-like beard, confident that the day would never come. It did, eventually, in October '69, when Rindt won at Watkins Glen, driving a Lotus 49B, coming home a convincing forty-six seconds ahead of another great pal, Piers Courage, in a Brabham. 'I genuinely hope Jochen gets success,' said Stewart, shortly afterwards. 'Not too much of it, but I hope he gets it.' A bitter Jenkinson duly shaved off the beard.

And then Chapman produced the Lotus 72. Well, how epochal do you like your Grand Prix cars? All right, it didn't have Cooper's paradigm-shifting insight of pushing the engine round to the back, but it was pretty close. Chapman (and his designer Maurice Phillippe) had taken the radiator off the front of the car and reconstituted it as two mid-mounted sidepods. This allowed them to locate a bit more weight within the wheelbase and at the same time shape the car like a wedge of cheese (an idea left over from the promising, but banned, 4WD gas turbine Indy car), and thus significantly reduce wind resistance. They also threw in torsion bar springing, inboard front brakes, anti-dive suspension geometry, an airbox for the fuel-injection trumpets (for the British GP) and a terrifically businesslike tripartite rear wing. It was the shape of the future, and Rindt had it in time for the 1970 Spanish Grand Prix.

It got off to an uneasy start. The fancy suspension was not to the drivers' liking, and Rindt, for one, was already in a state of mild paranoia about the lightness and fragility of the new car. 'I can't get on with this car,' he told his mechanic, Herbie Blash, 'it's going to break.' But then, according to Blash, 'He just had to drive it because it was so fast.' At Jarama, Rindt showed typical ingratitude (so far as Chapman was concerned), by spinning the car when one of the inboard brake shafts snapped in practice, stomping back into the pits and annoucing loudly that he wasn't 'going to get in that *bloody* car again'. At Zandvoort, a couple of months later, a driveshaft disintegrated at speed as Rindt was going past the pits. Bits and pieces went everywhere, all over the track and into the pit lane, a hailstorm of shredded engineering – one fragment actually hitting McLaren team boss Teddy Mayer – but left Chapman unscathed. Rindt couldn't believe it. 'What do you think?' he seethed, 'That car disintegrated right in front of Chapman's eyes, bits all over the place, and not one piece hit him.'

Nevertheless, Chapman stoically buttoned his lip and spent a good deal of time caressing and cajoling his star driver to use the brilliant machine at his disposal: with the required effect. As Graham Hill sagely observed, 'Colin will put his arm round Rindt's shoulder and lead him away for a friendly little chat . . . and Jochen will eventually get back in the car.' One particularly informative picture taken around this time shows old pals Rindt and Stewart, seated in front of the Lotus pits, grinning hugely at some private joke; with Chapman perched on the counter some way back, staring at his number one driver with fierce and undisguised suspicion.

Nevertheless, and despite all this, Rindt and Chapman were rewarded with four wins on the trot – Zandvoort, Charade (the French GP), Brands Hatch and Hockenheim – after the last of which Rindt cracked, telling Chapman 'A monkey could have won today in this car. Thank you.'

And the opposition? Stewart was temporarily marooned in a less-than-perfect March 701; Jacky Ickx in the Ferrari 312B was getting faster (and more reliable) all the time, but had probably left it too late in the season to overhaul Rindt; Ickx's team-mate, old-school wild man Clay Regazzoni, was too undependable, as well as being too far behind in the points.

Everything was set for Rindt to take the Championship, fulfil the potential he had shown in the past, silence the Denis Jenkinsons once and for all.

But Formula One was still a very dangerous place to be. Death kept stalking the circuits. John Taylor had died at the German GP in 1966; Lorenzo Bandini died at Monaco in 1967; Jo Schlesser was burned to death at the French GP in 1968. 1970 was turning into an even worse year. Bruce McLaren was killed at the start of June, testing a Can-Am sports car at Goodwood. Later in the same month, Rindt's great friend, the dashing Piers Courage, died in another ghastly fireball, this time at the Dutch GP. Rindt was so affected by the death of Courage that he started talking openly about taking the title and then giving up racing. For all his ambition and arrogance, he didn't want to stick around in a sport which had become an exercise in mourning.

Monza, therefore, became a crucial battle in the campaign. Rindt had retired at the preceding Austrian GP, allowing Ickx to pick up his first win for Ferrari. But a win in Italy would pretty much fix the Championship – and set Rindt free from the treadmill he now found himself on.

During practice, he decided to take off both the rear wing and the winglets on the nose, in order to get the maximum possible speed – over 200 mph – down the mindblowingly fast straight going into the Curva Grande. Maybe this was a good idea. Maybe not. Maybe it was Chapman's idea anyway. Rindt's team-mate, John Miles, flatly refused to drive the car set up in this way: wingless, it was hugely unstable at just about any speed. Chapman and Rindt, locked together by competitive desire, prowled around in the heat, stony-faced. Rindt went out on fresh tyres, going for an unbeatable lap. As he charged towards the Parabolica, a front brakeshaft failed; he ploughed into an imperfectly secured crash barrier, which broke, allowing him to smash into one of the barrier stanchions.

Not properly strapped in, Rindt shot forward in the cockpit and slid at 150 mph through his own safety harness: the buckle of which cut his throat. The car came to a halt in the dust, its front torn off, Rindt's legs protruding from what was left of the chassis. 'Rindt has stuffed it,' someone shouted in the silence which followed.

The mess was cleared up. Rindt's body was taken off to hospital in Milan. Practice went on in a desolate kind of way. The race went on, too, and Italian-Swiss Regazzoni won, in front of tens of thousands of screaming fans. Jacky Ickx then won in Canada and Mexico, but Rindt was not to be denied his macabre, posthumous Championship. He took it by forty-five points to Ickx's forty.

And Jackie Stewart? He was now losing motor racing friends and acquaintances at a rate of something like five a year, and was starting to get very slightly sick of the whole business. Speaking of those crashes which happened to other drivers, he once said, 'I isolate myself immediately. I lock myself into a numb condition, without any feeling or emotion until after the race. One has to do that.' But such strategies could only work for a while. Not long after Monza, he confessed that Rindt's death 'has had a profound effect on me, my attitude and feelings for motor racing, perhaps for ever.' In November, he had to present the widowed Nina Rindt with Jochen's World Championship trophy. After that, was it really worth going on?

1939: The Führer shakes hands with Tazio Nuvolari, four years after the Flying Mantuan's legendary win at the Nürburgring.

(*Left to right*) Karl Kling, Juan Manuel Fangio, Alfred Neubauer and Stirling Moss at the British Grand Prix, 1955.

Artistry: Fangio at Monaco, 1957, driving a Maserati 250F. Fangio
won the race.

The same year: Monza. Moss wins, and is almost reluctant to accept
Fangio's congratulations. Beba Espinosa holds the ring.

Peter Collins sits in a Ferrari 335 Sport, while Enzo Ferrari
establishes a point.

Unimprovable: Moss at Monaco, 1961.

Mike Hawthorn at Monaco, 1957, driving a Ferrari.

The Nürburgring, 1960s, in all its vast majesty.

Grim: Graham Hill with mechanics, 1965.

Guffaws: Hill is crowned 'Miss Earth', 1966. Bette (*left*) plays
the good sport.

Jim Clark, in pensive mood.

Clark and Colin Chapman, ecstatic, 1963. Clark has just become world champion.

Denny Hulme and Jack Brabham, in Denny's Championship
year, 1967.

Jackie Stewart proves his mettle, winning the Dutch Grand Prix, 1968,
with his right arm in plaster.

The beautiful couple: Jochen and Nina Rindt.

The ugly end: Rindt's crash, September 1970.

13

HAIR, HOTPANTS AND THE FIRST BRAZILIAN

Who was it who made Rindt's posthumous title safe? Emerson Fittipaldi: the first Brazilian to make it big in Formula One.

It was at Watkins Glen, October 1970, and Fittipaldi was making only his fourth start in Formula One. Team Lotus had now been whittled down to him and a Swedish driver called Reine Wissell. In just over two years, they had lost Jim Clark, Graham Hill and Jochen Rindt, to fatalities or major accidents – Hill having broken both legs horribly at the Glen in 1969.

Fittipaldi was twenty-three years old, brought up in the schools of hard knocks of Formula Ford and Formula Three, clearly a talent to watch, but not necessarily the person you would pick to defend prospective Drivers' *and* Constructors' Championships: especially with Jacky Ickx having won two out of the last three Grandes Épreuves and enjoying the clear mathematical possibility of stealing the prize out from under your nose. It was a situation as fraught as Jarama, '68, when Hill had dragged the team back into existence after Clark's death – the principal differences being that, in spring 1968,

Hill was a massively experienced Formula One driver; and there was no title actually on the line.

Fittipaldi was quick, amiable and laid-back. Nelson Piquet was a fan, and would remark, admiringly, 'Emerson was a fantastically quick driver, but he was very intelligent. He was soft on the car and even when he did not qualify very well he was usually at the finish. He was nearly always on the podium.' The Lotus 72 was still devilishly fast, but so were the Ferrari 312s; to say nothing of an extremely efficient new Tyrell being driven by Jackie Stewart. As it turned out, all the rivals (including Pedro Rodriguez in a surprisingly modish BRM V12) broke down or had fuel problems, and young Emerson, with his go-go sideburns and beaming grin, kept the slippery Lotus going and was rewarded with a sight he had only ever associated with Clark, Rindt and Hill: the spectacle of Colin Chapman jumping up and down in the pit lane, throwing his little Bob Dylan hat in the air as the car crossed the finish line and Tex Hopkins (as ever, in his lavender suit) threshing around with the chequered flag. Fittipaldi had won his first Grand Prix and secured the titles for his new team.

Fittipaldi's appearance also denoted something else: we were now definitely into the 1970s and as that untidy decade progressed, a highly typical mixture of hairiness, militancy and corporate fuddling began to fill the air.

Collective allegiances were being formed on all sides. On the one hand, the GPDA threatened to boycott circuits they considered unsafe; and started pressing the car builders to make safer cars – not an unreasonable request, given that the death rate showed no signs of slowing, with BRM alone managing to lose two key drivers in 1971 – Jo Siffert in a non-Championship race at Brands Hatch; and Pedro Rodriguez, in a sports car race.

On the other hand, big business was also on the rise, the leaden hand of commercial involvement becoming increasingly obvious.

Just take a look at the various corporate colour schemes on offer, on a 1971 grid. BRM, for instance, were now being sponsored by the tweedy Yardley cosmetics company (desperate to rebrand itself), and their handsome P153 sported a chi-chi white, gold, black and auburn colour scheme. All those years of doughty, determined, British racing green: gone overnight, in return for Yardley's money. The exciting March-Ford 711 not only had a kinky tea-tray spoiler on its nose (something of the Starship Enterprise, oddly, in the effect), it also had lurid red sponsorship from STP, the fuel and oil additives company that had been ubiquitous in American motor racing since the 1950s. Team Lotus were still dressed up as giant Gold Leaf fag packets. Tyrrell had ELF petroleum, their principal backers, plastered all over Stewart's car. New boys Surtees (started by the 1964 World Champion) were being funded by Brooke Bond Oxo, of all people: a car running on gravy. Only Brabham, Ferrari and McLaren were wearing much the same colours they wore in the past – although Ferrari were making plenty of their association with the Heuer chronometer company, and McLaren were about to thieve Yardley from BRM, for 1972. The relative innocence of a mere four years earlier – cars racing only in national or *écurie* colours – had quite vanished.

Then, again, motor racing was itself becoming a big, although disarticulated, business: around one and a half million people a year in Britain alone were reckoned to pass through the turnstiles at motor races; thirteen million watched it on the telly. And, as the sport grew, so the cars at the top end got more complex, and the personnel needed to create and service them grew more numerous, and, what with one thing and another, the cost of keeping a presence in Formula One ballooned. At the start of the 1970s, you needed around £140,000 a year to run a two-car Formula One team, of which at least £70,000 went on two cars and a spare, plus engines from Ford Cosworth. Transportation costs came in at another £20,000 per annum; the same, for engine rebuilds. The drivers themselves could hope to make an annual income of £15,000 and more from the sport, mostly from starting money and prize money. Of course, in Jackie Stewart's case, this was nearer £100,000, thanks to all his cunning business tie-ins; and the fact that he won a lot of races. But he was, as he would have been the first to admit, unusual.

Either way, everybody needed money, lots of it, and nobody cared terribly where it came from. At the same time, if you were a top-of-the line business and you wanted to put your name about, a Formula One car was an increasingly visible, internationally mobile and really quite glamorous kind of billboard to stick your name on. The BRM deal alone was believed to have cost Yardley £100,000. A new synergy was born: another little bit of the modern world.

Stewart, meanwhile, was not only reshaping the earnings potential of the average Grand Prix driver, he was also taking key steps in reshaping the sport's collective image.

Throughout the 1960s, the cars were beautiful, but everything else wasn't. Jim Clark wore his hair short, and kept a cardigan handy, in case his mother came round. Jack Brabham was a mysterious half-bearded pantomime uncle. Graham Hill was an RAF squadron leader, now retired on half pay. John Surtees looked like a cranky schoolmaster. Even funky, lordly, Jochen Rindt, in his early days, looked a bit like a boy scout without a whistle. The mechanics were worse: toiling grease monkeys dressed in the filthiest clothing you had ever seen. The fans and hangers-on were either boys wishing they were men, or men wishing they were more than the men they actually were. And Denis Jenkinson was a chipmunk in a tweed jacket.

But Jackie Stewart was, as ever, thinking ahead. He started to grow his hair. By 1969, it was down to his collar. By 1971, his second World Championship year – when he won seven out of eleven races and took the title by a runaway twenty-nine points, ahead of Ronnie Peterson in the March – it was past the collar and nearing the shoulders. He had been wearing a horrible Donovan/Dylanesque hat (in his off-duty moments) for some time, a bit like Colin Chapman, that eternal spiv. Now it became known as a Jackie Stewart hat, from which a tangled mat of barnet routinely emerged. He then teamed this up with some heavy flares and a pair of ludicrously outsized aviator sunglasses. The effect – especially when seen in partnership with Helen, his dishy wife – was simply electrifying. It was, at last, The Seventies.

A battle promptly broke out between him, Emerson Fittipaldi, Ronnie Peterson, and the insanely good-looking François Cevert – Stewart's team-mate – as to who could sprout the most uncontrollable haircut and densest sideburns. Almost overnight Formula One drivers started to look like first-division footballers, or roadies for the Moody Blues. Throw in the increasingly sexy prominence of their wives and girlfriends, plus the distant rumble of personality girls and female PR manipulators – courtesy of those new, non-traditional sponsors – and the sport was starting to look dangerously swinging.

Which was ideal, so far as Fittipaldi was concerned. Like so many racers on the up, he had been given sage advice by the exemplary Stewart: 'He was great with me,' Fittipaldi later said. 'He taught me how to behave with regard to advertising contracts, relationships with fans and agreements with sponsors. He was a real friend.'

But young Emerson was also a Brazilian – not the very first to drive in Formula One (that was probably Hernando da Silva Ramos, in the 1950s) – but certainly the first to make it big. And he brought a certain Brazilian flair to his work. Team Lotus had to get used to something called 'Emerson time', the time he thought it fit to turn up for testing, or sponsorial work, or whatever – sometimes completely punctual, sometimes an hour or more later than everyone else. He also liked, as the years went by, to travel with an increasingly colourful Latin American entourage: glamorous wife Maria Helena; his father; mother; kids. The air was filled with Portuguese, previously not much heard in and around the pit lane. Conventional Northern European reticence took a back seat. Beaming, hairy, benign, mildly exotic Emerson was introducing a new sense of other worlds.

And, to his lasting glory, he translated all this groovy, whiskery otherness into the World Championship in 1972. The Lotus 72 in which Rindt won the Championship in 1970 had been reworked into the 72D and given a striking new appearance, courtesy of Imperial Tobacco, who had decided that their latest brand of cigs needed promoting. So Team Lotus bowed to the inevitable: the cars were painted black and gold and renamed John Player Specials. They looked like flying coffins.

The season was basically fought out between Fittipaldi and Stewart, despite a couple of intrusions from Denny Hulme and Jean-Pierre Beltoise (the latter in a BRM, with the team's last-ever victory). Fittipaldi went on to win five GPs, Stewart, four. Crucially, Fittipaldi also picked up some seconds and a third in the first half of the season. This meant that he was able to wrap up the title by Monza. Stewart had, coincidentally, given himself a duodenal ulcer, scampering around in pursuit of fame and money, and was required by his doctor to calm down for the second half of the season – handing Emerson a small, but useful, advantage.

Which he took, and nailed the Championship in September, 1972. 'As soon as I was level with the pits,' he said, recalling this blissful Monza experience, 'I could see Colin jumping out over the guard rail and throwing his hat in the air.' This iconic vision, a revisiting of his first Grand Prix win, 'was the happiest moment I have ever had in my racing career! It was just the right thing to happen – I couldn't believe it.' And it made him, at twenty-five, the youngest world champion in the history of the sport.

But also it announced the eclipse of the Argentinians (Fangio, Carlos Reutemann, Froilan Gonzalez, Marimon) and the formal arrival of the Brazilians. Emerson Fittipaldi was the first term in an astonishing series, which would go on to include Rubens Barrichello, Carlos Pace, Felipe Massa, Nelson Piquet, Ayrton Senna. The likely lad from São Paolo was redefining the sport, reformulating the Latin American connection and giving it a completely new meaning. And what do you know, the first Brazilian Grand Prix was held in '72, although it wasn't part of the Championship. By the following year, it was.

And last but not least: it's worth noting that at Watkins Glen, 1972, despite the cool weather, girls were seen walking around in hot pants. Which will lead us, in the fullness of time, to only one thing. James Hunt.

14

ALL THE WORLD RACES FORMULA ONE - BUT THE CARS ARE MADE IN SURREY. OR THEREABOUTS

The major Formula One constructors, 1965–75.

England:

Cooper Car Company, Surbiton, Surrey

Lotus Engineering, Hethel, Norfolk

British Racing Motors (BRM), Bourne, Lincolnshire

Motor Racing Developments (Brabham), Milton Keynes, Buckinghamshire

Bruce McLaren Motor Racing, Woking, Surrey

Anglo American Racers (Eagle), Rye, East Sussex/Santa Ana, California

March Engineering, Bicester, Oxfordshire

Tyrrell Racing, Ockham, Surrey

Surtees Racing, Edenbridge, Kent

Shadow Racing Team, Northampton, Northamptonshire

Hesketh Racing, Easton Neston, Northamptonshire

Frank Williams Racing Cars (Politoys/Iso-Marlboro), Reading,
 Berkshire
Lola Racing Cars (Honda/Embassy-Hill), Huntingdon,
 Cambridgeshire
Ensign Racing, Walsall, West Midlands
Fittipaldi Automotive, Reading, Berkshire

Italy:
Scuderia Ferrari, Maranello, Modena

Japan:
Honda Racing, Minato, Tokyo

France:
Matra, Velizy-Villacoublay, Paris

15

JAMES HUNT: LAST TRUE BRIT

Emerson Fittipaldi won the title in 1972 in a version of the Lotus 72. The next year, Fittipaldi and Ronnie Peterson slugged it out at Team Lotus, their messy rivalry letting Stewart sneak through and steal the title.

There were all sorts of snippy little rumours going round about bad feeling between the two drivers – Fittipaldi being the number one, but Peterson the quicker and more charismatic – and Emerson duly promulgated the intelligence that 'If Ronnie has any problems he will talk to me, and if I have any I will talk to him. We will talk to nobody else.' Which was later modified, after Peterson's appalling death in 1978, to: 'Ronnie was a great team-mate. He was one of the best friends I ever had in racing.'

On the other hand, Lotus did win the Constructors' title in 1973, with seven wins to Tyrrell's five. And the following year, the Lotus 72E managed three more wins – at three contrasting circuits, Monaco, Dijon and Monza – in the hands of Ronnie Peterson, which was mildly extraordinary, when you consider that a car which had first come into being in 1969 was still winning races nearly five years on – and even managed a podium place in 1975, with Jacky Ickx at the Spanish Grand Prix. Yes, it had been tweaked and primped, with chassis refinements, aerodynamic changes, suspension modifications and so on; and the 72E that Peterson drove in 1974 certainly looked (and still looks) intensely menacing and purposeful, especially with its *Munsters* paintjob – but underneath, it was still the same 1969 brainwave that Jochen Rindt had alternately been terrified and entranced by.

Fittipaldi, meanwhile, took his second title in a McLaren M23, a car which looked remarkably like a Lotus 72 and, indeed, owed quite a lot to it: 'It's a car that's easy to make handle well on any circuit,' he said, brightly, 'because it's so simple.'

So Lotus and McLaren were doing the business as Great British constructors. But the drivers? Who did we find at the top of the table in '74? Fittipaldi, Regazzoni, Scheckter, Lauda, Peterson, Reutemann. What had happened to that Anglo-Saxon domination which had been going on since the start of the 1960s – Hill, Clark, Surtees, Hulme, Stewart, Brabham, all *those* names?

The fact of the matter was that it all came to end in October '73, when Jackie Stewart's team-mate, François Cevert, died in a particularly terrible crash during practice for the US Grand Prix at Watkins Glen.

Cevert was being groomed for stardom by the Tyrrell team. 'François can get past me whenever he likes,' Stewart said, indulgently, even though the twenty-nine-year-old Frenchman had only one GP win to his name. 'He's faster than I am.' What's more, Stewart was planning to retire from the sport after The Glen, his 100th Grand Prix, with his third Championship already in the bag: a typically neat and decisive piece of reasoning. Only Stewart and Tyrrell knew about this plan. It was all going to work out very nicely.

And then, in the last minutes of qualifying, Cevert lost control of his car, going through a particularly evil combination of bends known as The Esses. He smashed through a barrier, uprooting it, the car turning upside-down on the rail and destroying itself in a maelstrom of dust, GRP and metal. Cevert was more or less cut in half by the impact. Jody Scheckter was first on the scene and was so appalled by the destruction wrought on car and driver that from that moment on his views on racing changed fundamentally. From then on, he later confessed, 'My preoccupation was keeping myself alive.' Stewart and the Tyrrell team – 'distraught and disgusted', in Stewart's words – couldn't go on. They packed up and left, Stewart wretchedly forgoing his 100th race, the capstone to a brilliant career.

Indeed, it was another bad year for fatalities in Formula One – not least because of poor Roger Williamson's hideous death at Zandvoort. This has since become one of the more infamous moments in Grand Prix racing, not least because it was captured on Dutch TV: the crash, the burning car, David Purley abandoning his race to help – only to discover a couple of frightened and incompetent marshals unwilling and unable to assist the trapped Williamson, Purley's increasing horror and rage as he tries to manhandle the blazing car into an upright position, rupturing blood vessels in his arms, forced to listen to Williamson's screams as he burns to death. And the other drivers, in Purley's bitter words, 'just kept bombing through the accident scene.' Ronnie Peterson barely altered his racing line.

Stewart won that race. But first Williamson, and then Cevert – enough was enough. He hung up his crash helmet, winner of a record twenty-seven Grands Prix, and suddenly, the Brits dwindled to almost nothing. Graham Hill, absurdly, was flogging himself in his mid-forties round the back of the field, crocked up, greying, still nursing his injuries from 1969, but unable to quit. Jackie Oliver, a perennial trier, was, well, trying, without having much to show for it. David Purley, for all his bravery, was an unknown quantity.

Which left only one really viable proposition: James Hunt.

Hunt was, in many ways, a reincarnation of Mike Hawthorn – shagger, boozer, smoker, nutter, patriot, controversialist, blond. What had changed, principally, in the twenty years between Hawthorn and Hunt, were (a) the cars, (b) the publicity. And it was (b) the publicity which sealed Hunt's unique place in motor racing history, compounded with (c) his alarming frankness about himself and everything around him.

Hence, it is impossible not to warm to a driver who admits that, in the course of his first GP – at Monaco, 1973 – 'I was going well for the first third of the race, then suddenly it hit me: I couldn't drive at that pace any more. I was simply going to drive off the road. The heat plus the physical effort of driving the car had me completely knackered.' Equally, it is impossible not to be mildly repelled by the character he became at the height of his success – stupendously self-indulgent, boorish, arrogant, puerile. Hunt the world champion was often a creature without any grace whatsoever, lounging around in his motor home, smoking, holding forth to a bunch of sycophants, making fart noises, and taking the rise out of anyone who failed to amuse him. Racing journalist Maurice Hamilton was given the unenviable job of turning out *The James Hunt Magazine* – a fanzine for the credulous young – and had to spend hours being snubbed and derided by Hunt, in his search for quotable material. 'He behaved like a spoiled brat,' said Hamilton, 'and I thought he was a right sod.'

Like Hawthorn, Hunt came from the prosperous middle

classes of south-east England. He went to Wellington College, where he firmed up his vowels and his officer-class diction, before horrifying his parents by deciding to be a racing driver. He was mad, but genuinely committed – something easy to overlook in the general confusion of girls and partying that evolved over time. His father, a stockbroker, may have been well-to-do, but his parents detested his chosen career, and none of the family cash came Hunt's way. His early cars were hectic bargain-basement lash-ups, and it was only extreme determination which got him as far as Formula Three and the *Hunt the Shunt* phase of his life. Convinced about the rightness of what he did, he was nonetheless unnervingly candid about the contract he had entered into: 'Motor racing makes me come alive,' he avowed. 'But it also scares me to death.'

Scares me to death was an interesting admission. And *conflicted* would be another way of describing Hunt's relationship with his chosen career. His internal frictions weren't the same as Jim Clark's Jekyll and Hyde personality shifts. Nor were they equivalent to Graham Hill's jolly prankster/grim-faced battler dichotomy. They were more extreme than either. Hunt quickly became notorious for throwing up in the pits immediately before a race, and for trembling so convulsively with nerves that he made the whole car (in which he was sitting) shudder like a washing-machine. Peter Warr, team manager of Wolf Racing (where Hunt ended up later in his career), said, 'He was the most nervous driver I ever worked with. His eye movements would be rapid. He'd be snappy and almost quivering. When his car broke down, he'd jump out shouting "This car's a fucking heap of shit!" You'd just reel under the shock of this onslaught.'

He once physically attacked a driver called Dave Morgan, after both had got entangled in a Formula Three race at

Crystal Palace. Some years later, in 1975, Patrick Depailler nudged Hunt's Hesketh into the barriers at Monaco. Hunt immediately leaped out of his car and spent the next few laps loitering at the edge of the track, shaking his fist and yelling at Depailler each time the latter went by in his Tyrrell. More or less the same thing happened a year later, at the United States West GP at Long Beach, California, with the same protagonists, the same minor shunt, the same abuse and fist-shaking. Niki Lauda, friend and epic rival, claimed that 'Hunt was an open, honest-to-God pal – and one helluva driver.' Many others, conversely, thought he was a wastrel, a loose cannon and, to borrow Hunt's own phrase, 'Barking mad.'

Under normal circumstances, personality traits such as these would have condemned Hunt to burn brightly but briefly as a micrometeor trapped in one of the lower formulae. But his get-out-of-jail card arrived when eccentric British peer Thomas Alexander Femour-Hesketh, the Third Baron Hesketh, gallantly decided to manufacture an entire, fun-loving, team around him. As Hunt freely admitted, no one else was prepared to take a punt on him at the start of 1973. He owed everything to Lord Hesketh, a wheeler-dealer called 'Bubbles' Horsley and, surprisingly, 'Doc' Harvey Postlethwaite, a genuinely talented engineer who would go on to do great things for Ferrari.

Thus constituted, Hesketh Racing was every bit as implausible as the 1950 BRM team, but for wholly different reasons. Hesketh himself travelled around in a pinstriped Rolls-Royce and a flight of helicopters. Hunt took his Lordship's Porsche off one day, ostensibly to get it serviced, and never gave it back. They made a terrific fuss about the correct hanging of the Union Jack at race tracks and solemnly saluted it when raised. They prayed, loudly and in public, to a Chicken God. They got blind drunk, and on Champagne, at that. They had a lot of women around. 'They're attracted by fast cars, which have always been considered sexy,' Hunt confided, of the women. 'But most of all I think it's because racing drivers are nasty. Women always prefer nasty men.' Hunt, almost as an article of faith, eschewed all forms of clothing other than jeans and a T-shirt, apart from when he was working: in which case he would condescend to put on racing overalls. He also had a big dog called Oscar, who would eat with him in restaurants. Hesketh, Hunt and Horsley: to all intents and purposes, the *Commedia dell'Arte* of Formula One.

But unlikely contradictions are never hard to find in Hunt's career. The deranged Hesketh Racing *équipe*, using a modified March 731, did better in '73 than the works March team. Their home-brewed Hesketh 308 was better yet. Hunt managed three podium finishes with it in 1974 and famously won the '75 Dutch GP in an updated version of the same car. The nutters at Hesketh were far more competent than anyone had given them credit for; and Hunt was faster, too. With endearing modesty, he confessed that he didn't see himself as someone with an 'enormous natural talent. I'd put myself in the second rank, behind people like Peterson.' Ronnie Peterson, the Flying Swede, was unquestionably one of the heroes of Formula One: fast, aggressive, good for the sport. On the other hand, 'Maybe I can't do one-off banzai laps in practice like Ronnie, but I reckon I can get the job done over eighty laps or so. Even Ronnie has got to drive a race distance like the rest of us mortals, and a Grand Prix is quite a strain.'

Nevertheless, success was infectious. Master James began to take things seriously, to the extent of becoming something of a fitness fanatic, running, playing squash and tennis, training with the Chelsea FC players. Obviously, being tall, lean and muscular also did him no harm in the perennial search for sexual encounters, and fitness training at a professional level gave him a useful insight into the advantages of not being, say, a marathon runner: 'I can be chatting up a bird and were I a serious professional athlete I'd have to go off to bed at ten. But as a racing driver I can perhaps stay with her another hour, and that might make all the difference!'

And yet, at the end of the fraught British GP of 1976, he had barely got out of the car before calling into the crowd, 'Can I grab that cigarette off you?' and attaching himself urgently to someone else's half-smoked gasper. It was all most odd. He was smoking up to forty a day, boozing, he was a rowdy, posh oddball, racing for a team of posh oddballs, and yet he came eighth in the drivers' rankings in his first full season, fourth the next year, 1975, giving Hesketh Racing that first and only GP win; and he won the Drivers' Championship in '76.

Stranger yet: McLaren gave him a job. McLaren, the winners of the '74 Constructors' title with Emerson Fittipaldi, were, even then, a byword for good sense, hard work and dependability. They were well financed, with money from Marlboro cigs and Texaco fuel. The M23 had proved itself as an ugly, but very effective car. The only snag was that Fittipaldi had baffled everyone by abruptly quitting at the end of the '75 season, to form his own (monotonously ineffectual, as it turned out) racing team. A brief, dream-like moment was experienced, in which McLaren looked around to find that all the best drivers had got their places sorted out. Niki Lauda – 1975 world champion – was with Ferrari; ditto Clay Regazzoni. Jody Scheckter was at Tyrrell. Ronnie Peterson was at Lotus, although soon to return to March.

Carlos Reutemann was ensconced at Brabham; Carlos Pace, likewise.

That only left Hunt. Hesketh, meanwhile, were strapped for cash. Having been running high-mindedly without any sponsorship, they were in something of a transitional state and couldn't find a way to keep Hunt on. Early in '76, Hunt ran off to join McLaren, where, to the astonishment of many, he fitted in rather well. 'I think James worked at being an eccentric,' said Team Manager Alastair Caldwell, 'prancing around wearing unconventional clothes, doing crazy things and getting his name in the papers and so on. But it drew attention to the whole team, and everybody enjoys working for somebody who's important.' Or, as Teddy ('The Wiener') Mayer cheerfully pointed out, Hunt 'Certainly is quicker than Emerson ever was when he drove for us.' Who would have thought it?

And there was definitely something in Caldwell's claim that Hunt 'worked at being an eccentric'. Mike Hawthorn and Peter Collins partied because they were old-fashioned, instinctive fun-lovers. Hunt, on the other hand, was *driven* in all sorts of ways: it seemed at times as if the bad-boy *shtick* was willed, an attempt to mask, or at least deal with, the seriousness of his ambitions; a seriousness which McLaren tapped into.

And which was entirely necessary, given that Niki Lauda – determined, highly competent, not an easy person to get to know – was the man to beat. Lauda, at the end of 1975, was world champion – aged twenty-six, eighteen months Hunt's junior – and had been ensconced at Ferrari for two productive years. The ageing *Commendatore* himself didn't impress Lauda that much ('He would scratch himself in the most unlikely places, and hawk and spit for minutes on end, with obvious relish, into a gigantic handkerchief'), but the team, after years of humiliation at the hands of the *garagistas*, had pulled itself back together, had a brace of highly competitive drivers in Lauda and Regazzoni, and was now answering to the brilliant engineer Mauro Forghieri. Forghieri had designed the terrific 312B of 1970, with which Ferrari won the Constructors' Championship, and, with Lauda's help, produced the even more effective 312T for 1975.

Lauda himself was unquestionably a formidable driver: five wins in 1975, with nine pole positions. He was also, despite an ostensibly tricky personal manner, well liked. Nelson Piquet described him as 'a very straightforward person. He has nothing to hide. He never talks about you behind your back. He has a very good character.' Alain Prost called him 'a delightful person, once you get to know him, with a great sense of humour and a real lust for life.' Hunt liked him, too. Mauro Forghieri was somewhat in two minds: he and Lauda could often be seen yelling at each other in the pit lane and around the Ferrari garage, debating the pros and cons of the car and its driver. 'When the Ferrari went well,' said Lauda, 'he [Forghieri] considered me a very good driver, perhaps the best. When things went wrong, I was an idiot.' Still. The car was powerful *and* reliable; and the whole package was going to be better yet, in 1976.

McLaren, by way of contrast, were still consolidating their position as major league constructors; and had just signed a driver who spent much of his time barefoot and pissed, and who gave a good deal of his deepest thought (as ever) to the question of sex. 'I don't usually have sex before a race,' he said, earnestly, 'because I am very definitely concentrating.' On the other hand, 'If I have an hour or so to spare before dinner on the night before a race then I can enjoy the physical release. But I will only do it with someone who is fully understanding.' Just to make sure everyone understood his priorities, he actually took to having his electronic sex toys serviced by the McLaren mechanics. On paper, therefore, the gulf between Lauda and Hunt could not have been greater; and the need for strenuous application could not have been more marked.

The 1976 season certainly started off unpropitiously for Hunt and McLaren. Ferrari took five out of the first six races – four to Lauda, one to Regazzoni – even though Hunt won a disputed Spanish GP, and later added the French GP to his tally. But then there was the British Grand Prix, in July.

This was a shambles. A record crowd of 80,000 had turned up at Brands Hatch, wildly keen to see the new British hero close the gap on his arch-rival. And yes, he was on the front row of the grid, with Lauda on pole. Unfortunately, Regazzoni, just behind, went mildly berserk at the start, monstered Lauda on the first corner and caused a vast pile-up. Cars went everywhere. Hunt's and Lauda's machines were both damaged. As the debris was cleared away, Hunt, Regazzoni and Jacques Laffite (in a Ligier) scurried off to get their spare mounts. 'Then,' according to press reports, 'pandemonium broke out when it was announced that the race stewards had declared that no replacement cars would be allowed to start the race.' Outraged fans started to hurl rubbish on to the track, jeering and baying, in a fine British frenzy. 'At this point the RAC came closer than they have ever been of losing control of their own race.' In the chaos, meanwhile, the McLaren mechanics were bolting a new front suspension onto Hunt's car and struggling to get the thing back on the track before Brands Hatch turned into a battlefield. The organisers caved in. The race began with Hunt reinstated.

And what do you know, it was quite a thriller, with Lauda holding off Hunt until lap forty-five, when his gearbox turned sour, and Hunt breezed off to win. 'I was worried about the handling of the car,' he said afterwards, 'then it seemed to improve as things went on.' The sun shone, the crowd went nuts, and Ferrari lodged a protest. That, as it turned out, was the end of James Hunt's British Grand Prix. Lauda was handed the win, and all the detestation that so marks latterday relationships between McLaren and Ferrari was given a firm base from which to flourish. 'It seems these days that no Grand Prix would be quite right without a court of enquiry of some sort,' sighed *The Times*.

What happened next, though, put all the bickering into perspective.

The following Grand Prix was in Germany, at the Nürburgring. There was rain, on and off. Qualifying was a bit of a mess. There was more rain at the start of the race, but it looked as if it might clear up. Lauda started on wet tyres, came in to change to dry after one lap and dashed out again. Halfway round the circuit, he went hurtling through the left-hander at the Bergwerk, at which point his suspension collapsed, and he smashed into the banking on the right-hand side of the circuit, shooting back onto the track, his car in flames. Guy Edwards (in a Hesketh) managed to avoid him. Harald Ertl and Brett Lunger ploughed into him, one after the other. To their endless credit, Edwards, Lunger and Ertl, joined by Arturo Merzario, leaped out of their cars – doubtless mindful of the terrible Williamson crash – to try and rescue Lauda, trapped in the fireball. According to Edwards, 'Lauda was basically sitting in the middle of a fire and I would guess it would be about a minute before we managed to get the belts undone.' As Harald Ertl aimed a fire extinguisher at the centre of the cockpit to try and keep the flames under control, 'Lauda was conscious most of the time and was saying, "Get me out."'

A minute spent trapped in a petrol blaze, is a very, very, very long time. At last Lauda was extricated, helicoptered out, hospitalised in the trauma unit at Ludwigshaven. There were terrible exterior burns, especially to his face; but it was the damage to his lungs – those hideously toxic plastics, paints, mouldings, fabrications, at the heart of a Formula One car – which really threatened to kill him. He was given the last rites: on his way to becoming another casualty of the sport.

The ridiculous thing was that Lauda himself had for some time been trying to get a drivers' boycott of the 'Ring – what he called a 'Stone Age Circuit' – arguing that every driver there 'was taking his life in his hands to the most ludicrous degree'. As he said with unnerving prescience, a week before the crash, 'My personal opinion is that the Nürburgring is too dangerous to drive on nowadays.' When he looked at other circuits, 'Where the safety facilities provide much easier, much safer driving, and I compare them to the Nürburgring with 160 mph jumping – only God saves you.' At the 'Ring, 'If you have any failure on the car, one hundred per cent death! We're not talking if I make a mistake, but if I have a failure on the car. If I make a mistake and kill myself, then tough shit.' There was nothing timid about Lauda: he has gone into the record books as the only driver ever to lap the full circuit in under seven minutes, in 1975. But he wasn't stupid. He didn't want to die. And he really didn't want to race at the Nürburgring.

Chris Amon gave a typically thoughtful assessment at around this time: 'In its old form,' he said of the 'Ring, 'it was the supreme test of driving ability, the one course which separated the men from the boys. It was also very dangerous, but the one thing went with the other. But since the major changes in 1970, when some of the bumps were taken out and the track was made straighter, obeying the racing line a bit more, 'it has become much faster, yet in my opinion it no longer calls for the same supreme standards of driving skill that it did. Bravery, yes, but that is something different. I believe that the great dangers are no longer justifiable today because the track has lost its former unique qualities.' Jackie Stewart, who had unquestionably proved his credentials by winning there three times, also said, with discernible anguish, 'A circuit which can extend a driver's feeling so much has to be unique and therefore must not be allowed to die. Then I think of the terrible hazards and I can only have the utmost sympathy for all those who say it must be changed or abandoned. It is a terrible dilemma.'

The race itself? Hunt, impressively enough, managed to stamp his mark all over it by taking pole position and then, after the restart forced by Lauda's crash, keeping his head and winning convincingly, nearly half a minute ahead of Scheckter in the Tyrrell. It was a fantastically valuable win, sorely tainted by Lauda's terrible injuries.

About the only piece of good news that anyone would ultimately retrieve from the accident was the knowledge that Lauda had blotted the trauma out of his memory. 'Returning to the spot where it all took place,' he claimed, subsequently, 'stirs no emotions in me at all.' Chris Amon, on the other hand, was so demoralised by the experience that he never made the restart and retired from Grand Prix racing the moment the race was over. For him, the odds had just shortened too much.

Meanwhile, Hunt's season went on, in an increasing tangle of complexities. Ambivalent about the stroke of fortune which had taken his closest rival out of the contest, he was also staggering through the break-up of his first marriage. Suzy Hunt, the ultra-chic ex-model whom he had married in 1974, was now with film legend Richard Burton. She wanted to leave Hunt and marry Burton. The actual break-up probably didn't bother Hunt that greatly. When he spoke to Burton over the phone, the two got on unsurprisingly well. After all, two heavy-smoking, skirt-chasing, hard-drinking manic depressives would tend to see the world in much the same way, regarding women as amusing temporary possessions to be swapped about until their charm faded. But the publicity was a distraction he could have lived without.

Showing great sense of purpose, though, he took the Dutch, Canadian and US Grands Prix (the Canadian while suffering from tennis elbow), while Niki Lauda, having been brought back to life, disfigured and in appalling discomfort, staggered the world by getting back into the driving seat and scoring consistently from Monza onwards. It was a superhuman performance. And you don't have to have a very long memory to recall that Lauda and Hunt went into the final race – the Japanese GP at the Fuji Speedway, October, 1976 – separated by three points only. Hunt let it be known that, all things being equal, he would consider it fitting to share the World Championship with Lauda. Lauda just wanted to win.

Practice and qualifying took place as usual. The drivers lined up on the grid. And then the rain poured down, flooding the track. There was a long moment of appalled discussion as to whether the race should actually start. Eventually the organisers let it carry on, in unspeakable conditions. Lauda, partly casting his mind back to what had happened the last time he raced in the wet, and partly unable to see because he *had no eyelids with which to blink properly*, came in after one lap and retired. 'I could not see a thing ... Sometimes

I did not know in which direction the car was travelling. For me there is something which is more important than winning the world championship.' Mario Andretti, the winner, said, 'I have done a lot of twenty-four-hour races, but this was the longest race of my career. I thought it would go on for ever.' Hunt, when he staggered out of the McLaren at the end, was so disorientated and hysterical that Teddy Mayer had difficulty expressing to him the idea that, in coming third, he had secured just enough points to give him the title. A cigarette and a couple of drinks later, and he could more calmly aver, 'It was not so bad for me. I was in front most of the way. The cars behind were getting the wheel spray.' He then crawled away to celebrate properly.

Time passed. Suzy Hunt became Mrs Richard Burton. Hunt celebrated a bit more. In February, 1977, he was awarded the Tarmac Trophy by HRH The Duke of Kent. He turned up at the Europa Hotel, London, for the presentation, wearing jeans, a T-shirt and a windcheater. There was nothing anyone could do about it. Many hoped that, by the time he won his second title, he would have been to see a tailor.

Crazy Master James! You had to laugh!

No one could have known that they would have to wait another sixteen years before a Brit would be world champion again.

THE AGE OF BRAINS
1977-93

16

TURBOS, SIDE-SKIRTS AND ACTIVE SUSPENSION: TECHNOLOGY TRIUMPHANT

When James Hunt retired from racing after failing to finish at the '79 Monaco Grand Prix, one reason he gave for his decision was the overweening part played by technology – the need for the kind of research skills (and the money to pay for them) which seemed to be taking over the sport, leaving less and less for the driver to do except climb into an increasingly alien technological otherworld, hang on, and pray.

Plainly, having the best car had always been an indispensable part of taking a Championship. When Jim Clark pummelled the opposition in 1963 and 1965, or when Lauda did the business for Ferrari in 1975 and 1977, it was because the victorious drivers were driving cars which had the technical edge over the rest of the field. But the cars on the grid at least *looked* much the same, notionally obeying the same laws of physics and engineering. And that was a comfort to those who had come to see men race against other men, in the approved way.

At the same time, a false sense of security had crept in, thanks to the ubiquity of the Ford-Cosworth 3-litre V8. This powered most of the teams (Matra, BRM and Ferrari still holding out for twelve cylinders) and did create a certain consistency, even though Tyrrell's cutting-edge Ford-Cosworths were inevitably a bit gutsier than, say, Bellasi's, or Politoys'. It all helped to maintain the fiction that the cars weren't that far apart in sheer design terms, and that the driver was always at the heart of any team's success.

Then Renault won the French Grand Prix in July 1979 and changed everything.

With true Gallic indifference to perceived wisdom, the French car maker had started work in the late 1970s on a turbocharged $1^1/_2$-litre V6, as allowed under regulations which had been drawn up in the cheerful expectation that no one would actually take advantage of them. Well, the Americans had been using turbochargers at Indianapolis since the 1950s. Porsche had had great success with their turbocharged 917s in the Can-Am series in the early 1970s. The idea was not new. Nor was the size of the engine (in and of itself) entirely insane – think of Maserati and Ferrari, at the start of the 1950s, with their beautiful and effective little $1^1/_2$-litre V12s. What was different about the Renault challenge, what made it really problematic, was applying it to the incredibly varied circuits and intolerably challenging conditions of modern Formula One. That would be the hard nut to crack.

So for two seasons, the custard-yellow Renault RS01 squealed around the tracks, running its engine nearly up to 11,000 rpm (2,000 rpm more than the Cosworths), going like a bat, before invariably blowing up and settling at the side of the circuit in a pall of steam and smoke. It became a millstone round Renault's neck – they'd committed so much to it, they couldn't afford to back out. But they couldn't make it work, either. The other teams called the RS01 the 'Yellow Teapot' and jeered openly.

It took the arrival of the Renault RS10 in mid-1979 for the jeering to stop. This unnervingly potent device took pole position at the French GP and on race day stormed off into the distance with Jean-Pierre Jabouille at the wheel, winning handsomely, fifteen seconds ahead of Gilles Villeneuve in a Ferrari, and René Arnoux, driving the other RS10. It could not have been a more asssertive demonstration of *La Gloire de France*: it was the first time ever that the French Grand Prix had been won by a French driver, in a French car, with a French engine, using French tyres (Michelin) and French fuel (ELF). It was the first win for a turbo in F1. *And* the car was using the latest ground-effect techniques to keep the wheels stuck to the track. In fact, everything about it was deeply horrible, if you were a mainstream, *garagiste*-ethos British team with a mainstream British chassis and an off-the-shelf Cosworth V8 to play with. The Renault RS10 was the kind of car that could only have been produced by an outfit with industrial levels of commitment, finance and expertise behind it, and as such, was an evolutionary step up, even for a team as savvy as McLaren or Lotus.

FISA, the sport's governing body, and FOCA, the Constructors' trades union, were so frightened by the arrival of properly working turbos that they convened a special meeting in November 1979 to try to find a way to deal with the situation. Because, after all, if turbos were the way forward, then everyone would have to have one. But they were shatteringly complex in comparison with the Cosworth DFVs, and needed very serious money to develop. Renault could afford it; Ferrari, backed by Fiat's millions, were also starting work on a turbo, despite the *Commendatore's* disapproval of such things (as he said, darkly, not long after, 'A normally aspirated engine is an expression of the the total engineering efforts of all those who are responsible for the engine design, whereas with turbos you are in the hands of the turbo suppliers'). But if Renault and Ferrari were prepared to tip a fortune into turbochargers, where would that leave the *garagistas*?

And if the turbos weren't enough, what about all the other things the F1 manufacturers were having to spend a fortune on? Such as ground-effect, indeed – the creation of an area of low pressure beneath the car, using a mixture of airflow-management tunnels and side-skirts, to stick the car to the track.

Lotus (Chapman's genius, again) had got this working brilliantly in the 78 and 79, but it was difficult and expensive to get right, as well as being extremely alienating for many drivers, who had no choice but to scream through corners at insanely high speeds, hoping passionately that nothing would upset the workings of the airflow under the car. In these conditions, 'cornering', according to Niki Lauda, became 'a rape practised on the driver', in which 'something really terrible, unnatural and unpredictable' could happen at any moment.

But the scientists were in charge now: they had to be, or there was no point in being in competition. You couldn't just leave it to the driver and hope for sheer native skill to carry the day. It was the scientists who told the drivers what to do, not the other way round.

Brabham's engineers had therefore come up with an alternative approach to the ground-effect question: a 'FanCar' that used a large, well, *fan*, like an industrial extractor fan, driven off the gearbox, to suck the Brabham BT46B to the ground. Amazingly, this device worked, although it infuriated Mario Andretti, the 1978 champion, who complained that it was 'like a bloody great vacuum cleaner. It throws muck and rubbish at you at a hell of a rate.' The FIA bleated, 'At the moment we cannot find anything illegal about the car,' and Lauda used it to win the Swedish Grand Prix in June '78.

A couple of races later, though, the FanCar was withdrawn, only for Brabham to come back in 1981 with a piece of fiendish cunning in which hydropneumatics lowered the car's suspension, once under way, to enhance the ground-effect environment, given that side-skirts – integral to the original ground-effect systems – had just been banned. This also went down staggeringly badly with the rest of the F1 family. 'We cannot tolerate any longer illegal behaviour by other teams,' said a Ferrari spokesman, at the same time as he threatened to reinstate the skirts on the sides of his car, in retaliation.

Not that Brabham were fussed, this time. They took the '81 title, Nelson Piquet at the wheel.

Or was the real story at the start of 1981 the Lotus 88 twin-chassis car? And was this another work of genius or a piece of willed insanity? After all, Chapman, having given the world ground-effects, then felt he had to deal with their consequences as suffered by the drivers, not least of which were intolerable vibration, double vision, severe bruising and, occasionally, difficulty in actually keeping their feet on the pedals.

His answer was to build an almost completely rigid outer chassis, strong enough take the worst ground-effect batterings, with a softly suspended inner chassis in which the driver lounged, like a trucker in his sprung cab. It weighed a bit more than a conventional F1 machine, but the pay-off was that the ride could be brutally stiff and low (to keep the car stuck to the tarmac) without actually killing the pilots (Elio de Angelis and Nigel Mansell). 'It's a brilliant idea,' said a Team Lotus employee. 'It's so brilliant, it's scared everyone else.'

So brilliant, it never raced. At its first appearance at the United States Grand Prix West, the Lotus was met with official protests from eleven other teams at the track, even though no one could actually specify what rule or rules the Lotus 88 was breaking. The car was allowed to practise, but was then withdrawn from the race. At the Brazilian Grand Prix, two weeks later, McLaren, Osella, Alfa-Romeo, Ferrari, Williams and Ligier all complained again. This time, the stewards banned the car outright and effectively doomed Lotus' season.

Oh, but the cat was out of the bag, Lotus 88 or no Lotus 88. McLaren, with their inventive designer, John Barnard, had gone off to the wind tunnel at the Department of Industry's National Maritime Institute at Feltham, inserted a fake 'rolling road' and were using the setup to work on the new McLaren MP4, which, in turn, had its own major innovation, a carbon-fibre chassis. Brabham, meanwhile, had got their hands on a usable turbo, courtesy of BMW, with which Piquet took the 1983 Championship: the first to be won by a turbo car.

Ferrari, at the same time, had got *their* turbo working, and while Piquet won his Drivers' title, Ferrari, with Patrick Tambay and René Arnoux, took the Constructors' Championship. *And* Ferrari were about to acquire (they were pretty proud of this) a cutting-edge CAD package from the Digital Equipment Corporation, consisting of a VAX 8600 and four MicroVAX IIs, complete with a LAN to link them all together. That's how serious things were.

There was a deeper issue, though, deeper than computer software, engine hardware, wind-tunnel testing, composite materials, computer-aided design, or suction overkill. James Hunt's original despair at the way technology was usurping the role of the driver had touched on something fundamental about Grand Prix racing, something that made it unlike any other sport.

For the F1 enthusiast, how much of the pleasure lay in the talent of the sportsman, and how much in the technological appeal of the machinery? How important – to anyone's sensuous and intellectual enjoyment of motor racing – was the driver, really, when it came down to it? How much of the excitement of the track was located in the thuggish purposefulness of the machinery, the mind-blowing noise, the smell, the kinetic violence all around? Or again, was it all about the teams, anyway? Was one's allegiance to the *équipe* which enabled all the hardware to exist – charged with history and the culture of racing, like Ferrari, or provocative and brilliant, like Lotus, or rich and glossy and efficient, like Marlboro McLaren?

The early 1980s were, after all, a time when Formula One expended quite a lot of energy in tearing itself apart, just to see who really had the power: the drivers, the constructors, or the sport's governing body. What became known as the FISA–FOCA War, a battle between the *Fédération Internationale du Sport Automobile* and the Formula One Constructors Association, was partly a flare-up of Anglo-Saxon and French cultural differences, partly an extended protest by the smaller *garagistes*, who felt themselves being squeezed by the bigger corporatist Continental outfits (i.e. Ferrari, Renault and now Alfa Romeo), and partly a matter of extreme personal antipathy between Jean-Marie Balestre, the arrogant, absolutist, head of FISA, and Bernie Ecclestone, tough-nut business-headed owner of the Brabham F1 team and FOCA chief executive.

It was, however you looked at it, a vicious squabble. Balestre claimed that FOCA 'don't know what they are in to, they don't understand power, they're just little men playing with toys, making cars in garages: who do they think they are? They don't own motor sport!' Ecclestone's equally furious take on FISA was expressed thus: 'Who the hell is FISA? They are a bunch of nobodies, they appointed themselves and they think they own racing, when all they really have is a bunch of clubs around the world and self-important people living off the back of the sport.'

Things came to a head at the preposterous Spanish GP of 1980, in which FISA attempted to fine those drivers who had failed to turn up at the drivers' briefings for the previous two races. The drivers didn't pay. FISA threatened to suspend their licences. FOCA argued that FISA was acting beyond its authority and threatened to withdraw the FOCA teams from the race. The Spanish race organisers offered to pay a deposit on the outstanding fines – a gesture refused by FISA, unless the money could be proven to have come from the drivers themselves. In the end, the race was run with only the FOCA teams participating (and was won by Alan Jones in a Williams-Ford, first of six remaining runners) after FISA had declared the race illegal. Unsurprisingly, no points won counted towards either Drivers' or Constructors' Championships.

The conflict rumbled on for another year, until, in 1981, with the Concorde Agreement between FISA and FOCA, a working compromise was achieved. This did not, however, stop the drivers – under the aegis of *their* collective organisation, the GPDA – from organising a strike at the 1982 South African Grand Prix, to protest against new contractual restrictions.

And it was a real strike, too. For a while, everything ground to a halt. The big name drivers – Prost, Lauda, Rosberg, Piquet – sat around the pits or the hotel pool, cracking jokes, playing the piano. Only one car went out to practice – Jochen Mass in a March, for whom every team at the track held out a pit board. Days passed, and for a while it looked as if the Grand Prix was about to founder completely, until a solution was at last cobbled together, the offending contractual restrictions were lifted, and the drivers were promised that they wouldn't be punished for striking (but they were, as it turned out, by FISA).

The fact of the matter was that, on this occasion, both FISA and FOCA were so incensed by the drivers' actions that Bernie Ecclestone was moved to articulate a profound but unpalatable truth about the state of Formula One: 'We have been watching Ferraris for fifty years. Ferrari has had God knows how many drivers. They come and go but still all that people want to see is a Ferrari. They cannot see the bleeding driver anyway! Really, I ask you, what asset are they?'

It was a fair point: which was bigger – the sport or the driver? Teddy Mayer, of McLaren, had long espoused the view that drivers were 'light bulbs', interchangeable and replaceable, and Ecclestone was clearly thinking the same way. After all, if Manchester United could rebuild a whole squad after the Munich air disaster of 1958, how hard could it be to lose even a season's worth of drivers and start from scratch? There were hundreds of good drivers out there; and, as Bernie had so cogently remarked, the spectators couldn't see the bleeding driver anyway – a figure now reduced to not much than the brightly coloured pill of his own helmet, scarcely discernible at 150 mph, and, increasingly the mere plaything of the engineers' fiendish ratiocinations –

– Which had now come out with – fresh for 1983 – *active suspension*, courtesy of Team Lotus, again.

Lotus had been having a fairly dreadful time of it: when the 88 was banned at the start of 1981, it was said that Colin Chapman was so dismayed at this barefaced misappropriation of the rule book that he more or less lost interest in the sport. Then, in December 1982, he died of a heart attack (itself a by-product, possibly, of the ongoing De Lorean fiasco; quite probably a by-product of a lifetime of uppers and downers), and Lotus were never quite the same afterwards.

And yet, here they were with the Lotus 92, Chapman's last gift to motor racing, which boasted a suspension built round a computer and hydraulic jacks, instead of springs and shock absorbers. The system had initially been devised at the Cranfield College of Aeronautics, and, as Peter Wright, the Team Lotus aerodynamicist explained, 'The car's suspension works in much the same way as would a skier's legs on the slopes. As his legs react to different bumps and contours so his brain receives the message and instantly changes the posture of his legs. Our suspension receives its commands from the on-board computer and instantly obeys.' Nigel Mansell was the lucky recipient of all this brainpower and gamely announced, 'It's rather like having power steering, except that it works on all four wheels.' Which was great, except for the fact that Lotus's '83 season consisted mostly of retirements, with a solitary third place going to Mansell in the European Grand Prix at Brands Hatch. Indeed, it would take another few years before the active suspension principle would be properly exploited, and then not by Lotus. But the idea was there, which was all that really mattered. Progress was being made.

And yet, the sport's centre of gravity had shifted. The drivers had become very slightly less central to the way things were run. And the sponsors' names had got larger and larger. And the money talked louder. And the cars got cleverer and cleverer. And the engines became more and more powerful: in the mid-1980s they were turning out as much as 1,400 bhp, using a special fuel, the majority of which was toluene, a fantastically potent octane booster, capable of transformation into trinitrotoluene, or TNT. Technology was king. Finance was the First Lord. And no one ever again could jump into a racing car just for the sheer hell of it.

17

WHATEVER HAPPENED TO THE AMERICANS?

In the year 2000, who do you think was proclaimed Driver of the Century, by the popular autosports magazine *Racer*? Nuvolari? Fangio? Caracciola? Moss? Clark? Stewart? Senna? Villeneuve? Prost? Here's a clue: *Racer* is an American publication. And, yes, the Driver of the Century is none other than Mario Andretti, sports car racer, indy car champion, winner of the Indianapolis 500, and, in 1978, Formula One champion for John Player Team Lotus, driving the Lotus 79, the ground-effect 'Black Beauty'. What a trouper! He raced (for the last time) in the Le Mans 24 Hours in 2000: aged sixty! Hats off to him!

Well, if you're American, and you're going to pick anyone for Driver of the Century, Andretti is as sensible a choice as any. Still held in great esteem by the American racing public, Andretti embodies the Dream as much as anyone can. A humble Italian immigrant with an obsession with motor racing, he slogged his way, inspirationally, to the very top, starting with midget racers in the early 1960s, toughing it out in indy cars for a decade, before entering Formula One full-time with the Parnelli Team in 1975, all the while showing that gritty tenacity (as well as business acumen) which counts for so much in the States. Laconic, physically tough, laid back, determined, skilful, mechanically astute (an essential characteristic for getting the Lotus 78/79 working), affable, a family man, he had a certain craggy Mount Rushmore quality to his appearance, as well as an authentic American perma-tan and eerily tidy hair. Whenever he stood next to Ronnie Peterson – his Lotus team-mate – he looked like a good-quality US-made leather wallet placed next to a floor mop. He is, let's not be picky about this, a legend of the sport.

He is also the last American to become World Champion. Indeed, he may remain that way, given the startling paucity of North American racing talent in F1 nowadays. When Andretti retired from Grand Prix racing in 1982, he handed the job of Top American to Eddie Cheever, who drove for Renault, Haas Lola and Arrows, among others, achieving some success, before retiring from F1 in 1989. Michael Andretti, Mario's son, raced in 1993, keeping the flame alive. But between then and 2006, there were no Americans at all competing in Formula One. The encouragingly named Scott Speed did his best in 2006, but in 2007 Toro Rosso (for whom he was driving) let him go. And there, at the time of writing, the matter rests.

It wasn't always like this. Go back to 1960, and not only were Richie Ginther and Phil Hill highly active in Formula One, there was even an anomaly whereby points scored at the Indy 500 counted towards the F1 Drivers' Championship; an anomaly which ended in '61, but which nonetheless gestured towards some hopeful post-war proximity between the two racing culures.

It was '61, of course, when Phil Hill, native of Florida,

based in California, won the title for Ferrari, establishing his credentials, at the same time, as an exceptionally nice man. 'I'm in the wrong business,' he once said, 'I don't want to beat anybody.' Hill was also a thorough-going Europhile, who was 'completely captivated by the romance of everything I'd read about it, of the great Mercedes and Auto Unions, of Caracciola, von Brauchitsch, Tim Birkin.' He even did a training course with SU Carburettors, of Birmingham, which must have been an eye-opener.

Californian neighbour Richie Ginther was then persuaded by Hill to take up motor racing, and he too did the rounds of the Grand Prix season, joining Hill at Ferrari, before moving on to BRM and eventually Honda, to whom he presented their first GP win, at Mexico in 1965. He was solid, old Ginther, very technically aware, managing one win and fourteen podium places, but he simply walked away from motor racing at the Indy 500 in 1967, after getting drenched in fuel, not catching fire, but deciding that enough was enough, all the same.

Or, better yet, how about the great Dan Gurney? Gurney had many things going for him. He was a quick driver; he was extremely tall (six feet four inches); he had chiselled good looks, like a Burt Bacharach in overalls; it was said that he was the only driver Jim Clark ever confessed to fearing; and he helped design and build the Eagle-Weslake, still thought by many to be the most beautiful Grand Prix car ever made. He gave Porsche their first win in Grand Prix racing (French Grand Prix, 1962). He did the same for Brabham (French Grand Prix, again, 1964). And then he went and started his own team – All American Racing – initially planning to win at Indianapolis, but with the subsequent intention of showing the world that America could take on the smart alecs in Britain and Italy and win at Formula One.

It sounds almost endearingly high-minded now, to say nothing of being endearingly Eurocentric. And although the outfit was notionally based in California, in reality the AAR Eagle team was another British *garagiste* concern. The chassis was the work of the highly regarded ex-Lotus engineer Len Terry, while the sizzling V12 was designed by ex-BRM man Aubrey Woods and built by old-school Weslake Engineering in Rye, East Sussex. In due recognition of this state of affairs, Gurney changed the corporate name to Anglo-American Racing, and in 1966 he hit the tracks with the intensely dashing Eagle F1 car in midnight blue, complete with jetfighter radiator intake and sexy alloy wheels. A year later, and he had won the Belgian GP in fine style from both Jackie Stewart and Jim Clark, and was mobbed by cheering Belgians. And this a week after winning the Le Mans 24 Hours in another great Anglo-American co-production, a Ford GT40. It looked as if Dan's moment had arrived.

Unfortunately, that was it for Eagle in Formula One. It was a good car, all right, and Gurney was a good driver, and the two of them led handsomely at the Nürburgring in '67, before a halfshaft gave out. But that was the story, really: the car wasn't reliable enough (especially galling for a perfectionist like Gurney), and by 1968, he was driving for McLaren, before dropping out of Formula One altogether a couple of years later.

All right, how about Peter Revson? He too made a start in F1 in the 1960s, went back to the States for a few years, then returned in the early 1970s and won the British and Canadian GPs with McLaren in '73. He died in '74, practising for the South African Grand Prix and was a fine driver, and was indeed the last American-*born* racer to win a Grand Prix. Or how about . . .? Well, we've had Mario Andretti. Who else does it leave? Anyone?

*   *   *

There's something anomalous about all this, when you consider how much Ford, Firestone, Goodyear, Texaco, Esso, Mobil, Champion Spark Plugs, to name just the big ones, have contributed to Formula One over the years. So many millions of US dollars have flooded into the sport, and yet you can count the number of major American drivers on the fingers of one hand. Fair enough, the industry had no choice but to put money into Formula One, given its reach as a marketing tool throughout Europe and the rest of the non-US world. But why has the sport habitually meant so little, back in the States? Why has it gained so small a cultural purchase?

And why, for that matter, have the Americans had such a hard time of it, trying to find somewhere suitable to stage a Grand Prix?

The first couple of attempts, in the late 1950s, were at the Sebring track in Florida, and Riverside, California, with neither event generating a sufficiently big take at the gate to ensure a rerun. So the event moved on to Watkins Glen, which held its first United States Grand Prix in 1961, and which, as locus of the United States GP, was for a long while voted best-staged Grand Prix of the season (by the GPDA), very possibly in grateful recognition of the vast amount of prize money the Americans put on offer.

After all, in the mid-1960s, in Europe, it was starting money that kept many teams going – around £25,000 a race, split between perhaps ten outfits. That was the pot. And then they arrived at Watkins Glen, where, in 1966, instead of starting money, there was a single gargantuan bucket of prize money – over $100,000 in total, with $20,000 going to the race winner, all the way down to nearly $3,000 for whoever ended up in twentieth place. It seemed as if you couldn't lose. In fact, the $20,000 cash prize for race winner was more than all the first-place prize money of all the other Grands Prix *put together.* '$100,000 was a magic number at the time,' confessed Cameron Argetsinger, the race organiser, putting his finger right on it.

It should have been perfect, but it wasn't. The happy relationship didn't last. The 1960s were great, the early 1970s were okay, but by the end of the 1970s, the Glen had begun to turn from a fun-filled cash-cow into a slightly tawdry, behind-the-times hangover. There was a chronic lack of desire, somewhere in the system. The track wasn't kept up to date, with the result that it was too lumpy for the new generation of ground-effect cars. The facilities for the teams and the press corps were increasingly cramped and tatty. There was (amazingly, for the States) a shortage of suitable nearby hotel accommodation. And there was, apparently, 'hooliganism' among the well-beered-up young guns who liked to frequent motor races.

This last sounds unlikely, but it was true. Down in the infield of the Glen lay an area of badly drained land which, after rainfall, turned into a bog. It was, in fact, known as The Bog, and it was here that drunken auto race fans would periodically hijack vehicles and then set them on fire: the record for hijackings and torchings actually standing at twelve vehicles (including three buses), set in 1973. In fact, FISA intended to ban Watkins Glen as a venue altogether at the end of 1979, and it was only a last-minute reprieve (urged on by Mario Andretti and tens of thousands of petitioners in the States) which saw the 1980 GP take place there at all.

But FISA had their way, 1980 saw the last Glen Grand Prix, and thereafter the race became increasingly nomadic, shifting around from New York State, to Long Beach, California (where it had been running in tandem with Watkins Glen for five years, as the United States Grand Prix West), to the

Las Vegas Grand Prix (laid out in the car park of Caesar's Palace, run anti-clockwise instead of the normal clockwise, and drawing depressingly modest crowds), to Detroit (a relatively successful seven-year stint), to Dallas, to Phoenix, Arizona (where, in 1989 a pitiful 18,000-strong crowd turned out, causing the Formula One teams to depart in disgust, never to return), to Indianapolis, where a Formula One-flavoured track had been laid out, partly in the infield of the famous banked track, partly on the hallowed oval itself.

This, the most recent arrangement, got off to a terrific start in 2000, with a crowd of over 220,000 in attendance to watch Michael Schumacher beat Mika Hakkinen. After that, though, interest flagged, especially after Schumacher and Rubens Barrichello were reduced to trading places in 2002, and Michelin screwed up the tyre compounds in 2005, leaving only six cars able to take part in an authentic, modern, motor-racing fiasco. The last US GP took place in 2007 (Lewis Hamilton winning), and, at the time of writing, the United States *and* Canadian Grands Prix were in abeyance, leaving Formula One nowhere to go – apart from Europe, the Middle East, the Far East, the Antipodes, or South America, of course.

It's hard to know whom to blame for this state of affairs, or even if blame is the appropriate response. Formula One petrolheads are apt to cite chronic North American insularity, coupled with modest attention spans and a weak-minded, childish fascination with mere display, as the reasons why Formula One has never really fixed itself in the hearts of the Yanks. That, and the ingrained cultural solipsism which (to pluck an example at random) enables the States to take no real interest in football (as in soccer), a truly international game, while hosting an annual event called the World Series for American-rules football, which is played almost nowhere except the United States. Decades ago, we cry, America looked outwards, to Europe especially, for items of culture and recreation. But in the last couple of generations, any interest in the rest of the world has vanished in a kind of triumphal self-absorption – taking Formula One with it.

On the other hand, and let's be honest, here, a lot of Formula One racing can be breathtakingly dull. Back in the old days, it took real, priestly, dedication to post yourself as a spectator somewhere halfway round, say, the Nürburgring and consign yourself to an afternoon watching the occasional car roar past, often in solitary splendour, before it disappeared into the hills, where, for all you knew, something much more interesting might be happening. At Monaco, conversely, everything was/is a lot more compressed, but tended/tends to force drivers to tail one another around the narrow streets like slot-racers, with little overtaking possible. Silverstone, somewhere between the two, has its moments, but too often is familiar as a place where, once the pack has spread out, overtaking becomes a very distant possibility, and weary minutes can go by without anything of note happening. Even Monza suffers from *longueurs*. It's just the way Formula One is.

The American fondness (conversely) for oval tracks and stadium circuits, with primitive but relatively closely matched machines, may seem a bit dumb and retrograde in comparison with the endless complexities of the F1 scene, but at least you get a chance to watch most of the action, see plenty of wheel-to-wheel racing, catch plenty of overtaking, observe some smart pit work, and maybe encounter the odd crash. And it's no surprise that many of the newer Grand Prix circuits – Malaysia, Shanghai, Bahrain, as well as the redesigned Hockenheim – have strong stadium elements, while the old-school, improvised, somewhere-in-the-distance tracks like

Silverstone, are losing their grip. Stadium circuits are good (in theory) for the racing; they're good (in practice) for the TV; the punters (more or less) like them: they're the American way.

So there is at least a dynamic in action. But if Formula One has managed to accommodate something of the American ethos in its changing approach to circuit design and crowd entertainment, it still hasn't been enough to entice the Americans themselves back into the game. In fact, Andretti's retirement from F1 in 1982 may well leave him as the final term in a series which once seemed to have so much life in it. Which is a shame. When he went, he took with him the Stars and Stripes on the podium, the 'Star Spangled Banner' over the PA, the general noisiness of Yanks at play. It's a gap that still demands to be filled. And Phil Hill would never have wanted it this way.

18

JONES, PIQUET AND PROST: TWO GORILLAS AND A PROFESSOR

James Hunt may have packed it all in, not quite halfway through the 1979 season, but this did not mean the end of the larger-than-life, lock-up-your-daughters, racetrack character as a feature of the sport. There were, in fact, plenty to choose from; but the style had changed, become less flagrantly British, more intercontinental, more diverse. So diverse, in fact, that you hardly knew where to start.

Consider the Australian Alan Jones, the 1980 World Champion. Jones was a real tough guy: he once finished second in a race, despite having to drive with nothing less than a *broken hand* – the legacy of a punch-up in a pub, for God's sake. Patrick Head, the stupendously unsentimental designer at the Williams F1 team, called him 'a hard, competitive animal'. Frank Williams himself, one of the hardest nuts in a hardnut business, loved him, describing him as a 'man's man', and the kind of person who never 'needed propping up mentally, because he was a very determined and bullish character. He didn't need any babysitting or hand-holding.' Jones referred to himself when younger as 'an obnoxious little bastard' and despised those drivers who were less than entirely involved in their work, complaining that 'The car's taking them for a drive half the time.' He also referred to Australia, land of his birth, as 'the best country in the world', while, as a natural corollary to this, deriding all Frenchmen on sight. Alain Prost, terrified by these characteristics, reckoned that Jones was 'the most fiery, powerful, even violent, driver'.

Carlos Reutemann, Jones' team-mate at Williams, hated him, and he hated the moody Reutemann right back. Leading the Championship, halfway through 1980, Jones growled, 'The only time team orders come into it is if we are running first and second eight or ten laps from the end and are not under any threat. If Carlos is ahead under those conditions, *I would expect him to let me through.*' Which was exactly what failed to happen at the Brazilian Grand Prix the following year, leading to a fundamental collapse of relations within the team and, ultimately, to Reutemann's ignominious departure from the sport in '82. When Reutemann quite legitimately came second at the 1980 German GP, with Jones third (after a tyre disaster which robbed him of a sure win), Jones was so incredibly angry with everything he couldn't even bring himself to share the podium with Reutemann and Jacques Lafitte, the winner. 'This is just not possible,' he kept muttering, 'this is just too much. I was so close, and then this.' Everything was gruntwork, toil, aggravation, battle, the realities of cash, and the drudgery of testing. 'The sport,' he said, boiling it down to the bleak essentials, 'is work and money.'

At the same time, once Jones had won the Championship, he piously declared, 'All I want is a good rest and to go home to see my wife and child.' Which in turn made him the obverse of his great rival, Nelson Piquet.

While Jones wore his no-nonsense, uncompromised identity like a suit of chainmail, Piquet was devastatingly unstraight-forward and hard to pin down; fascinated by practical jokes and off-the-wall humour; highly sexed; occasionally over-whelmed by the demands of going the full length of a motor race (he collapsed on the podium after coming first in the 1982 Brazilian GP); and surprisingly sleepy. Apparently, even when Nelson was under extreme pressure – just before the last, and decisive, race of '83, in South Africa, for instance – his tendency was to go to have a nap. He was even known to do it when sitting on the grid, in his car, waiting for the start. So comfortable was he generally with the notion of relaxation (unlike Jones) that, according to Lauda, 'He used to tell me how he would take his boat out and fish, swim and skin-dive, how splendid it was spending a whole day doing nothing.'

Fair enough. You'd have to have a heart of granite not to admire him for being able to turn his back on the tiresome monomania of Formula One and show some true Brazilian commitment to pleasure. And his description of racing at Monaco as being 'like riding a motorbike round your apart-ment' has become part of the currency of the sport. But then it would also be hard to imagine (say) Alan Jones cheerfully admitting that 'Winning is a feeling which you cannot imagine. I sometimes piss my pants on the slowing-down lap.' Or, again, when Piquet got the drop on Carlos Reutemann at Las Vegas in 1981, causing an unnerved Reutemann simply to give up and *let* him overtake, Piquet's encapsulation of the moment – 'He just open the legs' – would have made Jones, or indeed, anyone else, squirm. Ditto his remark, on passing Nigel Mansell at the Canadian GP of 1991, and winning the race: 'I almost came!'

Oh, but this was all part of Piquet the rude boy, the joker, the shaggy-haired prankster with the goofy overbite. Because, if he wasn't going out of his way to provoke people verbally, he was playing around with them in other, equally satisfying, ways. He would habitually greet Professor Sid Watkins by trying to unzip his flies. He tipped the contents of a bottle of mineral water into Jean-Marie Balestre's jacket pocket while the magisterial head of FISA was delivering a lecture on track safety. And he once thieved all the toilet paper from the toilet, just before Nigel Mansell dashed in for an unstoppable crap.

Of course, the offbeat personal manner was a way of concealing personal ambition. Piquet wanted to win, and he wanted to win just as badly as Jones or Prost or Niki Lauda. Lauda, indeed, was almost effusive in his praise of Piquet's style: 'He seldom makes a mistake, he is always fast, he is always on form.' Gordon Murray, Brabham's – subsequently McLaren's – legendary designer, reckoned that Piquet was the most 'thinking' driver he ever worked with. Alain Prost – for some, the cleverest racer of them all – acknowledged the sheer consistency of his rivals, Piquet and Patrick Tambay, in the close-fought 1983 season, remarking, 'I climb up the podium and there they are alongside me.' Later that year, when Piquet had snatched the title from him by two points, he graciously admitted that 'The best car won the championship – and Nelson was the best man to drive it.' The fact that this remark would help to get Prost fired from his own team, Renault, is neither here nor there: Piquet commanded respect.

Respect, Alan Jones-style, too. He even went so far as to physically attack another driver, in front of the TV cameras, when he tried to lamp Eliseo Salazar at Hockenheim in '82, after Salazar had punted him off the track. Admittedly, Piquet's hand-to-hand combat technique was poor – a lot of pawing and slapping and airy high-kicks, not a style Jones would have admired – but his aggressive, unhinged engagement in the moment was there for a global TV audience of 800 million to see. He even threatened to do Jones over after the latter had bounced him off the track in the '81 Belgian GP – 'He's absolutely crazy! The next time he does that I'll kill him!' – but nothing came of it. Perhaps Iron Man Jones was just a bit too much to take on.

Later in his career, commentators (especially pro-Mansell British ones) beefed about his wavering involvement, his undependable form, his temperament. Piquet's response was invariably that there was no point in killing yourself if the car was never going to be competitive, and that titles were won by the steady accumulation of points, not by winning a handful of show-stopping races. He would also point out (after his retirement) that he got to be World Champion three times; won 23 Grands Prix from 204 starts; took 24 pole positions and 23 fastest laps – *and* was sufficiently well regarded to command a first-year signing fee with Williams of $3.3 million, when he joined them from Brabham, in 1986.

And the money was almost as important as the winning. At the time of his departure, he said 'The truth is that I moved to a similar team with the same potential, to make much more money. I told Bernie [Ecclestone, then Brabham boss] that I worked hard for him, so why couldn't I make the same money that Niki and Prost and everybody was making?' By the time he signed to Lotus for 1988, he had managed to extract a $6.5 million annual retainer from R. J. Reynolds, makers of Camel Cigarettes, some of which unbelievable lucre went on buying Nelson a 115-foot motor yacht with its own helipad. The money was an index of his significance and success as a driver as much as it was the key to a lifestyle of slobbing about in the Med, entertaining a succession of beautiful women, and siring seven children by four different mothers.

But was that all it came down to? Of course not. Piquet was a bit more frank about it than many others; but money, truth to tell, was now becoming the determining characteristic of F1 as a sport. It was the thing that made Grand Prix racing such an object of stunned fascination, worldwide – the fact that, now, such prodigious sums of cash were being poured into the game.

This was the 1980s, after all.

At the start of the decade, it was estimated that Formula One had a gross investment of around £100 million. It commanded 5,000 hours of international TV. It took a live gate of £15 million every year. By the time Piquet had signed to Williams – or rather, the Canon Williams Honda Team – the cost of a two-car team stood at about £8 million per annum, of which Canon paid £4 million, with Honda putting in £2 million for the engines, as well as supplying twenty-five full-time Honda technicians at the Williams HQ in Didcot; with over a thousand R&D technicians on call back in Japan. The upside for these big, big, players was in the incredible value of the TV exposure that went with the racing. In the States, the cost of advertising on primetime TV was put at $1 million a minute. Which meant that, viewed in this very specific sense, the 1986 British Grand Prix, won by Mansell in a Canon Williams Honda, repaid 50 per cent of Canon's investment in one go.

Piquet, a top performer in the sport, was only showing a

sensible awareness of his worth, just as Stirling Moss had done, twenty years earlier. It wasn't so much a question of greed; it was merely that the money was now swilling around so stupendously, you had to help yourself before it all went to a less deserving cause.

But while Piquet made an art form out of living large and fooling around, Alain Prost worried incessantly. According to his sometime team-mate Patrick Tambay, he used to bite his fingernails 'So deeply that it must be very painful for him. But he cannot stop it.' As well as being a nail-chewer at Jim Clark level, Prost was a brooder, an obsessive deep thinker. Brian Hart, the celebrated engineer, argued that 'Drivers like Prost think the race through on the Saturday night, think through the various permutations, where they'll be and when they'll be there, and it's locked in their brains.' Or, if not brooding on Saturday night, then obsessively churning things over with the chief designer – in this case, a suitably impressed John Barnard, who revealed that 'If you said to Alain, "Listen, I really need to talk to you all of the night," you've got it, no problem.' Or again, recalling Prost's mental clarity and retentiveness, 'You could talk about something a week after it happened and he'd still give you the exact picture.'

There was, of course, nothing sham about Prost's driving abilities. As well as being able to hold an entire race plan in his head and think with analytical precision about the various probabilities unfolding in front of him as a race progressed, he was quick. He admired Jackie Stewart's mixture of thoughtfulness and devastating speed – and Stewart returned the compliment: 'Prost is my kind of driver.' Lauda – likewise, a tactician and a hard racer – was another model. 'The only one,' said Prost, champing at his fingers, 'who taught me something, who dominated his subject, was Lauda.' In return, Lauda generously confessed to John Barnard, 'I don't know, I just don't understand this, I don't know how the guy does it', after Prost had just beaten him by half a second in qualifying. 'I must go away and think about it.'

It all sounds very grown-up. Were Prost and Lauda, then, locked in a state of mutual reverence for all that time in the first half of the 1980s, the period when their careers overlapped? Lauda was equivocal. He described Prost as 'a difficult character, to be honest. He's a moaner, he is not a good politician.' He also added, intriguingly, 'He has a lot of problems in his private life which I don't want to talk about.' Prost was a perfectionist, brilliant at setting up his cars and getting the most out of them. But this made him prickly, too – and his time at Renault, in the early 1980s, instead of being the realisation of a dream of harmony (French team, French driver, French tyres, French fuel), was filled with issues of temperament, *amour-propre* and national pride.

It was at Renault where they coined the title 'Professor' for him, and allegedly never saw him lose his mantle of thoughtfulness, except on one occasion, when René Arnoux failed to respect the team hierarchy and overtook him, as a result of which, Prost had 'a tearful tantrum'. At the same time, of course, there was a good deal of tricky Gallic wilfulness in the air – which came to a head in 1983, when Renault took advantage of Prost's fourteen-point late-summer lead in the Championship, to chuck posters all over France, hailing 'Our Champion', only for Piquet to nick the title in the last three races and leave the Renault team bent double with *chagrin*.

Prost complained that Renault were killing him with fatuous promotional and administrative duties. Renault said that their demands were scarcely onerous and that Prost should complain a bit less. Prost didn't stop complaining, however, but added to his litany of complaints by whingeing about the aggressive attention he was getting from the French press, later claiming that 'By 1982 I had become the bad guy . . . the French really don't like winners.' His declaration that 'The best car' – Piquet's Brabham-BMW – 'won the Championship' finally did for the relationship, as well as substantiating Lauda's claim that Prost was a moaner and not a good politican. The fact that he then enjoyed several untroubled years (until Senna arrived) back with his original team, McLaren, didn't mean that he was any more relaxed than before, but that the McLaren culture coped with him better.

Oh, and the sex. Whereas Alan Jones was a straight-up family man, and Piquet was a simple, uninhibited, lothario, Prost (according to a friend) was 'very romantic and he is very erotic and very sexy', and was prone to laying it so hot and heavy on the women he fancied 'that somewhere they are so aroused they have to give in'. Nothing wrong with that, except that Prost was so keen on amatory matters ('He spends a lot of time on it') that sometimes it seemed in danger of getting in the way of the business of actually driving cars. You could scarcely blame him: as Prost was the first to admit, he was small, not in the least conventionally attractive, and had a broken nose, dating back to his all-wrestling, all-football-playing, pre-motor-racing days. The problem was that, the more celebrated he became, the more distractions there were, such that even an intellect as stern as his had trouble dealing with them: in Prost's hands, skirt-chasing – as practised without a second thought by, say, James Hunt – became just one more thing that was perhaps more complex than it needed to be.

As a final touch, he detested the inescapable ground-effect cars, complaining that the net result of such fiendish technology was 'cornering speeds that were absolutely horrendous and completely inconsistent with track safety', leaving a car 'pinned to the track' and in a condition where driving skill was 'virtually an irrelevance'. Once the side-skirts were banned in '83, and the glue-like effects were mitigated, he was a lot happier. 'The pleasure of driving has come back,' he sang. 'For me the cars are more difficult to drive because they demand more concentration. They are more ... amusing. It is better now because it is the skill of the driver which counts.'

But in 1980 – when Prost was in his first F1 season, with McLaren – ground-effect was all the rage, and he had to live with it. He also had to live with the fact that McLaren were just starting to come out of a dismal losing streak, had only just formed a new partnership with Ron Dennis (who, clearly, was going to make a difference) and had a car which, while not without its interest, was really only a staging-post on the way to the all-conquering MP4 series. Prost managed to crash a fair bit. He then blamed the car for breaking, while at the same time blaming the team for blaming *him* for the crashes, before cutting short his contract and decamping to Renault, the land of promise. In the end, his rookie year was not particularly impressive. He came sixteenth in the Drivers' Championship, behind John Watson, Jacques Lafitte, Elio de Angelis, a whole host of mainstream contenders.

But while Jones and Piquet slugged it out at the top (the result: Australia 5, Brazil 3) Prost was working, thinking his way up to the next level. And for the next few years it would mostly be the likes of Piquet, Prost, Lauda and Ayrton Senna who would take the titles – complex, sometimes inscrutable characters, subject to dark motivations and inner conflicts.

Seen in this context, Jones was, in many ways, the last of the straightforward tough guys. Nigel Mansell did his best to keep the type from disappearing altogether (along with extra Mansell seasonings of suspicion and periodic complaining), but the real stars were far trickier, more labyrinthine, characters.

Which was great, if you were selling the sport to the rest of the world. A long time before there were Piquet and Prost, Grand Prix racing had traditionally been tucked away in the margins of the sports pages, a minority interest – except when Mike Hawthorn became champion, or Stirling Moss crashed. But now the teams and drivers were so big, so prominent, so international, that their media prominence called for constant new stories, personality angles, conflicts. Sportsmen were now *sports personalities*. The more diverse and troublesome they became, the better. It sold papers.

Two gorillas and a professor: a mixed bag for 1980, then.

19

FRANK WILLIAMS – THE TEAM BOSS AS RUTHLESS CEO?

It was the 1980s that saw the Legend of Williams begin to take shape. And what a legend it is: at the time of writing, the tally for Williams F1 stands at seven Drivers' Championships and nine Constructors' Championships. Compare this with McLaren (twelve Drivers', eight Constructors' Championships), Lotus (six Drivers', seven Constructors' Championships) or Brabham (four Drivers', two Constructors' Championships) and it's easy to see why people went around throughout the 1980s and 1990s declaring that Williams was going to become the most successful Formula One team ever – lining up to surpass even Ferrari, who, before the arrival of Michael Schumacher, had an eminently beatable eight Constructors' and nine Drivers' Championships to their name. If the last few years have seen a falling-off of form, it is nonetheless salutary to recall how staggeringly potent Williams were at the height of their powers.

It's also salutary to recall that, before he became so very successful, Frank Williams spent a decade not getting very far at all. Back at the end of the 1960s, he was scuffling around in a blagged Brabham with Piers Courage. These were madcap days, young men in love with the sport, the same intense friendship that bound Chapman and Clark, the affable, dashing Courage showing great promise, coming second at Monaco and Watkins Glen. And then dying an appalling death at the Dutch Grand Prix, 1970. Williams called him 'totally adorable', and, like Chapman after Clark, was never quite the same after his death: the iron entered his soul.

Unlike Chapman, however, he had the good fortune not to be a conceptual genius, but was instead an organiser, facilitator and strategist with rare talent, bottomless energy and, now, ruthless emotional detachment. Having survived the Scrounging Years which seem to afflict every team (apart from, arguably, Ferrari and McLaren) at some point in their evolution, he found himself at the end of the 1970s heading up a freshly reconstituted Williams F1, and poised to change the face of Grand Prix racing, once he and Alan Jones had got the Patrick Head-designed Williams-Ford FW07 to work properly.

Jones thought that Williams was The Man: 'Frank is the best bloke I've ever driven for,' he said. 'The trust between us was absolute . . . he would always give me the benefit of the doubt because I was the guy with my bum in the car.' Williams, in return, completely respected Jones, for his aggression, his commitment, his skills in testing and development, and the fact that he was entirely self-motivating, requiring almost no encouragement from his team manager. 'We had an enormous amount of respect for each other,' Jones claimed. 'And,' he added, unexpectedly, 'we enjoyed ourselves.'

Others felt the same way, whether a senior engineer, such as Bernie Jones – 'He's just brilliant to work for' – or Viv Orriss, who used to work for British Airways, and dealt with

Williams the passenger all the time: 'Everyone adored him . . . It was his smile which made you melt. It was devastating.' Even when young – and before his dreadful accident of 1986 – Frank looked pretty tightly wound: like a rogue Jesuit with more than a hint of Death's Head about the face. So the smile when it came must have been brighter than daylight.

Smile or no, he was also a lot better to work for than Bernie Ecclestone at Brabham, if Nelson Piquet was to be believed. 'Maybe I made the move to Williams because I wanted to screw Bernie,' Piquet said at the end of 1985, typi-cally upfront and smutty, 'because he is so clever: for the last seven years he's been able to screw me in deals in other ways. Now I want people to see he's not so clever. And he let go me [*sic*]. So now he's in the shit with the sponsors, in the shit with Pirelli and in the shit with everybody, because he's got no good drivers to put in his cars.' And it worked all right for Piquet, who, in 1987, collected his third and final Championship in the Williams FW11B.

By this stage, though, a title with Williams ought to have been a formality for just about any driver, the team being so strong that they had taken the Drivers' Championship in 1980 and 1982, and the Constructors' in 1980, 1981 and 1986. *So* strong, indeed, that one wondered if it wasn't doing something to their humanity. After all, chain-smoking, mous-tache-brandishing, keep-fit fanatic Keke Rosberg ('Takes himself so unbelievably seriously,' according to Lauda) had taken the Championship, in a Williams, in 1982, only to find that 'The attitude was: "Okay, well done. The next problem is next week." It was business.' Not that there was actually bad blood anywhere – 'The only time I ever had a cross word with Frank was when he told me Mansell was joining the team. I said I didn't want him and I was leaving'

– but, to Rosberg's way of thinking, the team, embodied by Frank Williams, had misplaced its emotions, or had somehow forgotten to acquire them in the first place. 'Frank,' said Rosberg, 'thought in his own mind that he was very caring and yet he seemed to forget to do it. It was a strange thing. He wasn't distant – and yet he was very remote.' To which Lauda scathingly (but indirectly) riposted, 'He [Rosberg] overlooks the really important things, the result being that he never seems to appreciate what is going on around him.' Which was the appropriate tough guy response, and one that Frank Williams would have endorsed. Formula One was a kind of protracted war, and the last thing you needed was bleating from footsoldiers like Keke Rosberg.

But there was something undeniably chilling about the setup. Jones took the title in 1980 and left a year later. Rosberg got it in '82 and was edged out after a couple of years. Piquet won the title in '87 and left immediately, to join Lotus. Mansell won it in 1992 and likewise left immediately to go racing in the US. Prost won it in '93 and retired at the end of the year. Damon Hill won it in '96, but was given the sack, two-thirds of the way through the season. Jacques Villeneuve got it in '97, and, a year later, was gone, to join BAR.

In other words, not only did no one ever stay on long enough to nail two titles for Williams, they were apt to depart with the briskness of someone being checked out of a hotel. It was the inverse of the kind of productive bonding that went on between Chapman and Clark, or Ken Tyrrell and Jackie Stewart. Alan Jones, determinedly loyal, insisted that Williams the man 'has always been extremely analytical rather than hard – and there is a difference.' But this was a nuance not always appreciated by other drivers.

After all, a team boss can be hard *and* soft, without losing effectiveness. Alfred Neubauer was quite rightly feared by the rest of the Grand Prix community – with his incredible cars, ruthless administrative efficiency, nightmarish physical presence – yet dedicated himself to providing his drivers with the tenderest comforts known to man. Yes, the Mercedes F1 experiment was short-lived, so Neubauer never had to face the chronic resentments that build up in a team over time; yes, he had two drivers who were not only geniuses, but who respected the team hierarchy; and the commercial pressures, although clear, weren't quite the same as those burdening teams in the mid-1980s. But he was, nonetheless, 'a mother hen with her chicks', as opposed to a shark-eyed obsessive whose only real ambition was to make the outfit that bore his name the most successful in the history of the sport. Neubauer could be more than one thing at a time.

But Frank Williams' insatiable need to prevail would lead a clear-eyed Eddie Irvine to muse (a) 'I would certainly not want to play a game of poker with Frank' and (b) 'He has always liked to prove that it is his car, rather than the driver, which does the winning, and I have to say he seems to have a point.' Peter Windsor, Williams team manager in the 1990s, saw it this way: 'Frank is a loner, but I wouldn't say he has a mean streak. I don't think there is anything mean about Frank.' No, Frank's remorseless behaviour obeyed this slightly pretzel-shaped logic: 'He's a very hard person sometimes but he is no harder on anyone than he is on himself. Therefore he is very fair as a result.' Cruel but fair. But also (Windsor again) 'The most unpredictable person I have ever worked for in my life. It was impossible to predict what he was thinking or how he would react to any situation.'

To recap: cruel, fair, completely unpredictable. An ethical despot, in other words.

Enzo Ferrari was pretty much the same, of course, and it

never stopped drivers wanting to sign for *his* team. And Colin Chapman was a notorious manipulator of other people. And no one would ever mistake Ron Dennis for Albert Schweitzer. But even former Williams press officer Ann Bradshaw had to confirm that, 'Frank has never been someone who engaged in social chit-chat. He isn't someone you would shoot the breeze with. He can be evasive.' And if that's what your own PR people say, then either you don't give a damn about how the world sees you, or you do give a damn, and you want the world to regard you with, basically, intimidated respect. Ferrari was a despot, all right, but his favouritism and moodiness could also be taken as marks of vulnerability, of humanity, even. Frank Williams, on the other hand, seemed to be the equivalent of the cold-blooded, highly successful, CEO. Damon Hill said of Williams: 'I have a soft spot for him. But I also know he is capable of doing despicable things – despicable in my terms.' Williams was so absolutely in charge of his emotions that, even after Senna's death, 'He did cry on the flight back from Imola,' according to the team's Iain Cunningham, but 'that was the only time I heard of any real emotion.'

Or would it be fairer to say that it is an intrinsic part of the appeal of Formula One, that it is so devious, multi-layered and conflict-prone – involving drivers, cars, designers, engine suppliers, tyre manufacturers, teams, team bosses, sponsors, a none-too-transparent governing body and some of the biggest egos on the planet – that it requires a different level of sophisticated, worldly, cynical, engagement on the part of the fan, the driver, the team boss? Only Scuderia Ferrari really inspire simple-minded football-fan levels of tribal loyalty – my team, right or wrong. All the rest is like an incredibly well-funded game of three-dimensional chess, cunning, intelligent, sceptical, dazzled by money and power, and capable of being thrown into disarray by the unpredictable exercise of human frailty or whim. Even calling Formula One a *sport* seems somehow wrong, given the physical and emotional distancing of the sportsmen from the fans; combined with all this extra intellectual and material tendency towards hyper-complication.

Would it then be fairer *and* simpler to say that Frank Williams in the 1980s and 1990s epitomised this modern state of affairs, that he wasn't a despot or a Machiavelli, but rather a highly developed and laudably candid incarnation of what everyone else was thinking, anyway? That he was the spirit of the sport, made flesh?

Or do we need to wait for the Mansell and Hill episodes to play out before we can reach a verdict?

20

MAY, 1982:
GILLES VILLENEUVE,
FERRARI, ANOTHER END

The harder-nosed an individual or a collective tries to be, the worse it is when sentiment does get through. You can only expend so much energy repressing your feelings. And when Formula One gets sentimental, it does so in a big way. In the case of Gilles Villeneuve, all the emotions got terribly overstimulated from the start and stayed that way to the end. As the death-or-glory, gladiatorially fixated Denis Jenkinson put it, 'Villeneuve just drove with tremendous spirit all the time. I loved him for that. He was a hero.' Such was the power of Villeneuve: bearded men fell in love with him.

Viewed rationally, of course, there was something not quite right about Gilles Villeneuve. This is true of many (if not all) top sportsmen, one way or another, but in Villeneuve's case, it's hard to escape the conclusion that he was a natural, both in the sense that he was fantastically gifted as a driver; and that bits of his personality were defective, or had simply gone missing.

When he signed for Ferrari in 1977, after two years spent trouncing the opposition in Formula Atlantic (plus a quick spell in a McLaren third car) he was twenty-seven-year-old, very nearly twenty-eight. He was Québecois with a wife and two small children. He was disarmingly honest and unaffected in his dealings with the rest of the world. He was completely culturally incurious. He lived in a motorhome, where he never smoked, drank or ate anything more adventurous than a burger with fries. He was pathologically addicted to risk, but was deeply conservative and even repressive when it came to family matters. Many times, he gave the impression of being incapable of rational thought; occasionally, he even came across as a case of arrested development. And about the first thing anyone said of him when they saw him on the track was that he was fast, but also an idiot: 'That boy's in too much of a hurry' (Carlos Reutemann); 'The man is a public menace' (Ronnie Peterson); 'That bloody red shit-bucket was all over me!' (Alan Jones).

To be fair, Jones didn't mind Villeneuve's immoderate need for speed as much as many other drivers. When Villeneuve smashed into him at the 1981 British GP, instead of going round to the Ferrari pit to fill Villeneuve's face in, Jones merely indulged him. 'Oh, it's just typical of old Gilles,' he said. 'You've got to give him credit because the guy never stops trying.' But Jones could afford to be relaxed, not least because he was the reigning world champion, while Villeneuve showed almost no sign of acquiring the kind of mental self-discipline which would get him to the same point. He was a loose cannon, in short, and much of what he did, on and off the track, seemed to be the expression of nothing more than a kind of ungovernable, shapeless urgency, a need to try and get his heart rate above its normal absurdly placid level and into the red zone, a place where he might be able to experience fear.

To this end, he sought out impassable mountain tracks to test his 4x4s to breaking point; he flew his helicopter around with marginal fuel levels or a defective electrical system; he routinely trashed road cars, whether they were Fiat 131s or Ferrari 400s, galvanising his passengers with a mixture of admiration and terror. 'Driving back to the hotel,' Peter Windsor (a passenger in Gille's Fiat) once remarked, 'Gilles would use handbrake turns as a matter of course.' And on the track, it was the same, only more so. He was either stationary or flat out. In 1979, 'The Prince of Destruction' (as he became known at Ferrari) led nearly a third of *all* the racing laps in *all* the races, but Jody Scheckter, his team-mate at Ferrari, became world champion that year.

Scheckter was the same age as Villeneuve and a hard driver too, but managed to keep his mind on the bigger picture. 'Gilles,' he said, 'wanted to win laps. He didn't really want to win races, he didn't want to win the World Championship. He was a very intelligent guy, but in my opinion he wanted the wrong things out of racing.'

The wrong things, but with the right degree of spectacle. Thus, at Zandvoort, August 1979, he famously went off with a puncture on the left rear tyre, reversed the car back onto the track, did – effectively – a whole lap at rather more than touring speed on two wheels, swerved back into the pits, where he yelled at the mechanics, 'Put a fucking wheel on there! Let me go out again!' And, like Alan Jones, everyone thought, 'It's just typical of old Gilles,' and loved him for this protracted moment of madness.

But why did he do it? If the suspension wasn't crocked up when he went off into the dirt at Tarzan, it was certainly a mess by the time he got back to his team. He was reputed to have a keen mechanical sympathy and was a good tester – but what red mist had come down so that he simply ignored the sparks from the undertray, the crashing, flapping wheel, the ruined suspension? It was as if he'd forgotten that the car *was* a car and had instead become something with infinitely lower engineering standards – a packing crate, or a brick wall. It was not rational behaviour.

Which was exactly what the crowd loved. Who, after all, wants to observe a careful conservation of the car with a view to a scrupulous amassing of points in order to calculatedly win a title, if instead you could watch someone who went bonkers and gave you a good time?

In this way, Villeneuve's 1979 season became a succession of dazzling, ultimately pointless, one-offs. At the French GP at Dijon, Villeneuve and René Arnoux, in a Renault, had a spectacular, *mano-a-mano* scrap in the closing stages, in which they fought like maniacs for second place, wheel-locking, running wide, bumping into each other, the essence of motor racing – at the end of which, Villeneuve came second (no one-two for Renault on their home patch), and Arnoux sportingly announced, 'Gilles drove a fantastic race. I enjoyed it very much!' To which Villeneuve replied, 'We didn't crash and it's okay. I enjoyed myself amazingly!'

Both drivers were gravely chastised by the Grand Prix Drivers' Safety Committee (President, Jody Scheckter) at the next race, the British Grand Prix, but it was all so much background noise to Villeneuve, who went on to pull his two-wheel stunt at Zandvoort, before creating another precedent for himself by seizing control of the American GP at Watkins Glen, where it poured with rain in the first practice session and rained heavily through much of the actual race.

It was the wet practice session which reduced iron man

Denis Jenkinson to a state of girlish adoration. 'Oh, he was fantastic! He was unbelievable,' Jenkinson said, overcome. Little Villeneuve had to be physically carried by a large mechanic across the puddles and strapped into his car. Then, in the torrent, he set out almost alone, to set a time *eleven seconds* faster than the next car down, Scheckter in the other Ferrari. It was (of course) an exercise in futility (the weather cleared up the next day and Alan Jones took a confident pole for Williams) but so startling a demonstration of skill and bravery that Jacques Laffite could do nothing but shake his head and ask, 'Why do we bother? He's different from the rest of us. On a separate level.' Scheckter thought him mad: 160 mph in a flood. But in the race the gods smiled again, Jones lost a wheel and retired, while Villeneuve (still glowing from his *beau geste* in practice) was rewarded with a win nearly a minute ahead of Arnoux, in spotty, rain-bothered conditions.

It was wonderful; it was miraculous. In the space of a season, Villeneuve had established himself among the other drivers as someone with excessive talents, endless verve and complete fairness in the heat of competition. Among the spectators, he was a show in his own right, a driver who uniquely justified the price of admission. So beloved was he that, riding as passenger in the new world champion's street car, he found himself more popular with Italian passers-by than Scheckter himself, the champ. Fans gathered round Gille's window, shouting, 'Hey! Villanova!' while Scheckter (filling up with petrol) was ignored. His celebrity was prodigious and immediate.

So, in 1979, Villeneuve took three wins, a pole position, four fastest laps, and came second in the Drivers' Championship, only four points behind his team-mate. Ferrari won the Constructors' title with their first attempt at a ground-effect car. Villeneuve's identification with the team was deep, grateful and heartfelt. To prove his commitment to the greater forces which owned the Scuderia, he even did a bit of rallying for Lancia, another part of the Fiat combine. And he felt a nervous warmth towards the *Commendatore*, revealing, rather sweetly, that, although Ferrari came across as a hard-bitten user of men, 'Maybe even a godfather,' nonetheless, 'He's a kind man and sometimes I think he sees himself as a father to his drivers.' Everything pointed to a harmonious and productive future together.

The problem was that Ferrari was just about to enter one of its darkest phases. Scheckter's title would be the last Drivers' Championship the team would see for over twenty years. The Ferrari 312T had been one of the most successful cars ever seen in Formula One, with Niki Lauda using it to win Championships in 1975 and 1977; Scheckter picking up the baton of initiative two years later.

But by 1980, the car – in its final version, the 312T5 – had become a turkey. It was the wrong shape to get the ground-effects to work really well (mainly due to its unhelpful flat-12 engine layout); and it stopped being deeply reliable, becoming, instead, as undependable as fairy dust. Villeneuve managed to rack up six retirements out of fourteen starts, with a total of six points for the whole season. The team as a whole failed to win a single Grand Prix. Villeneuve called the 312T5 a 'Wheelbarrow' and seethed at the way his fortunes had turned. 'When I won a race easily last year, people would say, "What a fantastic driver." Now they don't even notice that I'm battling twice as hard.' He also found himself having to grapple with the toxicity and paranoia generated by a Ferrari team in difficulty. According to Gaston Parent, his manager, 'Gilles thought that Forghieri and Piccinini –

[Marco Piccinini, the team manager] were afraid to blame the car. After the races they would phone the Old Man and tell him it was the driver or the tyres. It was never the Ferrari.'

It got worse. Scheckter packed it all in and went off to become, ultimately, an organic farmer. Didier Pironi, a classy, bumptious Frenchman, took his place. 'When one is praised and the other is forgotten,' Pironi philosophised of life as a driver in an F1 team, 'he feels wounded and resentful.' This was more than mere Gallic *de haut en bas*. It showed that Pironi was the kind of person able to take a suitably cool, worldly view of the sport's shifting dynamics. While Villeneuve was the new boy, he could only succeed. Now that Pironi – two years Villeneuve's junior – was on the scene, it was Villeneuve whose authority was open to challenge.

The year 1981 came along, and the car was still dreadful. The new Ferrari 126CK, had, on the one hand, a smart-as-paint V6 Turbo to keep up with the Renaults; on the other hand, it had the handling characteristics of, in Villeneuve's words, 'a fast red Cadillac'. The V6 suffered from routinely catastrophic turbo lag, which managed to combine with an ill-thought-through chassis to fill each corner with a kind of whiplash, and to transmit every bump and imperfection from the track surface directly up Villeneuve's spine. The car shook so badly, he actually found it hard to see; and he ended up with a headache every time he drove.

This left him with not much else to do except defy the odds and burnish his legend, rather than claim any Championships. He won by a margin of forty seconds at Monaco and followed that up with one of *those* defining drives (up there with Moss at Monaco, Fangio/Stewart at the Nürburgring), in the Spanish GP at Jarama, June 1981.

Everything was against him. His car still had the power,

and was still painfully unmanageable. He was stuck in seventh place on the grid. He had a Renault, a McLaren and two Williamses ahead of him, all infinitely nicer to drive, all eminently capable of winning. The pack formed up, Alan Jones and Carlos Reutemann took off in their Williams-Fords, and that should have been that.

But Villeneuve was in one of his transcendent moods. Less than a fifth of the way into the race, Jones had gone off the track, and Villeneuve had struggled into a hair's-breadth lead, where he sat, with Reutemann squirming around a few feet behind him. Reutemann was then joined by Jacques Lafitte (in a Ligier), John Watson (McLaren) and Elio de Angelis (Lotus), any or all of whom ought to have got the jump on Villeneuve in the second half of the race, leaving him somewhere around fifth place. But (with all that Ferrari power) he sprinted away from them in the straights and locked them in a train behind him on the rest of the circuit. This he managed to keep up, in intense heat, for over an hour – an exhibition of supreme cool-headedness, bravura and cunning; a display which only the greatest of drivers could have managed. The result was the squeakiest possible win for Villeneuve: the following four cars crossed the line within the next 1.24 seconds.

The press at once claimed that 'Villeneuve's race was something of a masterpiece.' Villeneuve himself, disarmingly modest, said that he had 'big problems around all the twisty bits, and it was a really hard race.' Mauro Forghieri, thinking, as ever, of purely mechanical advantage, started off by announcing that 'The best part of our car is the turbo. It was fantastic today.' Then he collected himself, and said, 'No, correction. The best part of our car today was Villeneuve. He was super, fantastic. What a driver!' Gordon Murray, his usual otherworldliness for once left in abeyance, was perhaps the most telling witness: 'I honestly think it was the greatest drive I've ever seen by anybody. His chassis is awful, worse by far than that of any other driver. His driving was just unreal.'

Oh, and Enzo Ferrari? 'Gilles Villeneuve on Sunday,' said the *Commendatore*, 'made me live again the legend of Nuvolari.'

Well, there it is. Ferrari himself said it; and it is impossible to imagine a statement more emotive, more resonant. Ferrari, the last link to the pre-war world, summons up the shade of the Flying Mantuan, his invisible presence creating the most powerful magic, the most numinous associations. Little Villeneuve, indomitable, fierce, brilliant and victorious: precisely a Nuvolari of modern times.

Which was fine for sentimentalists and historians; less so for Villeneuve himself.

The fact was that he was not taking the strain too well. It was fine and dandy being a folk hero, but Villeneuve was well over thirty by now; he was stuck with a car that might never come good; he was surrounded by go-ahead types like Prost and Lauda and Pironi; he loathed the new ground-effect tweaks which caused him (like everyone else) to rage that 'It's not driving, it's just a matter of aiming for the corner, flooring it and hoping you're on the right line. There's no satisfaction in these bloody things.' He started to dismiss other, less torridly committed racers, as 'parade drivers' or 'wankers' or '*chauffeurs de ballet*'. He also worried about his image. He shaved two years off the age he was prepared to admit to in public. He fretted over his diminutive height. He obsessed over his thinning hair, urgently smoothing it forward over his scalp the moment he took off his crash helmet. And he got meaner at home.

This was a real change from the original, unaffected, unpretentious Villeneuve, the one who had scratched a living in his early days, who preferred life with his wife and kids in a blue-collar all-American motorhome to a deracinated existence in expensive hotels and service apartments, who treated the world with constant, endearing candour.

Depressed, he went and boosted his self-esteem by buying an insanely fast and uncomfortable 36-foot powerboat, at the same time as he witheld spending money from his wife, Joann. He was painfully jealous and possessive when he was around her, but this didn't prevent him from starting a covert affair of his own. Rows broke out, and the kids, according to Joann, 'sensed there was a lot of tension and friction between us. It made them unhappy and unsettled them.' And young Jacques Villeneuve, ten years old, couldn't do anything right: 'Gilles was very demanding with Jacques.' Jacques 'would get very nervous just trying so hard to please his father'. Or, as one of Jacques Villeneuve's friends put it, 'When Gilles was racing, Jacques became almost a basket case.'

And there was still the problem with Pironi. When Villeneuve had gone full-time with Ferrari in 1978, there was everything to play for: his team-mate was Carlos Reutemann, quick but inconsistent, not an obvious threat to Villeneuve the brilliant new boy. With Scheckter in '79, he could give the more experienced driver a real run for his money, while still establishing his Nuvolari-of-our-times credentials and waiting for his chance to take the title. 1980 was a fallow year; Scheckter left, Villeneuve assumed the nominal lead driver position. And then in 1981, Pironi arrived.

Which was fine, at first. Villeneuve got on well enough with him. They could work to improve the car, rebuild the

Emerson Fittipaldi, winner at Brands Hatch, 1972, enjoying the moment.

And enjoying a joke with Jackie Stewart, while Ronnie Peterson, looking on, is mildly sceptical. Note the collective hair.

And doing what he does best, Silverstone, 1973, in the final version of the extraordinary Lotus 72.

James Hunt at work, United States Grand Prix West, 1976, with the Race Queen.

Niki Lauda, the same year, six months later.

Gilles Villeneuve, 1980.

Relaxed: Nelson Piquet, South Africa, 1982.

There they all are: (*left to right*) Ayrton Senna, Alain Prost, Nigel Mansell and Nelson Piquet, on the pit wall at Estoril, Portugal, 1986, every one a champion.

But, three years later, Prost and Senna are lost in their world of conflict at Suzuka.

And it shows.

Then Prost escapes in a Williams, while Senna has a go at
Damon Hill, Monza, 1993.

Senna before the San Marino Grand Prix, 1994, the site of his fatal crash.

A familiar arrangement: Michael Schumacher, winner at Brazil, 1994,
loves up Flavio Briatore; Damon Hill (second place) spectates.

Brazil, 2006: Schumacher after his last Grand Prix.

Brazil, 2008, with Lewis Hamilton after the Great Escape. Ron Dennis is suitably happy.

The story of 2009: (*left to right*) Rubens Barrichello, Ross Brawn and Jenson Button.

team's prospects. But there was always a profound cultural distinction between them, almost a generational distinction. Villeneuve was a romantic, a man who loved to drive, and who – for all his juvenile stunting off-track, and his death-or-glory madness on-track – was scrupulously fair in a fight: as testified to by René Arnoux after the '79 French GP performance. 'You can only race like that, you know,' said Arnoux, 'with someone you trust completely, and you don't meet many like him.' Villeneuve was, in essence, old-fashioned.

Pironi, on the other hand, was modern. He had worked his way up through the sport in a very French, *dirigiste*, semi-state-sponsored (ELF petrol) sort of way. He was ambitious, he was patriotic, he was a good politicker, he was determined to become the first French Formula One champion. He made it his business to handle the emotional complexities that permeated Ferrari. And his luck, his timing, were good. The powerful, nimble new Ferrari 126C2 was an altogether better car than the Red Cadillac that Villeneuve had struggled to tame. The 1982 season looked very promising for Monsieur Didier.

But worse for Villeneuve. His first two races ended in retirement. For the third, he was disqualified, owing – of all things – to the size of his rear wing. Pironi managed to extract a single point in this same period. Then, at San Marino in April, there was a FOCA-led boycott of the race, leaving the field open to Renault and Ferrari, plus one or two FOCA refusniks such as Tyrrell and Toleman. Fourteen cars started, instead of the usual thirty-plus. Ferrari had the place to themselves once the Renaults' engines had packed up, and Villeneuve led Pironi comfortably round the track for the closing stages of the race.

At which point, the trouble began. The two Ferraris were so far ahead of third-placer Michele Alboreto, floundering along in a Tyrrell, that the team hung out a SLOW sign, to make sure that the pair neither broke their engines nor ran out of fuel. Villeneuve took SLOW to mean 'hold your positions', as well as 'keep the speed down'. Pironi thought otherwise. A bit of dicing ensued. Villeneuve and Pironi swapped the lead, notionally in order to keep the crowd from dozing off; in actuality, as a portent of things to come. Villeneuve assumed that, whatever else happened, Pironi would stop overtaking shortly before the end and have the manners to cross the finishing line in a dutiful second place, younger driver yielding to the more senior, and so on.

But he didn't. Instead, he nipped past Villeneuve on the last lap, gave him no chance to come back, and stole the race.

Villeneuve was incandescent. His sense of affronted propriety, combined with his anxieties about his future in the sport, sent him clean over the edge: 'I haven't said a word to him [Pironi] and I'm not going to again – *ever*! I have declared war. I'll do my own thing in the future. It's war. Absolutely war.' The Ferrari team operatives made it worse by hemming and hawing. Pironi had made himself popular with the Scuderia, and his people were adamant that SLOW merely meant 'slow' rather than 'don't take the lead'.

Who had misunderstood the sign? Pironi or Villeneuve? After a while, Ferrari himself joined in, giving it as his opinion that Pironi had misinterpreted the pit signals and that he well understood Villeneuve's disappointment and agreed with him. But this was no use to Villeneuve. He was not in the most robust psychological state to begin with, and now, instead of merely vowing to get even (think of what Prost, Senna, Lauda, Schumacher, would have done in the same situation), he fixated on the loathed Pironi for two weeks, all the way up to the Belgian Grand Prix, unable to see past his monstrous, duplicitous form. He became obsessed.

And the rest is history: 8 May, Zolder, the Belgian GP, the last minutes of qualifying: Pironi had set fastest time. The session was coming to an end. Villeneuve had one fleeting chance to beat his despised team-mate for pole position. His tyres were shot; his steering was playing up. He was not thinking in the least rationally. The act of driving fast, the thing that gave him more pleasure than anything else, had become corrupted into an act of vengeance. He wanted to nail Pironi. He wanted to do him in. He flogged himself round the two-and-a-half-mile track, came up behind the hapless Jochen Mass, coasting in after his final lap, committed himself to the wrong overtaking manoeuvre. His Ferrari made contact with Mass's right rear tyre. It then launched itself into the air, before completely destroying itself, hurling Villeneuve clean out of the cockpit and throwing him into a catch fence. His neck was broken. He died later that day.

Ferrari withdrew from the race and went home to mourn.

It took a long time for them to win the Drivers' Championship again. They picked up a number of Constructors' titles; but there was a big gap between Scheckter and Schumacher. And, in August 1988, Enzo Ferrari died, aged ninety. There was an air of finality which hung about the team, all through this time. As Alain Prost would later remark, during his brief spell at the Scuderia, 'Crisis is the normal state at Ferrari. When you win, there is a crisis of optimism.'

But the crisis of optimism took a long time to arrive. And many people, inside and outside the team, never quite got over the death of Villeneuve: the last hero; the standard-bearer for an age which had produced Ferrari himself.

21

THE BOREDOM, PARANOIA AND OUTRIGHT MADNESS THAT IS MCLAREN, PROST AND SENNA

It was perhaps unwise of Ron Dennis, team principal at McLaren since 1981, to come out (as he did, once) with the nerveless observation, 'The problem with grey is that people immediately see it as a colour that goes with blandness. But I see it as a colour that works very well in mixtures and hues and responds to highlights. I like the flexibility of grey and I didn't choose it by accident. I think it's fresh, clean and has a tranquil effect, and it's also got dignity and class.' He was talking about the decor of his office at the McLaren HQ in Woking (the town itself a byword for dullness) but he could equally have been summing up the public image of the McLaren team during the 1980s and early 1990s: efficient, dull, ubiquitous, inescapable, really quite grey.

Once, long ago, there was a time when Ron Dennis wasn't Mr McLaren. He had started at Coopers, with the tiresome Jochen Rindt, moved on to Brabham, then decided to make his own cars. And at the start of the 1980s, he was running a successful Formula Two outfit called Project Four Racing. McLaren, meanwhile, were still under Teddy 'The Wiener' Mayer, but were stuck in a rut. Their last Drivers' Championship had been in 1976, with James Hunt; since when they had lost vitality and sense of purpose with the feeble M26 and M29 F1 cars, driven by slightly-less-than-Championship drivers John Watson and Andrea de Cesaris.

A connection was made. Ron Dennis was not only incredibly highly motivated and well organised, he also had sponsorship from the Marlboro cigarette people, and the services of top-of-the-line engineer John Barnard, with his clever carbon-fibre chassis designs. A kind of reverse takeover was duly fashioned, with Dennis becoming effective head of McLaren and establishing the foundations of the outfit we know and revere today. To an already strong financial/organisational/engineering mix, the team added a new engine in the form of the powerful and efficient TAG/Porsche turbo, and then a couple of absolutely first-rank drivers: Niki Lauda and Alain Prost. Lauda was making a comeback in '82 in order to scrape together some cash for his business enterprises; and Prost joined in '84 fervidly eager (after Renault) to reassert himself as a Championship contender.

And as a convocation of sheer brainpower and cunning, it was irresistible. In 1984, they collectively destroyed the opposition, taking the Constructors' title with twelve wins out of a possible sixteen. They also took the Drivers' title, with Lauda first and Prost second, a mere *half a point* behind his team-mate, but both of them with more than twice as many points as Elio de Angelis (Lotus) in third place.

Thus McLaren was established as the epitome of the modern British constructor, the apotheosis of the new *garagiste*, with a team of hundreds working at the gleaming shed of the Woking HQ, hundreds more at the TAG/Porsche engine works in Stuttgart, all in conditions as spotless and neurotically clinical as a NASA laboratory, all presided over by Ron Dennis: the team boss as omniscient, grey-loving stoneface. Thirty-odd years before, it was BRM, in a freezing shed round the back of someone's house, an air of austerity, desperation and unfeasible dreams, led by a romantic, culminating in an abject lack of success. Now it was McLaren. How far we had come in that time.

All of which was fine, so far as Alain Prost was concerned. He was doing everything just right. He won more Grands Prix than Lauda (to advertise his genius) but came runner-up (to show respect to the more celebrated driver). He also loved McLaren, whose crisp shirts, seriousness, lack of hysteria and Stakhanovite work ethic, suited him like a well-made set of overalls. So happy was he, that the next year, he took a highly efficient world title (his first), followed by another one in 1986.

Admittedly, the '86 title was achieved by dint of sneaking in between Nelson Piquet and Nigel Mansell, who had, un-believably, got themselves caught up in a cat fight at Williams, but Prost didn't care. 'I'm very sorry for Nigel,' he said, coyly. 'He deserved to be champion this year.' Prost was in the Land of the Blessed. He described the McLaren-TAG team as being 'Like my family, with a wonderful, friendly atmosphere.' He saw things completely eye-to-eye with John Barnard – and as for Ron Dennis, there was no praise high enough: 'Ron Dennis is a leader of men, a catalyst of energies, he is completely respected.' It was a world of sense and order. 'When I was at McLaren,' he sighed, later in his career, 'every remark was taken into account from Ron Dennis down to the lowest mechanic.' And in this manner, for three years in a row, McLaren won the Drivers' Championship.

They took a break in 1987 to allow Nelson Piquet and Williams-Honda to take the Drivers' and Constructors' titles (Nigel Mansell losing out again), before coming back in 1988 with the McLaren-Honda MP4/4, and the most eye-boggling display of competence ever seen in Formula One: fifteen wins out of sixteen races, with only Gerhard Berger's operatically sentimental win for Ferrari at Monza, just a month after Enzo Ferrari's death, breaking the spell. Ten of McLaren's wins were one-twos, at that – as often as not, a minute ahead of whoever had the unenviable job of coming in third. It was wonderful and terrible, the kind of ruthlessness that compels an awed respect at the same time as it threatens to send the observer into a light coma of boredom. It was Mercedes, 1955, all over again, but on a numerically far greater scale.

What stopped it from being completely tedious was the fact that it was now Ayrton Senna who just managed to pick up the Championship (as opposed to Niki Lauda), with ninety points to Prost's eighty-seven – the title chase thrillingly going all the way to Suzuka, the penultimate Grand Prix. To be pedantic, Prost ended the season with 105 points to Senna's ninety-four, but at the time only the best eleven results counted towards the Championship. Prost's steady accretion of points, which had worked well enough in '85 and '86, tripped him up this time. Senna won at Suzuka, and his eight outright wins to Prost's seven did the trick. Clearly, something needed to be done. The Professor went away to ponder his arithmetic.

He also went away to ponder the problem of Senna.

An awful lot has been written and said about Senna, over the years. The easy part is this: born in 1960 (which made him five years Prost's junior), to a wealthy São Paulo family, he rapidly developed an obsession with motorised transport, which evolved into an obsession with kart racing, which developed into a massively unfrivolous obsession with winning on the track, whatever the means of transport. As a childhood friend noted, Senna was 'very serious as a boy, I think too much serious. He seemed like a child who was thirty years old.' He duly moved to Europe and into the world of Formula Three, where he made a similar impression on his fellow competitors. According to one (the excellently named Calvin Fish): 'I'm not really sure he was enjoying himself,' and, 'People used to say "He's not really a happy kind of guy".'

Senna was, in fact, a bit different from the rest of the crowd, whichever continent he was on. He was introverted, not massively confident of his command of English, somewhat spartan in his personal habits (no booze, no fags, not a tremendous amount of womanising) and elementally committed to becoming F1 World Champion – really astoundingly so, even when compared with a conventionally single-minded, hyper-competitive F1 driver.

A drive at Toleman duly came his way: complete with an astonishing performance in a June downpour at the '84 Monaco GP. On this occasion, Senna exploited the great levelling effects of rain and Monaco to such effect that, even in the fairly feeble Toleman TG184, he saw off everyone on the track, apart from none other than Alain Prost, who was leading in his McLaren. More – Senna was actually catching him, and could very well have won the race, had it not been for Clerk of the Course Jacky Ickx stopping the race at the end of the thirty-second lap, citing the weather as reason enough to finish it there and then.

A degree of uproar followed, parties noting that Ickx had failed to consult with the stewards before halting the race; that he also worked for Porsche, who were supplying McLaren's engines at the time; that he was a Francophone, like Prost; and that the rain appeared to be easing off, anyway. Whatever the truth, he was suspended from race control duties, while an outraged Senna, having seen a guaranteed win snatched from his fingers, never forgave any of the chief protagonists. Toleman team leader Peter Gethin then did his best to interpret this new star to the rest of the world by claiming that 'Basically I think he's a nicer bloke than he appears to be,' but Senna had already instilled among his fellow F1 drivers the nervous awareness that he was not quite as other men.

Essentially, Senna took car control to a new level; and he could do it consistently, over the length of an entire race. He was the opposite of smooth – constantly on and off the throttle, stabbing at the brakes into corners, unsettling the car as if it were a go-kart, working it all the time, pinching out fractions of seconds. To take one observation from thousands: John Watson – no mean driver, five Grand Prix wins to his credit – said that to watch Senna in full flight 'was just mesmerising. Here was a man who is on a different level from anyone. Nobody was doing what Ayrton was doing in a car.' And when he stopped driving, his powers of concentration were such that he could analyse what he had just done in astonishing detail. When he moved to Lotus in the mid-1990s, Senna got Nigel Stepney as his mechanic. Stepney reckoned that 'on a debrief he could spend five or ten minutes telling you about one lap, every bump, every entry, every exit, every line he'd taken through the corners.' So boggling were his powers of recall that he even 'wore down' the Lotus designer, Gérard Ducarouge, with the sheer level of information at his command.

He served his apprenticeship: Toleman, Lotus, before arriving at last at McLaren, which is where the tensions really set in.

* * *

In calmer moments, even Prost would say of the Brazilian genius, 'The way he drives is very good and I must say he is fantastic, unbelievably quick, but for me he is driving too hard.' The same was said, not so long before, of Villeneuve; but Villeneuve's fair play on the track and saintly amiability off meant that people forgave him. Not so with Senna, who, at the age of twenty-eight, was just entering his most potent driving years, which were also the years when his ruthless, mystical arrogance was at its most baffling and infuriating. He managed to be both hot-tempered and inscrutable, and, indeed, the only person who seemed able to get under Senna's skin was – who else? – Nelson Piquet.

The rest of the time, however, he spent perfecting his already-extraordinary driving talents. It was in a qualifying session at Monaco, 1988, when Senna had his now-famous mystical encounter with pure speed: 'Suddenly I was nearly two seconds faster than anybody else, including my team-mate [Prost] with the same car. And I suddenly realised I was no longer driving the car consciously. I was kind of driving it by instinct, only I was in a different dimension. It was like I was in a tunnel.' Other drivers knew about this – the state of perception-altering self-hypnosis, shifting one's relationship with the car, speed, the track, into a new plane of consciousness – and were not always happy with it. Jackie Stewart rightly mistrusted it, arguing that it indicated the turning-point at which the car started driving *you*, rather than the other way round. But Senna somehow appropriated the moment of transformation, adding it to the mystique which was growing up around him.

All of which left Prost in the unhelpful position of being the nail-chewing, fussy, brooding, *older* driver, with no satisfactory way of dealing with Senna's Olympian aura of entitlement. At first, he tried to act the grown-up, comparing the newly arrived Senna with a 'pampered child', whose 'natural ability had always made him the focal point and centre of attraction in any team he had driven for'. Pretty soon, though, Senna was chewing up 1988's calendar of races (four wins in a row, from the British GP to the Belgian); and by the time they got to the Japanese Grand Prix at Suzuka, Senna had become a 'spoiled brat', who, according to Prost, was not only detested by him, but by most of the rest of the McLaren team as well. Apparently, there was 'a straw poll at Woking to establish who they wanted, deep down, to win the title, and I had come out clearly ahead'. Pointless, of course. Senna put in an imposing drive in the wet and the dry at Suzuka, took pole and fastest lap, beat Prost in the race and then came in second, behind him at the final Grand Prix in Australia, to take the Championship.

Were McLaren-Honda upset by the tensions between these two great drivers? No, they were as pleased as anything. The trophy cabinet was bursting, the sponsors were happy, the opposition was petrified. And Ron Dennis and co. were completely ecstatic when the positions were reversed in 1989, with Prost winning the title and Senna coming in as runner-up. What wasn't to like?

Everything, if you were Prost. By '89, the 'family' he had grown so fond of at McLaren had become 'awful. Senna didn't speak, didn't smile. The difference between us was that I worked for McLaren, while Senna worked for Senna.' Well, wasn't that to some extent true of everyone? Nobody in Formula One *wasn't* striving for their own glory, their own greater reputation. Wasn't Prost being just a little over-sensitive?

No, the problem was now one of *betrayal* – just as it had been with Villeneuve and Pironi, at Ferrari, seven years before. In the case of Senna and Prost, the great betrayal came at the San Marino Grand Prix, Imola, April 1989; and it was Senna who broke his agreement with Prost that neither driver would try to overtake whoever managed to lead into the first corner. As it happened, Prost made the better start and moved ahead right away, only to find Senna diving past him at the Tosa hairpin (all this after a race restart, incidentally, Gerhard Berger having very nearly come to grief in a fireball, half an hour earlier) then sitting imperturbably at the front for the rest of the race, while an incensed Prost wandered home in second place, forty seconds behind.

'It all changed at Imola,' Prost raged. 'We had an agreement and he broke it. What he did was dishonest and dishonourable. I knew then that I could never trust him again. I could have hit him.' This was *lèse-majesté*, after all. Prost was a two-time Champion, five years older than Senna, an international sporting figure, and if Senna thought that after Imola there could be any relationship between them other than on a purely technical level, he was barking up the wrong tree: 'I no longer wish to have any business with him. I appreciate honesty, and he is not honest.' Senna's riposte? 'Get fucked.'

And here's an odd thing: when trying to choose one of *those* definitive drives by which to remember Senna, well, you could pick his '85 win at Spa (pouring rain) or his 1993 victory at Donington (pouring rain, then less rain, then more rain), or his Spanish GP win in '86 (unbelievably close finish, Villeneuve-style, but with Mansell second), and let it stand for the whole of his achievement.

But it almost makes more sense to pick Imola, 1989, precisely because of the discord and rancour which accompanied it. That was the thing with Senna. However brilliant a driver he was, however much he embellished his reputation with his otherworldliness, his devotion to winning, his sheer conviction, there was something unwholesome, dangerously unethical, about it all. Fangio (still around, like a profoundly respected, but ageing, pope) summed it up by declaring that Senna was a great champion, but *not* a great sportsman. It was a slightly uneasy precedent that the Brazilian appeared to be setting: the notion that *winning* justified anything, anything at all.

The season went on, Prost and Senna grimly blanking each other in the McLaren pits. Senna took three GPs in a row (San Marino, Monaco and Mexico), but Prost, showing terrific cunning and toughness, fought back, with the US, French and British GPs. Back in '82, the wretched Villeneuve, unable to deal with Pironi's ethical depravity, had lost control of himself, with fatal results. Prost, however, turned out to be a steelier personality. By the time he won again, at Monza, in September, he was well in contention, having stashed away some useful second places to add to his wins – in contrast to Senna's dazzling but inconsistent assortment of pole positions, wins, retirements and out-of-the-points finishes.

And at Suzuka, for the Japanese Grand Prix, Prost very nearly had his third title in the bag. The pressure was showing (he had used his 'spoiled brat' taunt against Senna not long before the race), but Senna unquivocally *had* to win in order to give himself any chance of thieving the title from his team-mate. As it turned out, he was spectacularly on form: his pole position was a second and a half quicker than Prost's number two time, and, despite a crummy start and a duff pit stop, he managed to get back up through the field and right back behind Prost, well before the end of the race. He could sense Destiny working for him; his genius was at full stretch; the title shimmered before him.

Which is where it all went wrong. Senna, about to make history, lunged out to take Prost at the chicane; Prost moved over to cover; Senna, believing himself to have the advantage, refused to give way; the cars made contact, and the two drivers went off. Prost, thinking that it was all over, got out of his car and wandered negligently back to the pits. But Senna saw it differently. In a Villeneuve-like passion, he drove back onto the circuit, made it round to the pits, had his nose-cone changed, fell back into the race, and won it, from an absolutely flabbergasted Alessandro Nannini, driving a Benetton. And then, after all this, Senna was disqualified for missing out the chicane on the lap of the accident, and Nannini was handed the win in his place.

Senna appealed to the FIA. They reaffirmed the disqualification, suspended his licence for six months (although the suspension was, as it were, suspended) and fined him $100,000. Prost got to keep his third title, while setting his detestation of Senna in stone. 'Senna,' he said, 'is a man who just lives for and thinks about competition. He has abandoned everything else, every human relationship. He feels sustained by God and he is capable of taking every risk because he thinks he is immortal.'

It was all very odd. On the one hand, the McLaren team was so monumentally efficient at winning races, it was in danger of crushing the life out of the sport which gave it being (Australia, '89, being an event of real freakishness: neither McLaren finished). On the other hand, it had somehow allowed the two best drivers in the world to get to the point where they loathed one another so badly that they were in danger of destroying each on and off the track.

We have indeed come a long way from the effortless, strife-free superiority of Mercedes/Fangio/Moss/1955 – or, for that matter, from Lotus/Clark/Chapman/1965, when Jim Clark won five Grands Prix in succession and took the Championship by winning six out of a possible ten races. (The '65 season was so predictable that even *The Times*, normally 100 per cent patriotic, complained that 'The one-sidedness of G.P. racing in 1965 has tended to remove some of the tension and drama which one likes to associate with motor racing's *corps d'élite*'.) But then, Lotus had a clear team hierarchy (Clark's team-mate Mike Spence being there mainly to make up the numbers) with no room for argument (except, possibly, between Clark and Chapman) and a correspond-ingly clear sense of purpose. Mercedes were the same, only better. So how could McLaren have got themselves into a position where, at the height of their success, anarchy beckoned?

In a sense, Senna was doing no more than embodying the larger social changes that had taken place in the twenty-five years separating him from Jim Clark. The culture of defer-ence had gone comprehensively out of the window, while self-interest – the driving compulsion of unique personal destiny – was what made the world go round. At the same time, highly paid, commercially visible, sporting personali-ties (of all flavours) had become a lot more sensitive to the kind of authority they commanded. When Senna was being given his suspension and his $100,000 fine, he found it almost impossible to understand that there was a sovereign body – FISA – which actually had authority over him. Virtually in tears, he complained, 'I am supposed to be a lunatic, a dangerous man breaking all the rules, but people have the wrong impression.'

And then, just to add to this modern blend of dissent and autonomy-at-all-costs, there was a new element, specific to Formula One: the cars were now much harder to destroy in a crash. By 1990, it was possible to stand up for what you believed were your inalienable rights by taking a swipe at someone, at speed, and hope to walk away from the subsequent mess. Which was an altogether new, and sinister, development.

Incredibly, Senna and Prost did almost exactly the same thing at Suzuka in 1990 as they'd done in 1989 – the differences being that it happened on the first corner of the first lap, rather than in the final stages of the race; that Senna said it was going to happen; and he would be champion if it *did* happen. Boiling with petulance because he didn't like the side of the track on which the organisers had set pole position (which he held, by the way), and looking to avenge the crash of '89, he announced that he would lunge at the first bend *as if there were no other cars on the track,* in order to claim the advantage he believed to be his by divine ordinance. From there on, it was a case of *sauve qui peut,* as Prost might have put it.

So he did that, and Prost didn't give way, and the two crashed out of the race, and Senna took the Championship. Prost had finally had enough. 'I thought he was one of the human race,' he said of his team-mate. 'What he did is disgusting. I am not ready to fight against irresponsible people who are not afraid to die.' He then quit McLaren.

Senna, on the other hand, argued that Prost 'made a big mistake to close the door on me, because he took a chance that went wrong.' He admitted (with all the blinkered logic of a six-year-old) that 'I contributed to it, but it was not my responsibility.' He also claimed (despite having clearly won the psychological battle at McLaren) that Prost was 'always trying to destroy people. He tried to destroy me in the past on different occasions and he hasn't managed. He –' Senna by now could no longer bring himself to say the word *Prost*

'– will not manage because I know who I am and where I want to go.' When, in a TV interview, Jackie Stewart taxed Senna with the proposition that he alone had made contact on the track with more cars than the rest of the preceding world champion drivers put together, Senna bridled and then brushed the accusation off as it simply didn't matter: 'I find amazing [*sic*] for you to make such a question, Stewart.' It made you wonder what sort of monsters Formula One was creating. Away from the heat of battle, it was starting to look like this: Senna's egomania, his cataracts of paranoia, his monumental lack of concern for the interests of others were all permissible because he was a great driver. In any other walk of life, he would have been called a nut. But in Formula One, he was not just indulged, but fêted. Was this really the way forward?

Prost, meanwhile, having turned his back on Senna and McLaren, fell straight into the greedy arms of Ferrari: a poor decision for both parties. In his first year with the Scuderia (a year in which Senna blithely added the 1991 Championship to the one he took in 1990), he bitched away at team-mate Nigel Mansell, forcing him out of the team. In his second year, he bitched away at Ferrari itself, and got the sack before the end of the season. 'I've pointed out and underlined the defects of Ferrari throughout the season,' he said, by way of self-justification, 'but no one really listened to a word I said.'

He even managed to get into yet another asinine, contro-versy-ridden, crash with Senna, at Hockenheim. The usual story: both attacking a chicane, Prost tries to overtake Senna, Senna doesn't give way, Prost goes off, Prost complains vocif-erously, Senna replies with a protracted sneer. 'I think everyone knows Prost by now,' Senna explained. 'He is always complaining about the car or the tyres or the team or the mechanics or the other drivers or the circuit. It's always some-body else to blame. It's never his fault.'

Senna was triumphant, and apparently with good reason. So low had Prost sunk by the end of 1991 that he gave up racing altogether and took a sabbatical year, finding work as a pundit and commentator. Even then, he managed to get up people's noses. Max Mosley, head of the FIA – which had reabsorbed FISA early in the 1990s – growled that Prost 'really thinks he should be running everything', and that, during his sabbatical, he 'pontificated about things he does not under-stand and he describes the entire governing body in contemp-tuous and offensive terms.' Well, no one would ever accuse Max Mosley of mincing his words, but even so: is that any way to talk about a three-times world champion? McLaren, and all those victories, must have seemed a very long way away.

Just about the only thing to cheer Prost up during those fruitless years, was a win for Ferrari in Brazil, 1990, in front of Senna's home crowd. Senna had dominated both practice and the race, but banged into a back-marker (no surprise, there) about halfway through the race, and ruined his chances. Prost swanned through, finishing nearly fourteen seconds ahead of Gerhard Berger in the other McLaren. 'They don't come much sweeter than that,' crowed Prost. 'Beating Senna in São Paulo made it a fantastic day for Ferrari, but especially for me.' Team-mates, eh? And there the matter rested. For a while.

22

WHAT STRANGE NAMES ARE THESE? PART I

There was another world, somewhere away from Ferrari, McLaren, Williams – the dominant outfits of the 1980s and 1990s. Down in the pit lane and among the transporters and motorhomes were other names, other ambitions.

Such as?

Well, Lotus were still soldiering on, increasingly frayed at the edges, but working their way through some great drivers like an ageing *cocotte*, still just about able to attract virile young men, but unable to hang on to them. Ayrton Senna, Nelson Piquet, Nigel Mansell, Johnny Herbert, Mika Hakkinen all came and went, while Lotus dressed itself up in the sponsor's regalia of John Player, then Camel cigarettes, then Komatsu, the earth-mover company, and Tamiya, the plastic toy kit people – who once reverently produced 1/12th scale models of the Lotus 49, and were now doing their best to stop the team from collapsing altogether.

Brabham were in a worse state. Having enjoyed their final taste of success with Nelson Piquet, they had been sold off by Bernie Ecclestone at the end of the 1980s and ran their last Grande Épreuve in Hungary in 1992. Tyrrell, likewise, were living off their capital – Ken Tyrrell's prestige as Grand Old Man of the pit lane, past glories with Jackie Stewart – but were disqualified from the 1984 Championship as a consequence of various shenanigans involving illicit fuels and underweight cars topped up with lead shot (some of which escaped from the fuel tank vents of one of their cars, and came down like hail on the other pits). They never quite got over this and eventually disappeared into the maw of British American Racing in the 1990s.

Which left a mass of minor players, minnows, dreamers, struggling away in the lower half of the grid, battling for the odd point here or there, perhaps a podium place if they were really lucky. Consider the list: RAM (a mid-1980s British micro-outfit, best placing, eighth); Toleman (whose fame rests mainly on the fact that Ayrton Senna took second place at Monaco); Osella/Fondmetal (quixotic Italian chancers, lent significance by an engine deal with Alfa Romeo); Zakspeed (German saloon car racers by nature, using an engine out of Ford Capri in their doomed F1 car); AGS (a tiny French outfit with a legendary minuscule staff); Leyton House (short-lived reworking of the old March team); EuroBrun (Milanese team with a genius for failing to qualify – twenty-one starts from seventy-six entries); Coloni (still going in motor racing at the time of writing, but not Formula One, on account of being even less successful than EuroBrun – fourteen starts from eighty-two entries); Onyx (British team who actually took third place in the 1989 Portuguese GP, but were rapidly stuffed by the interventions of oddball car maker Peter Monteverdi); Life (yet another suck-it-and-see Italian outfit, who lasted precisely one season – 1990 – entered fourteen out of a possible sixteen races and failed to qualify for any of them).

*   *   *

Depressing, no? And yet, among these apparent down-and-outs were other, better-thought-through, livelier, more hopeful prospects, whose successes were the justification and inspiration for anyone who wanted to try their hand among the lower orders – the keepers of the flame, in fact.

Take the Arrows team. They started out in 1977, and were still (just) going at the turn of the century. Based round a group of refuseniks from the Shadow F1 team, they knocked out a brand-new Grand Prix car in less than two months, with a Ford Cosworth DFV engine on the back and Riccardo Patrese driving, and managed to get a second place at the Swedish Grand Prix in their first year, 1978. Patrese managed another second, two years later at the United States Grand Prix West, in Long Beach, and again, the following year, at San Marino. By 1988, they were using the preposterously named Megatron engine (actually a sensible BMW turbo) and had their best year, clocking twenty-three points in the season and coming an impressive fourth in the Constructors' Championship. Bernie Ecclestone's system of payments and rewards to racing teams – built round an occult formula involving the length of time a team had been in existence, and its past record of success – meant that, as well as getting money from their sponsors (USF&G Financial Services Group), Arrows were being kept afloat courtesy of Bernie, who made it his business to ensure a mixed grid at the start of every race, by helping the smaller teams to survive, day to day.

And, who knows, they could have made it as another Williams, if the chemistry had been right. The cars weren't too bad; the drivers – Patrese, Thierry Boutsen, Damon Hill – had promise. Money and management were always going to be tricky, that was a given.

But the real headache, as for so many of the smaller teams, was the engine.

When the Ford Cosworth 3-litre – the most succesful F1 engine ever, with 155 Championship wins to its name, the last being in 1983 – faded into the sunset it took with it one of the lifelines of the smaller constructor. We know that the DFVs being used by, say, the Politoys-Fords or the Bellasi-Fords, were not quite as peppy as those in the Tyrrell-Fords or the McLaren-Fords, but they were at least in a similar league. With that great leveller gone, however, an outfit like Arrows was forced into a much more rackety, contingent, situation. First, they had to blag a BMW engine; then an under-the-counter rebadged BMW engine; then a new 3.5-litre Ford V8; then a Porsche V12; then a Mugen-Honda V10; then a Ford again; then a Hart V8; then a Yamaha V10; and so on. With no chance to build up a relationship with an engine supplier (a new make every year, quite often), Arrows were forever doing their best just to keep up, let alone win.

Which was also the case at Jordan, the difference being that, somehow, Jordan Grand Prix (building on a sound base of success in F3 and F3000) managed to get competitive in their first season (thirteen points and fifth place in the 1991 Constructors' Championship), give Michael Schumacher his first F1 drive (same year), scrounge enough money together to keep going ('We've been through some horrific times': Eddie Jordan) and then, by the end of the, admittedly cash-drenched, 1990s, become poster-boys for the *Financial Times*, who swooned that Jordan Grand Prix had 'edged out established rivals on and off the race track', and that Eddie himself 'has been described as the king of the deal'.

Which was not far from the truth. Whatever else he may have had, Eddie Jordan definitely had a genius for promotion. He had his genial larrikin/madcap rock 'n' roller schtick worked out to a nicety, and gave it further definition with a tarty yellow paint scheme for the cars, plus nose-cone paintings like the ones on Second World War bombers, plus some breathtakingly underdressed girls dancing around the paddock, plus real partying after the races. In rock terms, he was Keith Moon to Ron Dennis's Chris Rea. At the same time (and proof that Jordan were only madcap when they needed to be), the team managed to hang on to Peugeot as engine suppliers for three whole years, before getting Honda engines, with whom they stayed for five seasons, in the course of which they clocked an extremely satisfying one-two at the 1998 Belgian GP (their first win, Damon Hill driving) and two more wins the next year. This put them a startling third in the Constructors' table, and caused the *FT* to break out in its rash of adoration. By now they also had serious sponsorship money coming in from Benson & Hedges and Deutsche Post and a staff of 250 people working for them. And the Jordan 199 was a nice car – conventional enough, with its carbon-fibre chassis, six-speed semi-automatic gearbox and high-nose aerodynamics – but it was reliable and reasonably good-natured, and it did most of what was asked of it. 'Our target has to be to make progress,' Jordan said, cautiously enough, 'but we have to be patient and see what other teams have done.'

Perhaps the most important thing about Jordan (cf. Williams) was that Eddie himself was not an engineer or former driver (cf. the begetters of Arrows, AGS, Zakspeed, Life) with all the intellectual and emotional baggage that entailed. He was, instead, a fantastic hustler, moneyman and irrepressible motivator of people. He was a pure fan of the sport who, having realised that he was never to be a great driver, let alone car designer, could give all his energies to the financial and human resources that his team would consume. The fact that the money gradually ran out as the twentieth century became the twenty-first, and that the team dwindled away with it is, was, in a sense, neither here nor there. 'At the end of the day,' as he put it, a couple of years after packing it in, in 2004, 'we delivered. Only five teams in the last twenty-five years have won multiple grand prix races. They are Ferrari, McLaren, Williams, Renault and Jordan. That's a fact. I mean, Jesus, Toyota and Honda now spend billions and can't even get on the podium.' Well, if you're prepared to overlook the absence of Benetton in this list (or merely regard them as an alternative Renault), you have to give him his due. The Jordan adventure was still an object lesson (of sorts) in how to be brave, and succeed at the highest level.

His comments about the competition were not misplaced, either. Because, now, who were the really bonkers minor teams? The start of the twenty-first century still saw Arrows, Minardi, Sauber, Prost (the old, successful, Ligier team given a makeover) fumbling around in the lower orders, getting by without the budgets or personnel of the big teams. But there were also these immense, blue-chip names – Honda, Toyota, Jaguar, BAR – commanding vast resources and yet, somehow, not doing much better than Fondmetal or Onyx, a generation earlier.

Which was sad and unsettling in its own right. The first division of motor sport now had its own tiny Premier League – three, four teams, inaccessible and aptly protective of their splendid isolation. Back in 1982, eight different Grand Prix teams won races in that Championship season. Only the brave would wager on that happening again, any time soon.

23

MANSELL - YOU ALWAYS HURT THE ONES WHO SUPPORT YOU MOST

Let us cast our minds back to the Dallas Grand Prix, July 1984. This was hosted by the City of Dallas, Texas, in order to demonstrate to the world that here was a genuinely great city, internationally minded, capable of hosting a top-flight sporting event, and not, contrary to popular belief, just a concrete dump full of oilmen which happened to give its name to a TV series.

Unfortunately, things didn't work out quite as the organisers had anticipated. The track was laid out in the Texas State Fair Grounds, 90,000 fans turned up, the temperatures hit over 100°F, and, as practice and qualifying went on, the track tarmac fell apart under the strain. It was generally thought to be the roughest circuit anyone had ever driven on. Alain Prost called the whole event 'at best a parody of a Grand Prix', noting that 'the circuit simply disintegrated', and that 'attempting to put on a Grand Prix in those conditions was absolutely scandalous. And the hit-or-miss organisation was also a disgrace.'

Still. Dallas had promised, so Dallas would deliver. With all those fans there, waiting, steaming in the sun, what else could anyone do? Despite loud complaints from teams and drivers, Larry Hagman dropped the green flag for the parade lap, the race went ahead and was won by Keke Rosberg in a Williams, with René Arnoux second in a Ferrari, after the majority of the field had spun excitingly off the loose-gravel track.

But the hero of the day – at least so far as the cheering Texans in the crowd were concerned – was Nigel Mansell. Having led for almost half the race, he found that his tyres were starting to fade. He pitted and came out again, trying to get back into contention, but, just before the end, bumped into the concrete wall and broke a half-shaft on his Lotus. So he got out of the car, and, in the appalling heat, started to push the damn thing towards the finish line. He never quite got there, collapsing like a landed fish on what was left of the tarmac, but was awarded sixth place, all the same. That was Mansell for you. The guy just never quit. *And* he was over thirty: quite a veteran by the standards of the time.

If there was an easy way to do things, Mansell didn't know it. And even if he did know it, he wouldn't have used it. Significantly, the contrarian-and-proud-of-it playwright Howard Brenton described Mansell as 'just a beautiful man. The quality that is most truly British is his bloody-minded-ness.' And in that statement, a whole nest of complications resides.

He was astonishingly committed to his craft, no question. At the very start of his career, he cleaned windows just to make enough money to keep going. In 1980 he raced, sitting in an agonising puddle of petrol, refusing to stop, when his Lotus sprang a leak. He pushed his car in the boiling heat of Dallas. He went toe-to-toe, wheel-to-wheel, at 200 mph with Ayrton Senna in Spain, 1991, which is pretty much at the top end of brave. The fans adored him. The Italians called him *'Il Leone'*; and when he won at Silverstone, 1987, a fabulous victory over Piquet, the crowd went bonkers and mobbed him. He was twice voted BBC Sports Personality of the Year. He became world champion, in 1994, eighteen years after James Hunt, setting records in that season for greatest number of pole positions and greatest number of wins. And when he quit Formula One, he went straight off and became Indy Car champ in the US, thus managing to be the first person ever to hold both titles simultaneously – a prodigious feat, given the world of difference between the two types of racing, and the fact that he was forty years old. What a man!

And yet, and yet. The sport had changed so much in the years since Hunt's Championship. Formula One had got vastly richer, more complex, more international in its scope. The new champions were cunning (Lauda; Prost); exotic (Fittipaldi; Piquet); exotic *and* cunning (Senna); but above all, not British. Grit and ability were not enough on their own. Britain needed someone cool, supercompetent, mediagenic, multinational in appeal, to make any impression against the current stars.

What it got was someone who looked like a policeman sounded like a policeman, and indeed *was* a policeman from time to time, on the Isle of Man. Had Mansell been enjoying his success in a quieter, less invasive age – 1957, say – none of this would have mattered. By the end of the twentieth century, however, it did. His turgid Upton-on-Severn vowels combined with a personality that seemed to alternate between stolid amiability and a drab pessimism. On-track, he managed to alienate people from all walks of life. Off-track, his detractors reckoned he came across as a bit of a pillock.

Was it entirely his fault, though, that Nelson Piquet so despised him, when they were both at Williams?

Mansell, having endured years of struggle, was now, in the mid-1980s, at last up among the big boys at a top team and was proving his gritty worth. He took his first Grand Prix win in 1985 at the European GP, consolidating this with a second win, in South Africa, at the end of the season. In 1986, he was better yet: five wins, plus a pole position and four fastest laps. Murray Walker, the BBC's hypervocal Grand Prix commentator, loved him. The fans took him as one of their own.

The big snag was his team-mate. In '85, he'd been paired with Keke Rosberg, whom he liked. For '86, of course, it was Piquet. And stolid Midlander became a walking target for Brazilian trickster, who, among other things, jeered in a notorious interview for the Brazilian edition of *Playboy* (well, of course) that 'The Englishman knows absolutely nothing about setting up a car,' explained how he went out of his way to hide from Mansell any improvements he'd managed to make to his own car, claimed that Mansell was argumentative and rude, and, as a Parthian shot, was thoroughly ungentlemanly by being rude about his wife.

Added to which was Piquet's gloating recollection of the '86 Australian GP at Adelaide. Mansell's talent for pissing people off was well attested by now (James Hunt had gone on record with the comment that 'at least 1,000 of the sport's insiders would be less than delighted' if Mansell won the 1986 title), but you still have to spare a thought for the poor guy when you read how 'Nigel,' as Nelson giggled, 'just needed third place to be champion. So I called the pits by radio and said, "Hey, get on to Nigel and ask him how much he will pay to let him pass. Tell him it's $250,000 to win the

Championship." I would have negotiated for sure.' *And* he hid Mansell's toilet paper.

Williams, naturally, did nothing to disentangle the two (although 1986 was the year of Frank Williams' road accident, so he did have other things to attend to), so Mansell and Piquet were left to squander the title in a long summer of squabbling, letting Prost thieve the prize at the end. But – and this is significant – while it may be perfectly acceptable to get on the wrong side of Nelson Piquet (or Alain Prost, or Ayrton Senna, or Frank Williams, or any of the other F1 prima donnas), how did Mansell manage to infuriate somone as affable as Mario Andretti, when he was over in the States racing indy cars in 1994? Andretti drove alongside Mansell in the Newman/Haas team and, while he managed to get on with the Brit for a while, ended up admitting, between clenched teeth, that he 'had a lot of respect for him as a driver, but not as a man'. The relationship between the two drivers started well, got worse, ended in acrimony. The sponsors took offence, race fans were disappointed, the press turned against him, Mansell quit Newman/Haas prematurely and stomped back to F1, his once-glowing reputation in America as a racer and title-winner now tarnished. How difficult do you have to be, to get on?

In so many ways, of course, he *was* an indisputably top racer, and not just because of his win-or-die-trying mentality. Like all the best drivers (and despite appearances to the contrary), he was a thinker: according to David Brown, his race engineer at Williams, 'He'd consider the race as the whole length of the race, and right from the beginning he'd try and plot his way through it.' Unlike James Hunt, he wasn't at the mercy of crippling nerves or existential waywardness, preserving, instead, an exemplary cool. Jonathan Palmer, one of his rivals in the 1980s, observed that Mansell 'didn't get tense on the grid. If anything, he was pretty relaxed.' And even Frank Williams couldn't ignore Mansell's constant drive for self-improvement. When Mansell returned to the Williams team in 1991, after a brief and painful holiday with Ferrari (and Alain Prost), Frank found him 'much more mature than he was, but at the same time he's every bit as aggressive as before'.

And the record speaks volumes: thirty-one Grand Prix wins out of 187 starts; thirty-two pole positions; thirty fastest laps. It is a fantastic achievement.

And yet, and yet, and yet . . . Even when he was on form, even when he was with the best team on the grid, even when everything was working out for him, he would win races with consummate flair and determination, and then complain afterwards about the handling of the car, or the meteorological conditions at the track, or the state of his tyres. The British media, heavily conflicted, desperate to boost their first chance of a champion in over a decade but unable to overlook Mansell's lapses, struggled to make sense of him. 'During interviews,' *The Times* complained, 'he can alternate between flippant superficiality and morose paranoia.' Elsewhere they said, 'How can a man who drives a racing car like that come across as so, well, *dull*?' James Hunt (jealous, perhaps, at the prospect of losing his position as Last Brit Champion) carried on being snippy on TV: 'Nigel must make up his mind whether his priority is to win every race or win the Championship.'

Meanwhile, he put his fans through the wringer in 1986 (losing the Championship by two points, to Prost); in 1987 (losing the Championship by twelve points, to Piquet); and in 1991 (losing the Championship by twenty-five points, to Senna). His rear tyre blew spectacularly, in front of a TV audience of tens of millions, at Adelaide, 1986, costing him the title; he did his back in at Suzuka, 1987, and couldn't drive for the rest of the season; he got *chickenpox* in 1988 and had to miss some vital races; he cheekily gave Ayrton Senna a lift back to the pits, having won the 1991 British Grand Prix, little suspecting that he was merely helping to conserve the strength of the man who would later pluck the title from his grasp.

He also scored some fantastic victories: 1987 British GP, carving off a twenty-second deficit in as many laps; debut win for Ferrari in Brazil, 1989, plus do-or-die victory over Senna in Hungary; first five Grands Prix of 1992, back to back, a new record. It was one damn thing after another, with Nigel. Triumph and disaster, hopelessly intertwined.

On his return to the Williams team in '91, he at last found himself in a position of relative strength. Frank Williams had spent the previous two years employing Riccardo Patrese and Thierry Boutsen – both okay, neither absolutely special – and had come to the conclusion that only a driver with Mansell's implacable desires would win another Championship for him. The negotiations were suitably crabby, but ended with Mansell getting the thick end of something between £5 and £12 million (depending on where you started counting) plus unconditional number one status within the team. 'I can speak with Frank,' said Nigel, comfortably, 'tell him things which aren't necessarily nice to hear without that affecting the confidence we have in one another. He knows he can tell me anything, too.' And Mansell delivered: five wins in 1991, followed by an incredible (and record-breaking) nine wins in '92, plus *fourteen* pole positions. And the Drivers' and Constructors' Championships.

Unfortunately for Mansell, Williams was still Williams, still thought the team was bigger than the driver (which it was), and stuck the knife into him in '92, his Championship year, by legging him over and replacing him with Alain Prost. And in the most convoluted way possible.

Ayrton Senna was used as the bargaining chip. He announced halfway through the '92 season that he was 'prepared to drive for Williams for nothing' – a extremely theoretical nothing, given that Senna could easily have kept himself comfortable with several millions' worth of sponsorship money, but nothing in the sense that Williams F1 wouldn't actually have to pay him. Shortly after the Hungarian GP in August – by which time Mansell had not only sewn up the Championship, but thought he was putting together a lucrative new deal with the team – Williams put the bite on him, telling him about Senna's offer and demanding that he settled for a smaller paycheque. 'Because Senna would drive for nothing,' Mansell complained, perhaps with some justification, 'I, the new world champion, had to accept a massive reduction in remuneration from the figure agreed in Hungary.'

As if this wasn't bad enough, it became clear that – for the time being, at least – the real target was less Ayrton Senna and more Alain Prost, kicking his heels in the middle of his sabbatical year, and still hungry for one more title. Prost was definitely up for it; while his thoughtful driving style, manic attention to detail and fondness for English teams made him a natural for Williams. In fact, a deal with the Frenchman had been on the cards since the very start of the season. More than that: he'd got Williams to agree *not* to offer the other seat to Senna, just to make sure that everything was as perfect as it could be.

When Mansell got wind of this, he went off the deep end, recalling his time with Prost at Ferrari, insisting that 'I am a better and more courageous racer than he will ever be if he is in Formula One for a lifetime or another ten years. He will be more of a chauffeur, making sure the car does the work for him.' Senna, too, was outraged. Although his McLaren-Honda MP4/6 had taken the '91 Drivers' and Constructors' titles, it was clear to everyone, Senna especially, that the Williams-Renault FW14B was a terrific car, and that McLaren could only go down, rather than up. He urgently wanted the Williams drive, and when Prost thieved it from him, he naturally enough, threw a tantrum, arguing that 'If Prost wants to come back and maybe win another title, he should be sporting. The way he is doing it, he is behaving like a coward.' Senna and *sporting* was always an unnatural pairing, but no matter, because, so far as he was concerned, he should be in exactly the same car as Prost in order for there to be a fair fight. 'He must be prepared to race anybody,' said Senna, high-mindedly, 'under any conditions, on equal terms.'

Frank Williams was at his most inscrutable, unpredictable and Dr Strangelove-like, throughout all this. The chances were that, in actual fact, he really *did* want Senna, and Prost was a chess move on the way to getting him. Equally, he *didn't* want Mansell, who was ageing, awkward and expensive. So Prost was both a convenient lever with which to remove Mansell, as well as being a likely world champion, just as the Williams Grand Prix car was reaching a peak of perfection in the shape of the FW15C. 'The bottom line,' according to Peter Windsor, 'is that Nigel was annoyed that Frank had signed Prost. The only way he was going to stay was if he got twice the amount of money Prost was getting.'

But that wasn't the only thing. 'No one appreciated where the team was when I joined them. The car was terrible,' Mansell protested. 'Prost has come to Williams to pick the fruit that I and the others in the team have sown and nurtured.' It was a fair point. Mansell had worked hard to perfect the FW15C – an astoundingly complex and brilliant machine, probably the most sophisticated car of its time, possibly the most sophisticated (given the   constantly changing nature of the F1 rulebook) there will ever be. It was his input that had helped get the computer-controlled active suspension, traction control, fly-by-wire systems, semi-automatic transmission, telemetry, and God knows what else working. The FW15C may not have had a turbo or ground-effects, but Alain Prost was so impressed by the gadgetry available, he called it 'a little *Airbus.*' And it was Mansell, partly, he had to thank for this prodigy on wheels.

Now, was there an irony in this – that if only Mansell had been a bit more like the car he helped develop (guileful, fascinating, packed with cutting-edge know-how) he could have driven it to another Championship? Was the car, on this occasion, smarter than the driver? Or, in seeking this irony, do we fall into the snobs' commonplace; the commonplace of poking fun at Mansell, just because it's easy? After all, Mansell was the one driver whom Ayrton Senna couldn't intimidate. The *Tifosi* called him a Lion. The mainstream British fans cheered him every inch of the way. And, in the end, will it be Williams F1 and its brilliant cars which stay in the memory, or the fearless, incredibly annoying Mansell?

THE MODERN AGE
1994-2009

24

THE END OF THE AFFAIR: SENNA'S DEATH

Time, the great leveller: by 1994, Ayrton Senna was looking at early middle age. Hard to think of Senna as anything other than sleek, self-contained and somehow ageless. But he was nearly thirty-four years old, and, like Jim Clark or Gilles Villeneuve – drivers whose talents sometimes appeared to place them outside the usual patterns of rise and decline – he was beginning to feel that his invincibility might not last for ever. Just as Clark had to watch the remorseless encroachment of young Jackie Stewart on his territory, and Villeneuve had to deal with the increasing presence of Alain Prost, so Senna now had Michael Schumacher (who had won his first GP at Spa, '92, in torrential rain – a classic way to advertise one's talent to the world) to remind him that nothing could be taken for granted.

Moreover, Prost, the Old Enemy, had taken his fourth title in 1993, cashing in delightedly on the opportunity thrown him by Williams, before retiring. Which meant that he, Senna, had one Championship fewer than the Frenchman.

Of course, Williams was there, waiting for him, the object of so much hope, so many ambitions. 'I feel comfortable saying this is a dream come true,' Senna declared at the time he joined the team. 'I've been waiting impatiently for this. I need it for motivation.' Frank Williams clearly didn't need to justify his wooing of one of the greatest drivers in Formula One history, merely noting that 'Quite apart from Ayrton's driving ability, I was very impressed with him as a businessman; his attention to detail is meticulous.'

Senna's godlike status with the fans had, meanwhile, been burnished by his relationship with God. Far from making him seem a bit weird, this had turned out to be another Senna USP. The aura of spirituality, of otherworldliness that hung around him somehow diverted attention from his rampant, and highly secular, egomania and made him even more special to the rank and file. 'I feel that I possess a kind of strength,' he had claimed, some years earlier, 'that brings me nearer to God. It is difficult to explain, but it is what I feel.'

This professed closeness to the Deity, with all its attendant seriousness of purpose, completely captivated Professor Sid Watkins, when he took Senna on a pilgrimage to the Loretto School, where Jim Clark had been a schoolboy. Senna gave a talk to the enraptured students, said Grace before dinner and debated theology with the Bishop of Truro, who also happened to be there. The following day, according to Watkins, the Bishop 'began his sermon with the confession that he had been spiritually and verbally outclassed by Ayrton Senna.' This was remarkable stuff, especially when you consider the venality and shallowness of your average bubble-headed footballer/athlete/tennis star/Grand Prix driver, and helps to account for the monumentality of Senna's legend, from the seething *favelas* of Rio, to the streets of Japan – where Senna was regarded with the greatest reverence. Indeed, his fondness for gnomic utterances – 'Wealthy men can't live in an island that is encircled by poverty. We all breathe the same air. We must give a chance to everyone, at least a basic chance,' or, 'Being second is to be the first of the ones who lose' – which, while they would have sounded ridiculous coming out of the mouth of, say, Alan Jones, merely confirmed Senna's place as the Thomas Aquinas of the race-track. His sincerity was unforced; and his faith was real.

But so was the pressure. Where, for instance, was Senna's Christian charity when he punched Eddie Irvine after the Japanese Grand Prix, Suzuka, 1993? Not that it turned him into an apostate, but there was definitely something unChristian in Senna's reaction to being unlapped by Irvine (who finished sixth) while leading the race. He screamed at Irvine: 'You're not a racing driver! You're a fucking idiot!' and followed this up with a resounding slap. Couldn't he have suffered Irvine as he would have suffered the little children? Or were things starting to get to him?

After all, even though Senna had always lived with pressure – generating much of it himself, much of the time – it was now coming too fast, too densely, not at his behest. 1993 was not an easy year. Prost claimed his fourth title at the Portuguese GP and announced his retirement, so there was nothing to be done about that. But Senna's future number two, Damon Hill, of all people, was threatening to take second place in the Drivers' Championship – as, indeed, was this horrible young German, Michael Schumacher, nearly ten years Senna's junior. When Senna won the last race of the season – at Adelaide, in November – he dragged Prost, who had come second, up onto the top step of the podium and tear-fully embraced him. He was overwhelmed, helplessly acknowl-edging that it was the end of an age, and that, while Prost was getting out with his dignity intact, Senna still had work to do, and not an awful lot of time in which to do it.

In theory, the move to Williams should have solved everything. In practice, it didn't. The fabulous FW15C of 1993 was *so* fabulous that, for the 1994 season, half of its gadgets were banned by the FIA, in an effort to normalise things on the grid. Traction control and active suspension were out, and, partly in consequence, the 1994 FW16 turned out to be an altogether dodgier car to drive. What then made things worse was the fact that rising star Schumacher's Benetton B194 suited him down to the ground and allowed him to walk the first two races of the season, in Brazil and Japan.

Still, all was not lost. Senna was still able to take two pole positions (albeit with some straining), the car was gradually improving, and there was a positive vibe in the Williams team, with Damon Hill dependable in the number two seat, and a powerful bond between Senna and Frank Williams himself. As Iain Cunningham observed, 'It was a very genuine friendship, and there is no doubt that Ayrton looked up to Frank.' It was with some optimism, therefore, that the team went to Imola, at the end of April, for the San Marino GP. Senna had simply blanked the first two failed races, arguing that he was now contesting a fourteen-, rather than a sixteen-race season. But, even with time running out and the season compromised, he felt that things might improve.

The fact that Senna's death, on 1 May 1994, can still generate reactions of upset and bewilderment is an index of how traumatic it was at the time. By the early 1990s, the Formula One community had got used to the idea that drivers didn't die in modern Grands Prix. The most recent death in a race had been that of Riccardo Paletti, in the 1982 Canadian GP, before most people's time in F1. Yes, Rubens Barrichello was badly hurt in a crash during qualifying at Imola, but he survived: it was reckoned to be an acceptable casualty. Then the hapless Roland Ratzenberger was killed during practice, two days before Senna's death, and an old, unfamiliar, dread resurfaced – a dread which, for some reason, seemed to attach itself most strongly to Senna himself. *Motoring News* recounted the uncanny detail that 'Several drivers reportedly felt the urge to go up to him [Senna] and touch his arm or shoulder at the drivers' briefing without being able to say why.' The Grand Prix Drivers' Association, which had been in abeyance for some years, was reconstituted, with a special brief to concern itself with safety. Senna, the most senior driver, offered to lead it.

Race day came around. Things got off badly, with a crash on the starting grid. The safety car came out while the wreckage was cleared away. Senna, who had been on pole, trailed round, with Michael Schumacher in second position. The safety car finally departed after five laps. The race was back on. Senna took off like a bat, desperate to leave Schumacher behind, desperate to reassert himself.

Too desperate. Lap seven, he went into the Tamburello corner, lost control and slammed into a concrete wall at something over 130 mph. The right front wheel of Senna's car was smashed back into his head; a piece of suspension penetrated the helmet. The red flags came out and the race stopped. The medical team – Sid Watkins in charge – got him out of the wreck, but it was a waste of energy. Senna died, lying on the track, the TV cameras watching him go. 'Every time I push,' he once said, 'I find something more, again and again. But there is a contradiction. The same moment that you become the fastest, you are enormously fragile. Because in a split-second, it can be gone. All of it.'

The race was restarted, Schumacher glumly won, and another kind of mystery took over: the mystery of the accident. Was it caused by a mechanical failure? A lumpy track surface? Tyres too cold after the period behind the safety car? Or a driver's error that brought with it the worst of bad luck? The endless to-ing and fro-ing of the manslaughter trials that followed merely served to make things darker, with rumours of missing accident video footage and many positive but unprovable assertions that the steering was seen to break seconds before the crash. As with James Dean, or Princess Diana: a crash, a death, and an enigma, all became inextricable component parts of the cult which then evolved.

Senna was buried in São Paulo, and Brazil went into three days of mourning. It was discovered that he had spent much of his personal fortune trying to alleviate conditions among underprivileged children: an activity which he had kept surprisingly quiet about. His legend kept growing. Was he like Rindt, or Villeneuve – too fast to live? Or like Clark – so far beyond other mortals that the jealous gods called him back? Then again, Fangio, Stewart and Prost were all still alive: no one had felt the need to impose a tax on *their* greatness. He couldn't, as Damon Hill would later argue, have simply made a mistake? Could he?

As if stung by a collective guilt, the motor-racing community at once decided to go to town on safety, attempting to forefend any more catastrophes. The Grand Prix Drivers' Association now had the ghost of Senna to compel it to new and bolder endeavours. The track at Imola was extensively reworked. Other circuits spent fortunes on redesigning crash-barriers and run-off areas. The next generation of cars had to meet far higher safety standards. The drivers eventually got to wear neck supports to reduce the potential damage from injuries such as those experienced by Senna. There was a tremendous air of sobriety about the place.

But the new striving for safety had an unintended, but not unrelated, consequence. Senna's predilection for driving in a fairly physical manner was given new room to breathe. As the cars and the tracks became visibly stronger and safer, so the opportunities for treating F1 as a contact sport became more various. You could go beyond the limits, more and more, and get away with it. It was an odd kind of legacy.

And it was music, of course, to the ears of Michael Schumacher, champion in the year of Ayrton Senna's death.

25

THE CURSE OF THE SON

How very odd: in 1996 *and* 1997, the Drivers' Championship was won by the son of a famous racing driver from an earlier generation. Damon Hill took it the first year; Jacques Villeneuve, the second. And they were in the same team. Since when did Formula One become such a family business?

Let's take a step back and consider the Ascaris. Antonio Ascari, a Mantuan like Nuvolari, started making a name for himself back in the 1920s, driving for Alfa Romeo. After a few tormenting failures in the Targa Florio, his career started to blossom when he won a brilliant victory in the Italian Grand Prix at Monza, 1924, driving a stupendous supercharged straight-eight Alfa P2. Next year, he was on even better form, demolishing the opposition at the first Belgian GP, at Spa, and was about to do the same at the French GP, when his car crashed massively while leading and killed him outright.

But he had a son, Alberto, who, undaunted by the fate that befell his father, went on to become one of the most successful drivers of the new age of Formula One. After starting out with Maserati, he fell in with the new Ferrari team, in time for the dawning of the Formula in 1950. A couple of second places put him fifth in the Drivers' Championship; next year, he won in Germany and Italy and came second in the title race. Then, in 1952 and '53, he absolutely wiped the floor with his opponents (Fangio, lest we forget, was going through his lean spell with Maserati and a broken neck), winning eleven out of a possible seventeen Grandes Épreuves in that time.

After that, Fangio was back in control with Mercedes, while Ascari dithered around with Maserati, before returning to Ferrari, and then moving on to Lancia. But it was in an impromptu test-drive of a Ferrari at Monza that he died, inexplicably turning the car over at the *Curva di Vialone*. Heartbroken fans at once made some sinister connections: Antonio Ascari was thirty-six years old when he died, on 26 July 1925; Alberto Ascari was also thirty-six years old when he died on 26 May 1955. Both died on fast left-hand bends. Both left behind a wife and two small children. If this was what happened when you followed your father into the sport, it didn't look like such a great idea.

Jump forward to the second half of the 1990s. Two Formula One drivers, Hill and Villeneuve, both sons of Grand Prix racers who died before their time, both orphaned, as it were, into motor racing, both bearers of a famous name – well, it was Ascari, doubled. It was guaranteed to provoke the anger of Destiny. And what made it worse still was this: however good Antonio Ascari had been, as a racer, there was no question that his son's achievements eclipsed his, whereas Hill and Villeneuve were in the less enviable position of having celebrated fathers whose reputations and personalities towered over them before they'd even had a chance to start.

In fact, growing up as the son of Racing Legend Graham Hill had the effect of marginalising Damon's ambitions, at the same time as it let him know that Formula One was a mixture of seedy showbiz as well as honest sporting competition. 'I was backstage when I was growing up,' he explained, wryly, 'and I could see the show and all the tricks that were used to convince the people in the audience that what they were seeing was for real.' Given the near-impossibility of making it as a mirthsome, friend-to-the-stars, larger-than-life racing institution like his father, Damon Hill did his best not to get into a car at all. Instead, he raced motorbikes, only sidling into four-wheelers at the relatively late age of twenty-three, when the temptation got too much to bear. Even then, having made his way through Formula 3 and got himself a job with Williams, he was happy enough being a behind-the-scenes guy, recording a fantastic number of solitary laps as a test driver and only being promoted into a proper drive in 1993 when Mansell left.

This put him in an invidious position, and he knew it. His only other Formula One drive had been with Brabham (at the point at which they were about to collapse), and there were plenty of other good British drivers around – Martin Brundle and Johnny Herbert, in particular – who might have seemed better fitted for the job. On the other hand, quite a lot of his life had already been spent dealing with fraught and intractable situations. Taking on a new, highly visible, job at Williams was easy, in comparison.

After all, when Graham Hill died in a plane crash in 1975, the Hill family not only lost their paterfamilias and principal breadwinner, they also found themselves more or less ruined financially, as the result of the ensuing insurance nightmare. Damon had to scuffle for work as a labourer and as a dispatch rider, just to pay the bills. Then, when he got into motor racing, his sponsorship deals kept imploding; he had to borrow £100,000 to keep himself in the business; Brabham went bust and never finished their final season. Everything he attempted was somehow in the teeth of adversity, like someone dragging a sled across the Arctic ice.

By the time he was properly in F1 and well into his thirties, he had acquired a reflective, self-deprecating style which was a long way from the self-adoration of many of his peers. 'I'm certainly one of the first people,' he said, ruefully, 'to pick up the paper and read about how wonderful I was.' Things hadn't come easily: anything that looked like a bonus was to be enjoyed as such, without false modesty.

And then Senna died. And in May 1994, Hill, after one full season in F1, got bounced up into the position of number one driver, with no one else immediately in place as number two. At Monaco, '94, the first race after Senna's Imola crash, Hill cut a very lonely dash in the solitary Williams on the grid. Worse, his race ended almost immediately in a several-car pile-up at the start, and Frank Williams could be heard gnashing his teeth.

Come the Spanish Grand Prix, at the end of May, he therefore found himself in a position unnervingly reminiscent of that occupied by his father, twenty-six years before, at the Spanish GP at Jarama: Graham Hill, suddenly leading Team Lotus, immediately after the death of Jim Clark. As for Graham, so for Damon. The towering genius had gone, the journeyman hack (wearing the same blue and white rowing-club helmet, even) trudging up to fill the unfillable place, a burden of cosmic proportions resting on his shoulders, all played out in the heat and dust of Spain.

And, like his father, he won the race. 'To win it is better than I expected to do,' he said afterwards, candidly enough. And it was a great win, just like Hill Senior's, even though it was to some extent handed Williams on a plate by virtue of the fact that Schumacher, in the Benetton B194, had to spend most of the race stuck in fifth gear – while *still* managing to keep in touch with Hill's Williams. On the other hand, this was Damon Hill's fourth Grand Prix win, in only his second full season; whereas Graham Hill's 1968 win came after he had already secured one World Championship, ten GP wins and the Indy 500. There was pressure, and there was pressure.

Which says much about Damon Hill. Pressure is one thing if you're a battle-hardened ex-world champion with an international reputation and the certainty that you've got the best car on the grid, another thing altogether if you've still got everything to prove, perhaps *not* the best car on the grid, a staggeringly gifted opponent (Schumacher) and a hypercritical team boss who clearly wouldn't have picked you as number one driver in a thousand years if fate hadn't sealed the deal for him. And yet, with all that on top of him, Hill tottered out at the Catalunya circuit and delivered.

His reward? To see Nigel Mansell being dragged back into the other Williams car, halfway through the season, at a vastly higher salary (allegedly £900,000 per race, as opposed to Hill's £300,000 for the whole year) and then to watch Schumacher (after a season of technological high-jinks and low track shenanigans) take the title by one point. He then made things comprehensively worse for himself in 1995, by failing to get the most out of the pretty good Williams FW17, having to watch Schumacher waltz away with his second title in a row (calling Hill 'a little man' in the process), and observe his new number two driver, David Coulthard (a young thruster in those days), take a neat victory over the German in the Portuguese GP.

Could it get worse? Yes, it could. By the start of '96, it was obvious that Frank Williams was only hanging on to Hill because his contract had another year to run. And just to emphasise his thinking on the matter, Williams had also got rid of Coulthard and signed up a new driver, a living reproach to the increasingly pained Hill, a real gunslinger in fact: Jacques Villeneuve.

Villeneuve was a bit of an exotic, even by the standards of Formula One. Not only was he French-Canadian, pointedly off-beat in his clothing and his personal manner, and a complete newcomer to F1, he was also Gilles Villeneuve's son and, as such, bathed in something of Villeneuve Senior's mystical aura.

Obviously, this could go both ways, given the well-attested nervous anxieties that Gilles had caused Jacques in his time. 'There wasn't much of a relationship,' Jacques confessed. 'I looked up to him because he was my father, but the few times I saw him we were on holiday or in the mountains for Christmas, stuff like that.' Or again, 'What exactly do they want me to do? Burst into tears at the thought of his memory every time I see the chequered flag?' Still, the inextinguishable glamour of the Villeneuve name – plus the fact that Jacques had managed some distinguished drives in North America, including a win at the Indy 500, which helped him to the 1995 Indy Car Championship – were unquestionably in his favour. Hill, of course, not only had to make endless apologies for his own shortcomings, he was still having to defend his father's reputation: 'It's a big mistake to assume that dad was a bit of a buffoon,' he said in '96. 'Anyone who could win five times at Monaco must have had some sort of instinct.' But for Villeneuve, eleven years Hill's junior and bursting with self-confidence, it was all jam.

And he helped himself to it. He described his new F1 car, in comparison with the simpler fare available in the States, as a 'big, powerful, very fast go-kart'. He also announced that he wanted to 'fight with the leaders' and that he didn't want to 'sit here and relax and just learn my trade'. To Hill's horror and his delight, young Villeneuve took pole position at the first race, Melbourne, March 1996. What's more, he led the race, set the fastest lap and would have won, but for an oil leak. And that pretty much set the tone. It only took another three races for Villeneuve to win his first GP, at the new, flavourless, purpose-built Nürburgring. As his racing career went on, and he took to wearing spectacles and doing odd things with his hair, Villeneuve began to resemble more and more an extremely powerfully built, wacky, Richard Dreyfuss. But on the podium in April '96, he just looks like a big kid whose birthdays have all come at once.

The only possible good news for Hill was that Schumacher, having moved to Ferrari for a king's ransom, hadn't quite got the F310 working properly and so wouldn't challenge, yet, for the title. The season played out: the scions of two legendary motor-racing families, driving for the same team, both in contention for the World Championship. Well, it reads like a Jackie Collins novel in précis, except for the fact that Villeneuve was a grinning outsider and Hill was a frowning, monobrowed father-of-three, who was officially and humiliatingly dropped by Williams before the season was over (at Monza, even) and who found himself snapping impotently at Villeneuve and Schumacher, who were being snotty behind his back at a press conference at the Japanese GP. 'Pay attention boys,' he said, brittle and angry. 'You might learn something.'

Schumacher and Villeneuve, young Turks together, had actually bonded at the penultimate race of the season, in Portugal, where Villeneuve, in the manner of his father, had pulled off a fantastic overtaking stunt on Schumacher on the parabolic curve leading into the main straight by clinging to the outside line, squeezing past a backmarker and breezing off into the lead. This bravura move went down fantastically well with just about everybody except Hill, who found himself driving carefully home in second place, with the Championship one point out of reach and his reputation as a bread-and-butter toiler in a great car mournfully re-emphasised.

There was, though, a happy ending, in true airport-fiction style. Hill showed what he was made of at Suzuka, last race of the season, by winning it, and the Championship, when Villeneuve's wheel fell off. A few spoilsports (Niki Lauda among them) reckoned that Hill should have done the job a lot more efficiently, on account of having far and away the best car from the start. But in modern motor racing, the best car is a prerequisite for the title. You *have* to have it – unless you're Denny Hulme in 1967, or Alain Prost in 1986. Hill had made a superhuman effort, was vindicated and validated, and his relief was absolute: 'I'd described it as like being let out of a room that you've been locked up in.' Frank Williams, having mercilessly shafted him in September, could afford to be generous in October. 'He controlled the Championship,' he said, judiciously. Then, with an access of something that might almost have been sentiment, he described Hill as 'a rare breed as a gentleman. I've hardly ever seen him angry and I've never seen him come out with any invective at all. Damon has climbed a mountain for four years and he thoroughly deserves to be at the top.'

On paper, Hill had done nothing less than dominate the season. He won half the races, took nine pole positions and set five fastest laps. More profoundly, though, his title had become a triumph of dignified resistance, a refusal to let his humanity become corrupted by the need to win. It was, in its way, a success every bit as dogged and deserved as any of those enjoyed by his father.

Then, to keep the Son Also Rises theme going, Villeneuve took the Championship in '97, in the Williams FW19, while Schumacher, having very nearly got the Ferrari to his liking, was disqualified from the entire Championship for deliberately trying to punt Villeneuve off the track at Jerez, the last race.

After which the whole Villeneuve project went into a decline.

In his first couple of years in F1 he had been cried up as a Gilles Villeneuve with sense, a 'tough little nut', who even impressed Stirling Moss. 'I think Jacques has got his father's skill – when he was dicing with Damon, he didn't give an inch,' observed the great man, 'but he's got an older head on his shoulders.' Trouble was, after his triumphs in 1997, he never won another Grand Prix. Williams went off the boil. Villeneuve then signed to BAR for the money (£13 million), but the team wasn't a McLaren or a Ferrari, nor was likely to be. Nor was it even a Jordan, where Damon Hill joyfully managed their debut Grand Prix victory.

Was Villeneuve possessed of an inordinate talent that went astray as the result of some dud career moves? Or was it a gift that was oversold in the first instance by being shown off in an unbeatable car? He certainly trumped his father, by winning a World Championship. But much of the rest of his time seems to have gone on squabbling with colleagues (he reduced Heinz-Harald Frentzen to 'a wreck'; Jenson Button was 'a weak team-mate'), making duff music albums (*Private Paradise*, 2007) and free-associating about fine wines ('You drink it and right away you know what is going in your mouth').

As a consequence – and despite Villeneuve Junior's consistently high profile – it's the fabulous Gilles, not the sometimes extremely good Jacques, who still claims ownership of the Villeneuve reputation. And it makes one wonder why, now, the offspring of famous names of the past choose to put themselves through it all. There's Nico Rosberg, son of Keke; Michael, son of Mario Andretti, and Marco, Mario's grandson; Nelson Piquet Junior (of whom more later); Geoff, Gary and David, sons of Jack Brabham, plus Matthew, a grandson; Christian Fittipaldi, nephew of Emerson; Markus Winkelhock, son of the late Manfred Winkelhock; Tomas Scheckter, Jody's son; Jean-Louis Schlesser, nephew of Jo Schlesser; Nicolas Prost; even Leo and Greg Mansell. Some of these have got as far as Formula One and made it stick; others, not. But since when did motor racing become a career option, mandated from one generation to the next? Since the cars got safer? Since the money got more appealing? Since sponsors became more likely to give you a hearing if your dad could put a word in for you?

And, given the relentless scrutiny, cheap nit-picking and quickfire opprobrium that encumbers most racing drivers, why would anyone want to give an extra hostage to fortune in the form of a famous antecedent, whose past glories you are extremely unlikely ever to match, let alone surpass? Michael Schumacher actually said, quite sagaciously, that if his son, Mick, ever wanted to go into motor racing, 'I would prefer to steer him away from a racing track on to some golf course because I have seen with Jacques Villeneuve or Damon Hill, or even with my brother Ralf, what a burden a name can be, and I would not want him to be constantly compared with me or to not be able to establish his own name.' And yet, they still come. The burning Oedipal need to defeat the Father must be stronger than one would have thought possible.

26

THE GLOBAL SPORT

By its very nature, motor sport is a tricky thing to participate in. You probably need a driving licence (unless karting), plus a competition licence, plus a car, plus petrol and oil and tyres to keep the car going, plus spare parts, plus maybe a spare engine, plus a man (or men) to work on the car, plus a way to transport the car and its peripherals to the sporting venues, plus an expensive crash helmet and driver's overalls ... For tennis, on the other hand, you need a tennis court and a racquet. For football, you can get by with just a ball and a piece of level ground.

This may account for the fact that maybe a quarter of a billion people worldwide participate in the Beautiful Game. Perhaps a billion will play volleyball (*volleyball?*), and half a billion basketball, but these are heavily skewed towards some countries and away from others; their appeal is dense but patchy. Football, on the other hand, has genuinely global reach (apart from in the States, home of something called *soccer*), and if you do a loose, fairly unreliable calculation, you may determine that the sport attracts $3^{1}/_{2}$ billion fans worldwide. Which is about half the total world population.

And Formula One? This senselessly overpriced, overcomplicated, elitist technosport, where they change the rules on a weekly basis, where you can't even see who's in the cockpit, the races are processions, and the whole thing is a racket, anyway? Another figure, take it or leave it: the Grand Prix season will garner, on average, an annual cumulative TV audience of *50 billion*. It will also be shown in over sixty countries. Total annual team expenditure, 2006–7: nearly $3 billion. World's highest-paid sportsman, including wages, product endorsements, merchandising and other emoluments? Michael Schumacher at his peak: around $80 million a year.

Does any of it make sense? No. Not really.

27

SCHUMACHER, SENNA AND THE ART OF TAKING NO PRISONERS

Say what you like about Michael Schumacher, whatever he did, he did 110 per cent. He got the most Championship titles; the most Grand Prix wins; the most poles; the most fastest laps; the most races won in a single season; the most money. And, just to round off this cavalcade of attainment, he was the most ethically problematic champion in the history of an already ethically challenged sport.

How do you solve a problem like Michael Schumacher?

Schumacher himself has never gone out of his way to clarify things for the benefit of others, preferring to compile, instead, a Schumacher Dictionary of Dullness with which to deaden future generations. Some random entries: Having punted Damon Hill out of the Australian GP in 1994 (and thus secured himself the Championship), he noted that 'It took me a long time to realise I have become World Champion.' Having attempted to do the same thing to Jacques Villeneuve at the European GP in 1997 (which led to his being retroactively disqualified from the entire season), he mused that 'It was a mistake.' When he won his first title with Ferrari, 'It was a real explosion of emotion.' When he took his *fifth title in a row*, coming second at Spa, 2004: 'You can't always be the winner, but in my eyes I also emerged a winner today by taking the World Championship.' After coming second to Jacques Villeneuve at the Nürburgring in 1996: 'It has to be said that, if Damon Hill hadn't experienced problems, I would have finished not second but third.' In an interview, 2003: 'I'm just like everyone else, I just happen to be able to drive fast.'

At times of deep emotion, he might go a bit further. On winning the 2001 Championship for Ferrari, he radioed to his team, 'It's so lovely to work with you guys. I love you all, I love you all, thank you.' And, on contemplating the fact that he had equalled Senna's tally of Grand Prix wins (at Monza, 2000) he burst into tears at the post-race press conference and couldn't speak at all. But the rest is a toneless non-commentary, a compulsive shrinkage of events, as though he were an airline pilot talking you through a spot of turbulence. 'This season,' as he sagely remarked, when he joined Ferrari, 'I think we have to concentrate on developing reliability.' And who would disagree with that?

Of course, it's the facts that do the talking. When Ferrari agreed to pay Schumacher $50 million (or 15 per cent of the entire team budget) over two years, they were acting perfectly rationally. Schumacher was outstanding, back in 1996, not just for his speed on the track, but for the incredible energy and commitment he brought to the job as a whole, and which he made his business to transmit to everyone else around him. Jean Todt, brought in to head the team, started to describe Schumacher as a 'reference point': the person whose remorseless work ethic, whose focus and whose relative unflappability (by the standards of F1) became a benchmark for the most junior mechanic, the most senior engine technician, for Todt himself.

You could see this even when Schumacher was starting out in karts at the start of the 1980s. Video footage reveals Michael not only winning, over and over again, but tirelessly urging on his younger brother Ralf, who was also out on the kart track. It wasn't enough for Michael to win; Ralf had to, as well, or what was the point? The image is persistent and unshakeable: Michael with stonewashed jeans, mullet and chin, *willing* achievement out of somebody else, out of the ether.

Thus, the supercompetitive young Michael Schumacher thrashed the opposition in karting, moved up to Formula 3, thrashed the opposition again in 1990, jinked slightly to one side by going sports car racing, but then, at the age of twenty-two, got into a Jordan at the '91 Belgian Grand Prix and took things from there. Benetton promptly snaffled him up; he won his first GP in 1992 (Belgium, again), managed another win in '93, and then got what he most wanted in the 1994 season, taking eight wins and the title, by one point, from Damon Hill.

His relationship with success was, however, already beginning to seem curiously Faustian, as if darker forces might be involved. He managed to be disqualified from not one but two races in his first Championship year – a surprising tally, even for the modern age. The first disqualification came at the British GP, for being cheeky on the parade lap and overtaking pole sitter Damon Hill. The other, more sinister, was for excessive wear on the skid block underneath his car, indicating possible malpractice in the ride height settings. This was then followed by a two-race ban given as punishment for appealing against the first disqualification. At the same time, the Benetton team as a whole was befogged by rumours that it was using a form of traction control: comprehensively outlawed, but a lot harder for race officials to put their fingers on than, say, the lead shot pouring out of the hapless Martin Brundle's Tyrrell, back in '84. So the rumours went on, and no one could prove anything. And then the season was wrapped up with Schumacher driving Hill off the track at Adelaide, and driving himself into his first Championship. Yes, Schumacher was very, very good: but did he have to seem so, well, *iffy* into the bargain?

He didn't care, either way. One Championship down, and another scooped up in 1995 – keeping a fairly clean sheet this time, with the nice, reliable Benetton B195, and Hill screwing up his own chances on the way. And then he went to Ferrari.

This was a move so bold, so pregnant with the twin possibilities of triumph and disaster, it was almost statesmanlike. Ferrari were locked in a world of despair. Their last Drivers' Championship had been in 1979; the last Constructors' Championship in 1983. Whole seasons had gone by without a single win. Gerhard Berger had won in Germany, 1994; Jean Alesi in Canada, 1995. The rest was terribly slim pickings, and the team, despite a few recent improvements, had slumped into a condition in which they more or less expected not to succeed.

Fortunately, at the start of the 1990s, the FIAT board had put international business hotshot and expediter Luca di Montezemolo in charge of the Ferrari team. Montezemolo, being something of an organisational genius, could see the wood for the trees. He set about dismantling the old pasta-and-politics Scuderia, creating a new, thoroughly pan-cultural Ferrari team, embracing designer John Barnard, manager Jean

Todt and engineers Gustav Brunner and Osamu Gotu. English became the *lingua franca*. He killed off the sentimental Ferrari dependency on V12s and stuck a modern, professional, soulless, V10 at the back of the new F310. And he got Schumacher.

To this refreshingly meritocratic pick 'n' mix, Schumacher himself added his old Benetton friends, designer Rory Byrne and technical director Ross Brawn, just to make sure that everything was as right as it could be. And then – the *reference point* – he compelled them, all of them, from Montezemolo down to the last cleaner, the last office gofer, to work and work again for glory. As Jackie Stewart averred after one of Schumacher's Championship triumphs, 'No matter how good Jean Todt is, no matter how brilliant Ross Brawn, no matter how clever Rory Byrne is, the one thing that has brought this to pass is that they all want to work for Schumacher and they know that, given what they can provide, he will deliver.'

At the same time (it went without saying), if you were Eddie Irvine, Schumacher's new team-mate, you were not much more than a spare coat hanger in the changing-room of Destiny. Schumacher was so comprehensively involved in the business of creating a viable car that every minute of the day went on shaping it to his desires, his strategies, leaving Irvine with plenty of time to iron his overalls, watch TV or chase girls. Like Senna, Schumacher drove his cars slightly over the edge, with a great deal of twitching and balancing and fighting. Unlike Jim Clark, who just got into whatever was available and made it his own, Schumacher had to have his cars tweaked and prinked until they were hysterically nervous. Which made them increasingly difficult for anyone else to drive.

Thus, after half a season of pummelling the F310 into shape, Schumacher was starting to make progress, while Irvine, who had begun the year by going faster than the German, now routinely found himself a second and a half slower, every lap. Everything bent itself towards satisfying Schumacher's desires. Paolo Martinelli, one of the Ferrari technical directors, said, unsurprisingly, 'Michael is able to be very clever when he is doing laps in the car: which are the points that must be addressed first?' The point being that, whichever point *was* addressed first, it was only ever one of Michael Schumacher's points.

Much of which good work was then eclipsed by the fact that he tried to bounce Jacques Villeneuve clean off the track in the final (and deciding) Grand Prix of 1997, at Jerez – so far failing to bump his way to the Championship that he was, instead, disqualified from it entirely.

There they were, entering the Dry Sac corner, Villeneuve ahead in the Williams, holding the inside line, perfectly properly, when Schumacher, half a car's length behind, simply drove his right front wheel into the Williams' radiator side pod. 'The hit was very hard,' Villeneuve said, subsequently. 'It was not a small thing.' Martin Brundle, commentating for ITV, nailed it right away. 'That didn't work,' he said: a professional racing driver spotting a professional foul. 'You hit the wrong part of him, my friend.'

Then came the fall-out. The *Frankfurter Allgemeine* called Schumacher 'a Kamikaze without honour'. *La Republicca* said the whole thing was 'Shameful'. Villeneuve himself (who had once upon a time shown Michael who was boss) got on his high horse, complaining that, with Schumacher, 'You don't know if the track will be wide enough, you don't know if he has seen you and it is very difficult to judge.' The British press went to town, heaping contumely on the charmless German (*Serve Schu Right*, etc.). In fact the only person who seemed unconcerned was Schumacher himself. He just put 1997 behind him, rallied the team and went on with the '98 season as if nothing had happened.

There seemed to be something of a contradiction in Schumacher's personality.

On the one hand, he was an exemplary worker, a true inspiration to the team, a storming driver, yet modest in his habits away from the track, placidly married to long-term partner Corinna, starting a family, not even especially interested in getting his face all over the papers, the epitome of virtue. On the other hand, after five brief years in Formula One, he had racked up two race disqualifications, two race suspensions and one complete Championship disqualification. Stirling Moss was a fan at this time, and, relishing the fact that Schumacher was a proper *racer* rather than a percentage player like Prost, generously declared that 'If Schumacher had raced with us [Moss and his contemporaries] he would have driven with the ethics of people of our era.' Which was nice of him to say. As it was of Niki Lauda, to claim that 'The only thing I would criticise him for is that he does not admit to mistakes.' But even as Schumacher went on his way, hanging Irvine out to dry, bludgeoning the Ferrari team to suit his own ends and regarding the track as his first, everyone else's second, you wondered whether old Stirling (or old Niki) had quite got it right.

Indeed, when Schumacher crunched his Ferrari at Silverstone in 1999, badly breaking a leg, some took this as a Karmic intervention, a sign that he needed to rethink his priorities. 'I suddenly felt my heart beat slowing and then completely stopping,' Schumacher revealed afterwards. 'The lights went out.' Irvine promptly rethought *his* priorities, emerging brightly from the Master's shadow, setting the car up to his own liking, taking four victories that season and not quite winning the Championship. He ended up a mere two points behind Mika Hakkinen. And that would have been some kind of irony: all that work, all that stupendous team-building, all that Teutonic dedication, only for fun-loving, girl-chasing, wild-card *Swervin' Irvine* to take the prize at the end. How Villeneuve, Hill, Brundle and, in probability, Irvine would have laughed.

But we all know what really happened. History was duly made in 2000, when Schumacher walked all over the opposition and became Ferrari's first world champion for twenty-one years. And then did it again. And again. And again (only just, though, two points clear of Kimi Raikkonen). And *again.* 'It means a lot to me to win my seventh title here in Spa-Francorchamps,' Schumacher mused, blandly, in August 2004, 'and especially as this is Ferrari's 700th GP. Quite remarkable really.'

As an unintended consequence of this bludgeoning supremacy, the worldwide viewing figures for Formula One started to tank. 2002 was particularly bad: the year that Ferrari won every Grand Prix bar two. True, McLaren had very nearly whitewashed the 1988 season; which was bad enough in its way. But at least two of the greatest drivers of the post-war era – Prost and Senna – had spent that year locked in a remorseless struggle which didn't resolve itself until the end of October. Schuey, on the other hand, had 2002 all wrapped up by July, leaving him nothing much else to do for the next three months except find some fresh records to chase and lob an occasional win in the direction of his latest team-mate, the gentlemanly Rubens Barrichello.

Something was clearly up when ITV, who had bought the rights to show Formula One for an estimated £30 million back in 1997, started to complain. Viewing figures had held up reasonably well until the French GP, when Schumacher clinched the Championship. After that, audiences fell by 600,000 a race, on average. Over the season as a whole, ITV reckoned they lost some 5 million viewers.

Bernie Ecclestone was at first high-mindedly dismissive: 'It's difficult for anyone to fight against Schumacher, but that isn't the fault of Michael or Ferrari.' The chorus of complaint grew louder. Bernie began to get nervous. By October, he had reassessed the situation so fundamentally that, instead of letting Schumacher and Ferrari simply get on with things unbothered, he reckoned it might be a good idea to bung some extra weights into Schumacher's car in order to slow him down. 'After what has happened with Ferrari this year,' he announced, 'we have to put a cap on it. We have to do something to keep the sponsors and the viewers happy.' A kilo of lead, it was reckoned, should add 0.3 of a second a lap to Schumacher's time – enough to let the others catch up.

Not that all embarrassments were of Schumacher's making. In the 2002 Austrian GP, at the imaginatively named A1-Ring, Barrichello made the running – pole position, a comfortable lead in the race – only to be told by Ferrari to give up the lead to Schumacher at the last second, so that Michael could take maximum points. Barrichello, seething, but having no other option, did just that at the finish line, to the boos, catcalls and massed thumbs-down of the crowd. On the podium, the Austrian Chancellor duly gave the vast silver winner's trophy to Schumacher, who at once handed it over to Barrichello with as much finesse as if it were a plastic replica at a karting event, and pushed Rubens up onto the top step. Alan Jones reckoned that Schumacher should have said, 'This is his race, I'm going to let him have it,' no matter what instructions were coming from Jean Todt.

The FIA reckoned that Schumacher and Ferrari were showing insufficient respect to the protocols of podium behaviour and fined them $1 million.

It happened again, same year, at the US Grand Prix at Indianapolis, even though Ferrari had forsworn the use of team orders. This time Schumacher let Barrichello past (just) at the finish line, and settled down to endure the contumely of others. And again, at the US Grand Prix, in 2005. Ferrari wandered home one-two in front of a hail of booing Americans, not least because all the other top teams had pulled out, owing to problems with their Michelin tyres.

Schumacher was, on these occasions, an innocent victim of the agencies of others. There was something graceless and ridiculous about the way he sometimes picked up his points – emphasised by the glazed stoicism with which he dealt with any subsequent complaints – but it wasn't *all* down to him. But then, somehow, he managed to cap a career of providential shamelessness in his final season, 2006, by parking his car across the track at Monaco during qualifying – either as the result of a genuine driver error or in order to make sure that Fernando Alonso couldn't snatch pole position from him.

This was especially important as he wanted to set himself up to take his sixth win at Monaco and thus equal Senna's record there, another vital number to add to his collection. So he went into the Rascasse corner, just as qualifying was coming to a close, drove slowly and incorrectly round it, and ended up stationary. According to one of the stewards, 'He performed some absolutely unnecessary and pathetic counter-steering, and that lasted five metres, until there was no more chance of going through the turn normally.' His speed at the point at which he lost control? About 10 mph. 'That's completely unjustifiable.' For Keke Rosberg, it was 'The worst thing I have seen in

Formula One. I thought he had grown up. He is a cheap cheat. He should leave F1 to honest people.' Benetton boss Flavio Briatore said, disgustedly, 'It was unbelievable. This is Monaco, this is Ferrari, so nothing will be done. It's a disgrace.' Even Jackie Stewart, choosing his words with care, reckoned that 'It was an unfair advantage. I am sure he knew Alonso was on a fast lap. It reflects on him and Ferrari.'

Schumacher, naturally enough, stood his ground. 'No, I didn't cheat,' he argued, 'and I think it is pretty tough to be asked if I did. I don't care what other teams think. You saw me lock up and run out of road. Initially I didn't stall the car but I hesitated to reverse because of the traffic coming from behind and then I did stall.' It did him no good. After seven hours of headbanging with the race organisers, Schumacher found himself stripped of his pole position and was obliged to start, in disgrace, from the pit lane.

Ricardo Patrese, Schuey's Benetton team-mate back in 1993, was one of the few to speak up publicly for him. 'What's happening against Schumacher is something from the days of the Inquisition,' he protested. 'How can you decide that Michael stopped in the middle of the track deliberately?' But then he made a most interesting comparison: 'In 1990 Ayrton Senna crashed into Alain Prost at the first turn in Suzuka. Afterwards, he clearly said he did it on purpose. Does it look like Ayrton is less respected because of that? That he isn't a legend in F1?'

This was the unnerving thing: disgrace didn't mean that much to Schumacher. In fact, he used it as a kind of leverage to greatness. By refusing to be put off by his very public demotion, and by fighting his way up from the pit lane, the worst starting-place imaginable, he drove his way into fifth place; and at Monaco, the circuit where overtaking is impossible and grid position is everything. It was a magnificent performance, a display of the unremitting racer mentality that so appealed to Stirling Moss, and which all great drivers have had – the need to keep fighting, keep moving up, never submitting to Fate. So he was shameless and indomitable and brilliant, and still, at the remarkable age of thirty-seven, as fast as anyone on the track. What *were* we to think?

And he did it again, only more so, and without the controversy, in his very last Grand Prix – Brazil, October 2006.

By now, he had decided to quit Formula One. Up to the Japanese Grand Prix, he was in with a shout for his eighth title. But his engine blew up at Suzuka and, with an unusual air of *gravitas* about him, he announced, 'This year, it wasn't to be,' even though, given unbelievable good fortune, he could still have taken the title in São Paulo. Plainly, he didn't get his eighth Championship – Fernando Alonso, everybody's new favourite, got his second Championship instead – but Schumacher went out with real, unquestionable style.

Having qualified a feeble tenth, he nonetheless started to carve his way through the field, before getting a puncture, trundling back to the pits, enjoying a leisurely eleven-second stop, and coming back out, absolutely last on the track and in danger of being lapped by Felipe Massa, his twenty-five-year-old team-mate, and now, the race leader.

What he showed then, was a kind of greatness. He simply refused to be beaten. From the absolute back of the pack, he fought his way, fair and square, no illegal moves, past the makeweights (Sato, Speed, Albers), past Barrichello, Fisichella, Raikkonen, setting fastest lap on the way, and was closing in on third-place Jenson Button and second-place Fernando Alonso, when the chequered flag came out and it was all over. It was, simply, a wonderful, even generous, performance: a treat for the fans, a piece of pure driving for its own sake. He seemed to have enjoyed himself, too. 'We were driving an amazing car today,' he said, either in recognition of the part played by Massa in *his* car, or because he was entitled by then to use the royal first person plural. 'These wheel-to-wheel duels are the highlight of Formula One, especially when you can see the track opening up ahead, you're driving a good car, you've sussed your opponent and you're ready to make your move. Generally, you just want the race to be over, but today I would have liked it to go on a bit longer.'

It was as if he had finally calmed down enough to do something because it was a joy to do, rather than because it would enlarge his already overweening reputation and put some extra silver in the trophy cabinet. It made him seem human, again. It made one want to recycle a bit of *Macbeth*: nothing in his racing life became him like the leaving it.

So then you turn back to Senna, to try to put some kind of perspective on Schumacher's history. Ayrton Senna didn't exactly make it *acceptable* to turn the desire to win into a kind of Holy War; but he did seem to shift the ethical framework of the sport to the extent that supreme talent became a validation of any behaviour on the track that didn't result in death or injury. And he got away with it by combining idiosyncratic cow-eyed intensity with an unlikely spiritual loftiness and the sort of talent that was pointless to complain about. He also won three World Championships – a terrific achievement, but one which he had to share with Jackie Stewart, Jack Brabham, Niki Lauda and Nelson Piquet, and which was beaten by Alain Prost's four titles, trounced by Fangio's five, and hopelessly eclipsed by Schumacher's seven. He was fallible, in other words. He didn't get everything he ever wanted. He died still yearning for something beyond his reach.

Schumacher, on the other hand, had none of Senna's charisma, none of his otherworldliness. For all his dedication, genius and off-track straightforwardness, he ended up coming across as a train-spotter (all those numbers, all those records), but a train-spotter with a fantastically ruthless streak and a marked talent for self-deception. His colossal, monomaniacal success single-handedly threatened to kill off Formula One's popularity with both the public and the sponsors, as well as alienating anyone with a sentimental reverence for fair play or the sporting spirit. The more he won, the less it seemed to be worth.

Yes, this tends to happen to players or teams who like to win whatever the cost to the fans, or whose personalities radiate dislikeability: from John McEnroe at his most adolescent, to Douglas Jardine, captain of the England cricket team in the Bodyline Series, to Arsenal in the George Graham years. Your sporting invincibility has the effect of making you personally vulnerable. We know this, and live with it. Yet the existence of these people, these nagging, conflicted presences, leads one back to the same question: what exactly is sport for? Or, more directly, what *is* sport?

Is sport, in fact, what Michael Schumacher made his living at? Wouldn't he have been just as happy running Siemens or BASF? Or was that never really the issue, all those years ago, when he took his first drive in a proper racing car? Was it just the means to an end?

28

ECCLESTONE, MOSLEY AND THE RISE OF THE TECHNOCRATS

In a way, Schumacher's insistence on getting the job done, no matter what it did to his reputation, was no more than a recognition that Formula One was big business, and that if he was going to become the Microsoft of the race track, there was no point in being half-hearted about it. Two generations had been and gone since the days when Peter Collins gave up his car to Fangio at Monza in '56 (costing him the Championship), or Stirling Moss got Mike Hawthorn's points reinstated in 1958 (ditto). New rules applied.

And it wasn't as if the sport's supremos could complain. Bernie Ecclestone and Max Mosley had spent years turning F1 into one of the biggest cash-generators on the planet. As Mosley himself admiringly said of his colleague, Bernie Ecclestone was the man who in thirty years had transformed 'a niche sporting contest with a worldwide following and virtually no television coverage into a world-famous branded competition with a global following plus a television audience rivalled only by the World Cup and the Olympic Games'.

On a good Sunday in the late 1990s, it was reckoned that 350 million people might sit down all around the world and tune in to a Grand Prix. Ten years on (with the Far East now tuning in), it was nearer half a billion: a potential audience which made multi-national companies frantic to buy twenty square centimetres of logo space on Michael Schumacher's overalls, or an inch or two on a McLaren sidepod. And if Schuey occasionally overstepped himself with regards to the laws of the sport, it scarcely mattered so long as Shell and Vodafone got their names clearly reproduced across all media, paper and electronic.

Which, in itself, was fine. If there was a snag, it was that very few people could account for Ecclestone's and Mosley's quasi-imperial positions at the head of Formula One's bureaucracy; nor for the fact that they seemed to have been there for so long.

Bernie Ecclestone in particular was really amazingly old – seventy-five in 2005 – and his diminutive form, complete with immutable Byrds-era haircut, had been patrolling the paddock for decades. Despite being so familiar, he was, at the same time, oddly mysterious. What was definitely known about him was that, long ago, he had been a car dealer and an amateur racer (in Cooper 500s) just after the war, that he could 'value an entire showroom of used cars in one glance', and that he had owned the Brabham team in the 1970s. This in turn had given him an entry to what would become the Formula One Constructors' Association; and in 1978, he assumed the position of FOCA's Chief Executive.

In those days, there was still enough laissez-faire about the sport for race organisers and competing teams to leave it to Bernie to sort out the money so that they could get on with something else. The organisers didn't pay out according to a published scale: they just handed the cash over to FOCA and let Bernie Ecclestone distribute it among the members according to his special formula. And while many queried the covert nature of FOCA's cash transactions, others were curiously grateful – not least because Ecclestone had a genuine passion for motor racing and made it his business to keep struggling teams afloat so they might live to race another day. 'First you get on, then you get rich, then you get honest,' was one of Bernie's more famous maxims; and he kind of meant it.

He was joined, meanwhile, by his alter ego, Max Mosley, son of Sir Oswald Mosley, and, like Ecclestone, a racing-driver *manqué*. Mosley, a tall, patrician, Oxford-educated barrister, was more or less an inverse of the diminutive Ecclestone, but as soon as their eyes met at a Constructor's Association meeting (Mosley was running the March team at the time), both realised that they could achieve much together. Ecclestone took charge of the moving and shaking; Mosley the lawyer handled the fine print and man-management, alternately terrifying and charming those in FOCA's path.

Time passed. Ecclestone and Mosley consolidated their positions. After all, the Formula One teams just wanted to make cars and race them: the nagging, chronic business of paying for everything, sorting out relationships with the outside world, managing the interests of the sport as a whole, never went away, but was at the same time deeply unsatisfying. They were mostly delighted to leave it all to the Odd Couple. And, by the early 1990s, what had happened, but Mosley was President of the FIA, having removed the prickly Jean-Marie Balestre, while Ecclestone had seen to it that the TV contracts to show Grand Prix races passed through FOCA. This stroke of entrepreneurial genius – accepting the centrality of TV to the success of any sport and exploiting it – made him not only extraordinarily powerful, but also staggeringly rich. Famously, in 1996, he drew Britain's biggest known pay packet: £55.9 million. His net fortune in the early years of the twenty-first century was guesstimated to be around £3 billion.

All in all, it created an impression of consistency and capability. British teams felt comfortable with the fact that two Brits were in charge of things. Ferrari felt comfortable with the fact that, as the biggest and most glamorous team, they still had to be placated, whatever Williams and McLaren said. Everyone else just went alone with the status quo.

And yet the tough, technocratic combined front that Bernie and Max liked to project was only partly real. It was a little bit like the building of the British Empire. Ecclestone and Mosley had fought a determined and resourceful campaign to seize power and territory. Having seized power and territory, however, they were then faced with the problem of what to do with them: a question to which they didn't always have an answer. Ecclestone had his brilliant coup for the TV rights. The rest of his time, though, seemed to be mostly spent putting together ideas that didn't come off: digital pay-per-view TV; gold and silver medals at Grands Prix; weights in Schumacher's car. Mosley, on the other hand (to take the most recent example), spent the end of 2008 and the start of 2009 disastrously trying to bludgeon the F1 teams to accept an unfeasible new budget-capping scheme, and very nearly created a rival, breakaway, F1 circus by way of response. This contained echoes of the attempt made by the Grand Prix Manufacturers' Association in 2001 to start their own rival GP World Championship, which, in turn, harked back to the incredibly divisive FISA–FOCA wars of the 1980s. At the end of which, Mosley had to fall on his own sword and give up his FIA presidency.

As an example of the measured and rational exercise of

authority, in other words, the Ecclestone/Mosley axis has sometimes failed to impress.

But then, for such a macho pastime, Formula One can be quite hysterical, fractious and queeny when it wants to be. And, as such, it persistently leaves itself wide open to exploitation by a more determined entity (such as the Ecclestone/ Mosley two-headed monster). Any change to the rules and regulations is still met with cries and complaints and disorderly threats to leave the sport. Teams run out of cash and have to be bailed out by one of Bernie's unsung subventions, or just fold, leaving an ugly gap on the grid. In times of recession (early 1990s, now) or other financial crisis (after 9/11) everyone scrambles around panicking and trying to cut costs. As soon as the money flows again, everyone buys themselves a motorhome the size of a department store. There is no consistency, except within the fiefdoms of the very top teams. At the time of writing, the money has dried up again, *and* the regulations are being tweaked. 'Formula One,' according to Ron Dennis, 'tends to be the last into a recession and the last out.' The UK, still the centre of F1 technology, was, until recently, enjoying an annual turnover in Formula One of over £600 million. Any threat to this is apt to create mild panic. Who will survive? Will anyone survive? It will be interesting, to say the least, to see how it pans out.

And Bernie and Max? Max lost some of his poise when revelations about his private life were splurged all over the tabloids, which was followed by his unconnected decision to give up the FIA presidency. Bernie, meanwhile, was attracting opprobrium, first over his efforts to finesse the disappearance of cigarette sponsorship, then by claiming that Hitler 'wasn't a dictator'. In the middle of which, his intensely glamorous wife decided to leave him, somehow gloomily confirming what one of Ecclestone's biographers had written about him at the start of the decade: 'Do people want to know him or his money? He cuts a lonely and incomplete figure. The curse of Ecclestone's life is that he has ended up getting what he wanted.'

There is an end-of-an-era feeling about Bernie and Max. They have had a good run, but things must change. And what will future historians make of them? Altogether, there is something authentically, messily Anglo-Saxon about the two technocrats and the world they have made. It is a world of muddle and improvise, as well as shrewd exploitation and clever insight. It has done the job, but it is a bit of a dog's breakfast. And it generates the question: how would it have been different if a crisp Teuton had been in charge? What would F1 look like with Michael Schumacher running things?

29

WHAT STRANGE NAMES ARE THESE? PART II

One might ask: while Michael Schumacher was winning an unprecedented, and probably unrepeatable, five Championships in a row, what, exactly, were the other teams doing? How had they let this happen? In the year 2002, for instance, Schumacher won eleven races; Rubens Barrichello (also Ferrari) won four; Ralf Schumacher won one, for Williams-BMW; David Coulthard won one, for McLaren-Mercedes. It was the usual suspects, in other words, but the sharing-out of victories was frankly bizarre.

Was anybody else even involved? Yes – serious names, at that: Renault, Jordan, Toyota, Jaguar, BAR-Honda, plus those stalwart triers Sauber (who never won a Grand Prix), Arrows (likewise) and Minardi (ditto). Between them, they scrounged together sixty-four points, spread over seventeen races: an average of eight points a team, for the entire season. Of course, 2002 was an exceptional year, and Renault and Jordan had already proven their credentials as race and, in Renault's case, Championship winners. But even so.

For many, it was Jaguar who were the worst failures, not least because they were so unbelievably, ostentatiously spendthrift in the way they went about failing. They were the perfect exemplars of the new phenomenon of Formula One As Speculative Bubble.

Having convinced themselves that the vast reach and international glamour of F1 were worth getting into in a bigger way than just by funding Cosworth engines, Ford – owners of Jaguar at the time – bought the promising Stewart Grand Prix team in 1999. This had been started by Jackie Stewart three years earlier and already boasted a GP win, courtesy of Johnnie Herbert, at the new Nürburgring. Ford paid an eye-watering $154 million for the outfit. They also signed Eddie Irvine, hot from Ferrari, and put him on, it was rumoured, a £15 million contract. And they bought themselves a vast travelling circus of hospitality suites and motorhomes, finished in a ditzy pearlescent reworking of Jaguar racing green, and stuck them dauntingly among the trailers and trucks of the existing Formula One teams. This was the high point.

For there on, it was a monotonous flop. Year one of competition saw them pick up four points. At the start of year two, Irvine announced that they would 'deserve a good kicking', if they didn't make significant progress. 'It will be difficult to do that badly again,' he said, and, what do you know, they picked up nine points in 2001. Panicking, they sacked some people and brought in Niki Lauda to beat sense into what was left of the team. Lauda found that 'The whole car was from beginning to end a disaster,' ordered the building of a new wind-tunnel (at fabulous expense) and generally made his presence felt. 'With our works team, Jaguar Racing, we are in Formula One to stay,' boasted the Ford Motor Company's chief operating officer. They scored eight points in 2002, one less than the year before.

For 2003, Lauda was sacked, and the team did marginally better, but in 2004, some kind of nadir of vulgarity was reached when a jewel merchant allowed Jaguar to stick a £100,000 diamond on the nose of each car at the Monaco GP: as a promotional gag, not, presumably, to improve the handling. When (new) number two driver Christian Klein crashed on the first lap, the diamond came off, went missing, and Jaguar were reduced to scrabbling around at the track edge, looking for it, before asking if anyone who might subequently have found it would hand it back to them. The season ended on a grand total of ten points, and Ford, who were now losing hundreds of millions of dollars on their Jaguar investments generally, pulled the plug on the team and put it (and Cosworth Racing) up for sale for £1.

Once upon a time, Jaguar Racing was being cried up as the answer to a nation's prayer, a British racing green Ferrari. Now, it was like BRM and the V16, only fifty years on, with a budget the size of a small country's GDP, and far more people watching. Then again, nobody ever got paid much (least of all at Ford) for their sense of history. Wise old farts shook their heads and said that it was typical of an American-owned effort – all flash and noise, no substance, and that the great days of the Cosworth DFV and the GT40 could never be recaptured.

Harder to understand, though, was the under-performance of the Toyota F1 team. Having plunged into Formula One in 2002, they weren't expected to start winning straight away, but they could at least have done better than two points in 2002; sixteen in 2003; nine in 2004. After all, Toyota, at the time of writing, are the biggest car company in the world – by whatever measure you choose to employ – have an army of clever and diligent engineers to draw on, a tradition of thoroughness behind them, serious and deep-pocketed sponsors (i.e. Panasonic) plus mind-boggling industrial wealth: their total assets in 2008 standing at around a third of a *trillion* dollars. Yes, in 2005, things brightened a bit with a couple of third places for Ralf Schumacher and fourth place overall in the Constructors' table. And they have managed some poles and some fastest laps. But seven years of trying and no Grand Prix win. Renault, with less money to hurl at the sport, won two World Championships in those years. What was Toyota's problem?

Worse, what was Honda's? This was even more pressing, given Honda's reputation for engineering excellence, their Championship-winning engines (McLaren and Williams), their recent experiences with the BAR team, a competition history of their own (forty years earlier, admittedly), and a decent flavour of savvy aggression about them. When they relaunched themselves in 2006 as Honda Racing, they had all the right qualities, to say nothing of a brace of decent drivers – Jensen Button and Rubens Barrichello – as well as the good wishes of race fans everywhere. Three years later, they had given up in tears, with CEO Takeo Fukui wretchedly announcing that 'Honda Motor Co. has come to the conclusion that we will withdraw from all Formula One activities, making 2008 the last season for participation.' The team was costing £150 million a year to run, the sponsorship was not all it might have been, Button had done well in 2006, with a pole position in Australia and a win in Hungary, but after that nothing, nothing to speak of. And, in mid-2009, BMW announced that they, too, were going to give up Grand Prix racing. It was all so sad.

But if Toyota were on the brink of quitting and Honda and BMW (to all intents and purposes) had already bailed out, what hope for the rest? Minardi, who had been limping along on a £30 million budget, sold out to Toro Rosso. Jaguar sold out to Red Bull. Sauber, bless them, kept going, and even won the 2008 Canadian Grand Prix. Arrows went bust halfway through 2002 and were never heard of again. Super Aguri, a kind of Arrows/Honda spin-off, went bust at the end of 2008. Force India may stagger on for a while.

One would have said that really, now that the bubble has burst and the bling and spangles have been lobbed into the dumpster, it was all down to the old, irreducible hard core: Ferrari (with a budget that reached, at one time, £250 million), McLaren, Renault, and a Williams team which seems very slightly to have lost its mojo. It's unnervingly like the mid-1950s, when Ferrari and Maserati (after the disappearance of Mercedes) had the place to themselves, with only distant rumblings from Vanwall and Connaught to disturb their ambitions.

One would have said: until some unnerving rule-changes for 2009 wrong-footed the big players and what do you know, Ross Brawn, Schumacher's go-to guy at Ferrari, bought Honda's cars and kit for a song, fitted Mercedes engines and, with yesterday's man Jenson Button at the wheel, won six out of the first seven races of 2009. While Red Bull, with Renault engines, came good, and started a serious push for victory in mid-season. And then McLaren came back to life, and ...

To continue the positive note: whatever the states of the various teams, the number of *places* in which you can hold a Grand Prix race has ballooned in the last decade, thanks to the tireless promotional work of Bernie Ecclestone, the Colonel Tom Parker of the sport. Ecclestone realised a while back that it was no good leaving the circus to trail around Europe, with occasional excursions to the English-speaking colonies (and Brazil). The market was heading eastward.

Which meant the sudden arrival of some strange new circuits: Malaysia, Bahrain, Turkey, China, Singapore, Abu Dhabi – with South Korea and India waiting to join in. Thus, Formula One got some fresh destinations to visit; the destinations, by virtue of the arrival of Formula One, announced to the world that they were places of some importance. Everybody was a winner.

Except that, as is the way with these things, a gap has opened up between the modernisers and the traditionalists. The old, hairy, mad, circuits have either gone or been carefully spayed. No more Nürburgring, Zandvoort, Watkins Glen or Estoril. Hockenheim has been tamed. Monza and Suzuka are habitually being tinkered with. Spa and Monaco, opposite ends of the spectrum, still exist to terrify and infuriate, but they have something of the quality of difficult elderly relatives: impossible to ignore, but not quite what the younger generation wants to hang out with. What the world wants now is something more like the Sepang Circuit in Kuala Lumpur, Malaysia.

This prodigy is thought by many to be the best track in the world, and you can see why. It opened in 1999, cost $120 million to build, has a mass of thrill-packed corners of all flavours, as well as a couple of straights down which a modern F1 car can hit 186 mph. It has terrific grandstand views, and terrific grandstands, some with exotic inverted-parasol canopies. The facilities are excellent, the track is wide, it can hold 130,000 paying spectators, and the sweltering heat and humidity generate useful and entertaining extra levels of stress among the teams and drivers.

Only two small things militate against the all-round greatness of Sepang. One is that the track may be sinking in places, on account of having been built on a reclaimed swamp. The other is that it crowned Hermann Tilke as the doyen of circuit design, the Yves Saint Laurent of the modern stadium race-track.

Is this really such a bad thing? German-born Tilke, having already had his way with the Österreichring and Hockenheim – doctoring and reducing them, according to his detractors, to disinfected pastiches of their former selves – set out his stall at Sepang, and most of the world was pleased. Bahrain, Shanghai and Istanbul all followed. Having raced in the European Touring Car Championship, Tilke reckons he knows what racing is about – 'This has given me a feeling and a heart for motorsport' – and that the fans should not only be able to see and hear the cars, but also 'smell them'. His fond-ness for having a long, high-speed straight ending in a brake-boiling hairpin, cannot be gainsayed. Nor the gallimaufry of twiddles around the rest of the circuit. Nor the king-sized run-off areas, so vast that the fans often see the cars as so distant and dwarfish, they might be radio-controlled models. But there it is. 'Safety is always the first aim,' according to Tilke.

You have to move with the times; and however pregnant with history and character somewhere like Britain's very own, very old, Silverstone might be, it is often a terrible place to view a race; and the facilities can be distinctly Welfare State. Hardly surprising, then, that (a) the British Grand Prix was being tipped to move to Donington, and (b) Hermann Tilke was given the job of buffing up the legendary circuit – where Auto Unions once thundered through the trees – making it safe for the twenty-first century, turning it into the Sepang of Leicestershire, in fact. It is only sour grapes, surely, to complain that, if hairy Donington is ever given a Tilke makeover, it will be a bit like all the other tracks. And that all the other tracks, Tilkified or not, are already increasingly alike. And that to complain about modern safety features, modern spectator facilities, well-equipped pit lanes, however depressingly similar they may be, is to mark you down as a closet Jenkinson.

30

THE BEAT GOES ON

What was so special about 2006, then? For a start, Schumacher retired. Secondly, the Championship was won by Fernando Alonso, the first Spaniard to win the Drivers' Championship, in 2005, and now the youngest person, at twenty-five, to win titles back to back. Thirdly, the season as a whole ran the risk of becoming interesting, once Schumacher had got his dander up and started to chase Alonso down in the second half of the year. Fourth, no native British team, no *garagiste*, won a single race: the first time since 1956 that this had happened. Everything went to Renault, Ferrari and (once) Honda. All right, Honda and Renault both had substantial specialist presences in the English Midlands, like so many others. But their souls lay elsewhere. In other words, there was a pleasant scent of insurrection in the air.

And Alonso was good, no two ways about it. After juvenile successes in the inevitable karting, he got into a Formula One car – a test with Minardi – and found himself immediately going more quickly than the established drivers. 2001 saw him compete in the Australian Grand Prix, the youngest driver ever to start an F1 race. 2003 rolled by, and in Hungary, at the wheel of a Renault, he became the youngest driver ever to win a GP. The 2004 season was all about Schumacher's war of attrition against the rest of the world, but in 2005, using a mixture of cunning strategy and get-ahead hard charging, Master Fernando became the world's youngest champion. He memorably asserted that 'Spain is not a country with an F1 culture, and we had to fight alone, every step of the way, to make this happen.'

The next year was even more absorbing, with Schumacher going for final glory, and Alonso starting to fray at the edges. When he lost his Championship lead to the German in October, he claimed that 'The whole team is gutted, apart from the handful who don't want me to take the number one to McLaren.' Really? 'Some others are happy because we went past Ferrari in the team battle,' he added, darkly alluding to the fact that Renault wanted the Constructors' Championship first, the drivers' second. 'They are not helping me as much as they could.' Renault at once replied with a frosty 'There is no problem at all with the relations between him [Alonso] and the team,' but it was clear that Fernando, in the manner of a champ who understands his own worth, was not going to hang about where he wasn't wholly appreciated. So, having taken his second title, he went off, in a marked manner, to McLaren –

– Who had just had a frightful year of it. Not a single victory for a British team! Neither Williams nor McLaren could make it onto the top step of the podium. It was an index of how the world had changed. Britain was still pretty much at the centre of Formula One – maybe 350,000 people were directly employed by F1 teams in the UK, with Renault alone taking 600 of them – but the *garagiste* tradition, gamey, individuated, embodied in Brabham, Lotus, Tyrrell, March, McLaren, Williams, was dying. Indeed, McLaren only enjoyed its pre-eminence thanks to the investment and authority that came with Mercedes.

Nevertheless. The new McLaren MP4-22, lined up for the 2007 season, looked infinitely better than its 2006 predecessor: dazzling silver, dementedly aerodynamic – like a lobster on steroids – it compelled respect. The McLaren team as a whole, having had a mild crackup in 2006 with various key players defecting to other teams, was strong again. A new number two driver, Lewis Hamilton, was going to do all the right things to keep Alonso happy. There was no question of settling in, of spending a season getting to know people. The point, according to Alonso, was 'to win the Championship'. That was all. 'It's for this reason that I switched to McLaren Mercedes. We both want to be world champions.'

How could he have known that it would turn into a revisiting of the Williams/Piquet/Mansell nightmare? How could he have foreseen that Hamilton was some kind of prodigy? What was it with McLaren? Six months after telling the world that he was going for a hat-trick of titles, Alonso found himself publicly griping away at the McLaren ethos. 'Well, right from the start I've never felt totally comfortable,' he announced in a radio interview. 'I have a British team-mate in a British team, and he's doing a great job and we know that all the support and help is going to him, and I understood that from the beginning.' In an attempt to make his complaint sound like something else, he added, 'I'm not complaining,' and, 'I would be worse if I were at Renault, or Honda, or any other team.' It wasn't a big thing, really it wasn't. 'I'm calm, I'm fine, but I know there's a certain impatience to return to the top and dominate.' The only problem being that the impatience was his, mostly: everyone else was staring in disbelief at Lewis Hamilton.

After all, Hamilton's time in F1 could still be measured in weeks, rather than years. And yet, halfway through the racing calendar, he had been on the podium *in every single race*, had won twice and grabbed two pole positions. People were cracking up at the very mention of his name. Fantastically talented, hard-working, a tale of virtuous hard graft to the very top, good-looking, self-deprecating: Hamilton had the oldsters fighting to praise him. Sir Stirling Moss reckoned that 'He's the best thing I've ever seen,' that 'I can't think of anybody who has shown that much talent,' and – reaching for the very top drawer of greatness – 'Lewis certainly has the qualifications to be up there with Fangio.' Sir Jackie Stewart, equally aglow, claimed that Hamilton had 'been able to accomplish more in a shorter time than any driver I've ever seen.' Nigel Mansell drizzled on the whole thing by pointing out that 'Lewis has lucked into a fabulous car,' and 'What he's done has been very impressive but it's what he should have been doing anyway.' But no one cared. Hamilton was an absolute sensation. And (what a riposte to 2006) he was a British driver, in a British team, with the first real chance at a Championship since Damon Hill, ten years earlier.

Of course, it didn't work out like that. For all his petulant gloom at the way McLaren refused to give him, the twice-champion, absolute and categorical first billing, Alonso kept toiling away, winning at Monza and collecting a third in China, where Hamilton managed to break the hearts of millions by falling off the pit lane and into a gravel trap.

Who, though, was the real beneficiary of all this? None other than the fiendishly composed, often outlandishly fast, Kimi Raikkonen. Let's be frank: the Finns are not as other people. They have produced more Formula One world champions, as a proportion of their population, than any other country. There are just over 5 million of them, but they've turned out Keke Rosberg, the great Mika Hakkinen (champ in 1998 and '99) and now they have Kimi Raikkonen, who crept like a thief in his Ferrari among the McLarens and hung the wretched Alonso and the bedazzled Hamilton out to dry.

Known as 'Iceman', Raikkonen was being paid something over £20 million at Ferrari in 2007 and was, apart from an occasional tendency to party too hard, too cool for words. According to his compatriot, Mika Salo, 'Things like family stuff and so on are not close to us. During my time in F1 my grandfather and grandmother died, and I never even went to the funeral. It was not a big thing for me, and I believe it's the same here [Finland] for everybody.' There you go. He also revealed that Finns were 'very stubborn, jealous and selfish people. So you'd rather do well yourself than let somebody else do well.' It was perfect for Raikkonen. Fatally for the two McLaren drivers, he won three out of the last four races, in a Ferrari so bristling with aerodynamic aids, it was impossible to count each separate flange and flap without getting a headache. Alonso was deeply frustrated: four wins came his way, but so did four seconds and four thirds – Raikkonen, or Hamilton, or Massa, forever scuppering his chances.

'I just like to be alone, or to be with my friends,' Raikkonen said, writhing in the glare of fame. At the wheel? 'I just go out and try to go as fast as I can.' The pressures of competition? 'I don't think about too many things too much. I just do it.' A £20 million salary, big house in Switzerland, former Miss Scandinavia as a wife? 'I can't complain.'

*   *   *

On the other hand, Max Mosley was belatedly fretting over what he called 'the Schumacher effect', the lurking problem that Hamilton might soon be so unreasonably successful it would cause people to 'start writing to me saying can't you do something to slow him down'. This, shortly after Hamilton had effectively lost the title. But was he right to worry?

Probably not. The 2008 season turned out to be an exercise in – yes! – thrills, with Hamilton locked in a struggle with Felipe Massa, Raikkonen getting some hot action at the start before fading in the points (although setting an inordinate number of fastest laps – ten in all), and Alonso coming back on form in the second half of the year. Having moved back to Renault, he was typically touchy and plaintive at first, but brightened once he picked up a win at the teeming, floodlit Singapore GP (of which, more later). He subsequently felt so good about things, he could even bestow a kind word on his former boss, Ron Dennis, declaring that 'There is respect for each other,' and that 'There are not many people like Ron any more.' By the time everyone arrived in China, it was almost preposterously exciting, with twelve points separating the top three drivers, Hamilton getting edgy after crashing around in Japan ('What can I say? it was a bad day'), and Alonso beaming over the improvements in his Renault ('The feeling I have now is that we can do anything').

And then Hamilton did his nut in China (on Hermann Tilke's squiggly Shanghai circuit), taking pole position, setting the fastest lap, and winning the race, fifteen seconds ahead of Massa. This, after six Grands Prix without a win, one of which was in Belgium, where the stewards bumped him down from first to third, following an infraction of the rules. 'Another step towards my dream,' he said, before driving the British viewing public into a collective nervous breakdown by nearly winning, then nearly losing, then finally winning the Championship, on the last bend of the last lap of the Brazilian Grand Prix. 'I was shouting, "Do I have it? Do I have it?" on the radio,' Hamilton later revealed. 'It was only when I took the chequered flag and got to turn one that the team told me I was world champion. I was ecstatic.'

You can bet he was. The youngest-ever world champion, at twenty-three. No wonder Alonso looked pissed off after the race. And as for poor Massa . . .

Stefano Domenicali, Sporting Director at Ferrari, went straightaway over to Hamilton at the end, to congratulate him. 'I did my job. I think this is correct,' he sighed. 'At the end of the day he won by one point and it means he was better by one point. He is a world champion. He lost last year by one point. And next season? We will see.'

31

AND ON

Another interesting year in F1? What are the chances? Amazingly, 2009 gave us, among other things: teams back from the dead, a world champion from out of left-field, the disappearance of Max Mosley, back-to-front starting grids, plus at least two hand-wringing scandals and one almost career-ending accident.

First things first. The superhumanly clever Ross Brawn, one-time technical director for Ferrari and Benetton in the Schumacher years, took over what was left of the Honda F1 team after the original owners had bid a tearful farewell from the sport, taking their engines with them. Brawn promptly renamed the team after himself, fitted some Mercedes power units at the backs of the cars and, thanks to a millimetre-close reading of the season's new rule book, attached a rear diffuser which worked an awful lot better than the other teams' rear diffusers.

The result? Jenson Button took his six GPs and was transformed from a likeable has-been skirt-chaser into a driver whose substantial talents had at last been rewarded with the right kind of vehicle. Nigel Mansell did an impersonation of a damp fog, by reckoning initially that it was the car that the won races, not the driver ('That car looks just amazing. I mean, the balance of that car'), before yielding enough to say that Button 'is not letting this go, he is staying focused. He is more focused than I have ever seen him and better than ever. It's his Championship.'

Which it was, in a slightly minor key. For the first few months of the season, it was indeed nearly always Button's Imax grin that met the press at the end of each race ('It's a very special feeling to have got this win . . . To win here is fantastic . . . You guys are absolute legends'), while tough guy Mark Webber declared that Button was 'on another level', confirming that the 2009 Championship was already a foregone conclusion.

But then the project started to lose vitality. Other teams caught up. Button was infected by inner hesitancy. Red Bull, by Jaguar out of Stewart, turned out to have the next Michael Schumacher driving for them – a guy called Sebastian Vettel, distinguished by having even more teeth in his head than Jenson Button, and who, like Schumacher and Senna before him, was 'blindingly fast from the start'. As a consequence, he broke Button's winning run at Shanghai, scoring Red Bull's debut win on the way. He did it again, to everyone's horror, at the British Grand Prix, while Webber took the German GP. Worse: McLaren, having started the year with the wrong sort of car, got it working by July, when an exultant Lewis Hamilton won the Hungarian GP ('It's an incredible feeling to be back here'), and suddenly Button was looking less than magisterial.

Did he panic? As it turned out, he played a thoughtful game, consolidated his points and secured the title by driving like a bandit at Brazil and battling his way up from fourteenth on the grid to fifth place by the end: a fantastic drive. The only snag was that, overall, Button's year seemed to lack the terrible ruthlessness that a Schumacher or Clark or Fangio would have commanded. He could have wrapped it up by August, but didn't. Nor did he manage a grandstanding final win; settling instead for a grandstanding fifth. There was, retrospectively, something about it of the just-caught-the-bus feel of Hawthorn's title (one race win, one point ahead of Moss) or James Hunt's (one point, Lauda injured), or even Lewis Hamilton's (except that Hamilton was given the benefit of the doubt, because he was obviously such a racer at heart). Was this somehow expressive of the English condition?

In the scheme of things, it won't matter. History will record that Jenson Button took the Championship with a healthy six wins, four poles and two fastest laps, *and* will have been the first back-to-back British champion since Jackie Stewart (1969) took over from Graham Hill (1968).

And where, for that matter, was the great Fernando Alonso in all this? Or Kimi Raikkonen? Or Felipe Massa? Where was the opposition? Well, poor Massa ended up badly hurt after being hit by an errant bit of Barrichello's suspension and slamming into a tyre wall at 130 mph. 'I thought we'd seen an end to all this sort of thing,' Bernie Ecclestone muttered, after visiting Massa in hospital. 'It's mad.' Barrichello was in tears, and Ferrari as a whole continued the decline they had gone into after having the title thieved from them by Hamilton, seven months earlier. Raikkonen did get a win at Belgium, yes, but by the end of the season they were in fourth place in the Constructors' Championship and *100 points* behind Brawn, those hilarious upstarts. Gloomier commentators ended the year with much head-shaking and numerous predictions that, without Schumacher (fleetingly earmarked to fill in for Massa mid-season) and all his startling energies, the Scuderia was about to enter one of its periodic Dark Ages again.

Or would Fernando Alonso turn it all round? 'Driving a single-seater from the Prancing Horse is everybody's dream in this sport, and today I have the opportunity to make this dream come true,' he gushed, on signing a three-year deal. 'I can't wait to start working with my new team.' But then, whoever he drove for, it could hardly be worse than working with Renault – who had not only failed to get their R29 working (third place in Singapore the best they could manage), but also found themselves at the centre of a race-fixing scandal of scarcely credible dimensions.

This was, of course, the Nelson Piquet Jr/Singapore 2008/Premeditated Crash fiasco.

The wretched Piquet, having repressed his guilty conscience for nearly a year, found, on being dropped by Renault in August 2009, that he was at last free to blow the gaff on an authentically scandalising piece of news: that Renault's team boss, Flavio Briatore, had, at Singapore the previous year, told him to stick his car into the circuit wall so as to force out the safety car and allow Alonso to capitalise on a surprisingly prescient pit stop. Which, as it happened, enabled him to go on and win the race.

Formula One has become fairly inured to moral shoddiness by now, what with Senna stuffing Prost at Suzuka (1990), Schumacher crashing into Villeneuve (1997), McLaren being found guilty of thieving technical information from Ferrari (2007) and getting a severe reprimand for misleading the stewards at the Australian Grand Prix (2009). But Piquet at Singapore seemed to be taking us into a new world of crazed duplicity. How could he be sure he wouldn't total himself as well as the car? How could he be sure he wouldn't total someone *else's* car? 'I bitterly regret my actions to follow the orders I was given. I wish every day that I had not done it,' he announced, before attempting to place the blame on his boss, Flavio Briatore. 'All I can tell you,' he argued, 'is that my situation at Renault turned into a nightmare,' and Briatore, according to him, was the man responsible. The FIA promptly held an inquiry. Piquet was granted immunity by the FIA for fessing up. Briatore and Pat Symonds, the Renault team engineer, were not. Symonds was given a five-year suspension. Briatore didn't turn up at the hearing and was banned from the sport indefinitely. He then disappeared from view, before re-emerging to appeal against the judgement, at the same time claiming €1 million in compensation from the FIA.

Piquet's strategy may yet backfire. On the one hand, pushing Flavio Briatore into the frame hasn't actually done Nelsinho's standing much good with other players in Formula One. And, on the other hand, Briatore is well armed and extremely formidable. Painting him as some kind of titan of fallibility and blaming him for 'The lowest point I had ever reached in my life' is a risk. At the time of writing, we have no idea what evidence Briatore will adduce in the course of his appeal. But, by God, it ought to be interesting.

After this, the graceless removal of Max Mosley from the Presidency of the FIA came as something of an anti-climax. This had nothing to do with the recent newspaper revelations about his sporadically off-beat private life; nor, specifically, was it a riposte to the hand-in-glove, two-headed autocracy he had run for so long with Bernie Ecclestone. But it was to do with Mosley's not altogether unreasonable attempts to shrink the costs of Formula One and reduce the amount of money hurled at technical problems, mainly by the larger teams. He saw budget caps; he saw a sensible use of resources at a time of international financial strain; he saw a slightly more level playing field; he saw new teams being able to afford to come into F1; he saw himself getting his own way.

The trouble was, instead of creating consensus, he managed massively to alienate most of the big F1 players – who announced that Mosley (due to retire from his job at the end of 2009, anyway) could go whistle, and that they were prepared to set up their own breakaway F1 series if he didn't come to his senses.

Mosley had been around too long, was what it came down to. His writ no longer ran. His ability to get things done was now being seen as mere bossiness. Ferrari's Luca di Montezemolo called him 'a dictator'. Seething, Mosley let it be known that perhaps he wouldn't pack his job in, but instead seek re-election, just to see who really had the power: 'There was no need for me to involve myself further in Formula 1 once we had a settlement,' he told di Montezemolo, but, 'I now consider my options open.' The summer wore on. Then, suddenly, he capitulated. He gave up on the budget question, leaving the teams to assure the world that they'd try to cut back, somewhere. His job at the FIA came up for re-election. He didn't stand – but he did have the satisfaction of seeing his preferred player, Jean Todt, take over from him. Was it age getting to him (he was sixty-nine, after all), or had he decided that life was complicated enough, without the headache of Formula One to deal with?

Whatever the cause, the era of Max Mosley ended, just like that – a figure from the days of Jackie Stewart, Emerson Fittipaldi, Nelson Piquet, Niki Lauda, Alain Prost, Gilles Villeneuve, Ayrton Senna, just gone. Change was in the air. And when the last race of the season took place at Abu Dhabi, on a man-made island, under artificial light, overlooked by an immense futuristic hotel building that electronically changed colour in the night sky, and was won by a Red Bull, with another Bull second, and a Brawn third, you couldn't help but wonder where the sport would be in another ten years' time. Perhaps Mosley reckoned that at last the scenery was changing too fast for him too keep up.

We will see, indeed.

Appendix I

GRAND PRIX CHAMPIONSHIPS

(Note: Constructors' Championships began in 1958)

1950
Drivers' Championship
Nino Farina
Juan Manuel Fangio
Luigi Fagioli

1951
Drivers' Championship
Juan Manuel Fangio
Alberto Ascari
Jose Froilan Gonzales

1952
Drivers' Championship
Alberto Ascari
Nino Farina
Piero Taruffi

1953
Drivers' Championship
Alberto Ascari
Juan Manuel Fangio
Nino Farina

1954
Drivers' Championship
Juan Manuel Fangio
Jose Froilan Gonzales
Mike Hawthorn

1955
Drivers' Championship
Juan Manuel Fangio
Stirling Moss
Eugenio Castellotti

1956
Drivers' Championship
Juan Manuel Fangio
Stirling Moss
Peter Collins

1957
Drivers' Championship
Juan Manuel Fangio
Stirling Moss
Luigi Musso

1958

Drivers' Championship	Constructors' Championship
Mike Hawthorn	Vanwall
Stirling Moss	Ferrari
Tony Brooks	Cooper-Climax

1959

Drivers' Championship	Constructors' Championship
Jack Brabham	Cooper-Climax
Tony Brooks	Ferrari
Stirling Moss	BRM

1960

Drivers' Championship
Jack Brabham
Bruce McLaren
Stirling Moss

Constructors' Championship
Cooper-Climax
Lotus-Climax
Ferrari

1961

Drivers' Championship
Phil Hill
Wolfgang von Trips
Stirling Moss

Constructors' Championship
Ferrari
Lotus-Climax
Porsche

1962

Drivers' Championship
Graham Hill
Jim Clark
Bruce McLaren

Constructors' Championship
BRM
Lotus-Climax
Cooper-Climax

1963

Drivers' Championship
Jim Clark
Graham Hill
Richie Ginther

Constructors' Championship
Lotus-Climax
BRM
Brabham-Climax

1964

Drivers' Championship
John Surtees
Graham Hill
Jim Clark

Constructors' Championship
Ferrari
BRM
Lotus-Climax

1965

Drivers' Championship
Jim Clark
Graham Hill
Jackie Stewart

Constructors' Championship
Lotus-Climax
BRM
Brabham-Climax

1966

Drivers' Championship
Jack Brabham
John Surtees
Jochen Rindt

Constructors' Championship
Brabham-Repco
Ferrari
Cooper-Maserati

1967

Drivers' Championship
Denny Hulme
Jack Brabham
Jim Clark

Constructors' Championship
Brabham-Repco
Lotus-Ford
Cooper-Maserati

1968

Drivers' Championship
Graham Hill
Jackie Stewart
Denny Hulme

Constructors' Championship
Lotus-Ford
McLaren-Ford
Matra-Ford

1969

Drivers' Championship
Jackie Stewart
Jacky Ickx
Bruce McLaren

Constructors' Championship
Matra-Ford
Brabham-Ford
Lotus-Ford

1970

Drivers' Championship
Jochen Rindt
Jacky Ickx
Clay Regazzoni

Constructors' Championship
Lotus-Ford
Ferrari
March-Ford

1971

Drivers' Championship
Jackie Stewart
Ronnie Peterson
François Cevert

Constructors' Championship
Tyrrell-Ford
BRM
Ferrari

1972

Drivers' Championship	Constructors' Championship
Emerson Fittipaldi	Lotus-Ford
Jackie Stewart	Tyrrell-Ford
Denny Hulme	McLaren-Ford

1973

Drivers' Championship	Constructors' Championship
Jackie Stewart	Lotus-Ford
Emerson Fittipaldi	Tyrrell-Ford
Ronnie Peterson	McLaren-Ford

1974

Drivers' Championship	Constructors' Championship
Emerson Fittipaldi	McLaren-Ford
Clay Regazzoni	Ferrari
Jody Scheckter	Tyrrell-Ford

1975

Drivers' Championship	Constructors' Championship
Niki Lauda	Ferrari
Emerson Fittipaldi	Brabham-Ford
Carlos Reutemann	McLaren-Ford

1976

Drivers' Championship	Constructors' Championship
James Hunt	Ferrari
Niki Lauda	McLaren-Ford
Jody Scheckter	Tyrrell-Ford

1977

Drivers' Championship	Constructors' Championship
Niki Lauda	Ferrari
Jody Scheckter	Lotus-Ford
Mario Andretti	McLaren-Ford

1978

Drivers' Championship
Mario Andretti
Ronnie Peterson
Carlos Reutemann

Constructors' Championship
Lotus-Ford
Ferrari
Brabham-Alfa Romeo

1979

Drivers' Championship
Jody Scheckter
Gilles Villeneuve
Alan Jones

Constructors' Championship
Ferrari
Williams-Ford
Ligier-Ford

1980

Drivers' Championship
Alan Jones
Nelson Piquet
Carlos Reutemann

Constructors' Championship
Williams-Ford
Ligier-Ford
Brabham-Ford

1981

Drivers' Championship
Nelson Piquet
Carlos Reutemann
Alan Jones

Constructors' Championship
Williams-Ford
Brabham-Ford
Renault

1982

Drivers' Championship
Keke Rosberg
Didier Pironi
John Watson

Constructors' Championship
Ferrari
McLaren-Ford
Renault

1983

Drivers' Championship
Nelson Piquet
Alain Prost
René Arnoux

Constructors' Championship
Ferrari
Renault
Brabham-BMW

1984

Drivers' Championship	Constructors' Championship
Niki Lauda	McLaren-TAG
Alain Prost	Ferrari
Elio de Angelis	Lotus-Renault

1985

Drivers' Championship	Constructors' Championship
Alain Prost	McLaren-TAG
Michele Alboreto	Ferrari
Keke Rosberg	Williams-Honda

1986

Drivers' Championship	Constructors' Championship
Alain Prost	Williams-Honda
Nigel Mansell	McLaren-TAG
Nelson Piquet	Lotus-Renault

1987

Drivers' Championship	Constructors' Championship
Nelson Piquet	Williams-Honda
Nigel Mansell	McLaren-TAG
Ayrton Senna	Lotus-Honda

1988

Drivers' Championship	Constructors' Championship
Ayrton Senna	McLaren-Honda
Alain Prost	Ferrari
Gerhard Berger	Benetton-Ford

1989

Drivers' Championship	Constructors' Championship
Alain Prost	McLaren-Honda
Ayrton Senna	Williams-Renault
Riccardo Patrese	Ferrari

1990

Drivers' Championship
Ayrton Senna
Alain Prost
Nelson Piquet

Constructors' Championship
McLaren-Honda
Ferrari
Benetton-Ford

1991

Drivers' Championship
Ayrton Senna
Nigel Mansell
Riccardo Patrese

Constructors' Championship
McLaren-Honda
Williams-Renault
Ferrari

1992

Drivers' Championship
Nigel Mansell
Riccardo Patrese
Michael Schumacher

Constructors' Championship
Williams-Renault
McLaren-Honda
Benetton-Ford

1993

Drivers' Championship
Alain Prost
Ayrton Senna
Damon Hill

Constructors' Championship
Williams-Renault
McLaren-Ford
Benetton-Ford

1994

Drivers' Championship
Michael Schumacher
Damon Hill
Gerhard Berger

Constructors' Championship
Williams-Renault
Benetton-Ford
Ferrari

1995

Drivers' Championship
Michael Schumacher
Damon Hill
David Coulthard

Constructors' Championship
Benetton-Renault
Williams-Renault
Ferrari

1996

Drivers' Championship
Damon Hill
Jacques Villeneuve
Michael Schumacher

Constructors' Championship
Williams-Renault
Ferrari
Benetton-Renault

1997

Drivers' Championship
Jacques Villeneuve
Heinz-Harald Frentzen
David Coulthard

Constructors' Championship
Williams-Renault
Ferrari
Benetton

1998

Drivers' Championship
Mika Hakkinen
Michael Schumacher
David Coulthard

Constructors' Championship
McLaren-Mercedes
Ferrari
Williams-Mechachrome

1999

Drivers' Championship
Mika Hakkinen
Eddie Irvine
Heinz-Harald Frentzen

Constructors' Championship
Ferrari
McLaren-Mercedes
Jordan-Mugen-Honda

2000

Drivers' Championship
Michael Schumacher
Mika Hakkinen
David Coulthard

Constructors' Championship
Ferrari
McLaren-Mercedes
Williams-BMW

2001

Drivers' Championship
Michael Schumacher
David Coulthard
Rubens Barrichello

Constructors' Championship
Ferrari
McLaren-Mercedes
Williams-BMW

2002

Drivers' Championship
Michael Schumacher
Rubens Barrichello
Juan Pablo Montoya

Constructors' Championship
Ferrari
Williams-BMW
McLaren-Mercedes

2003

Drivers' Championship
Michael Schumacher
Kimi Raikkonen
Juan Pablo Montoya

Constructors' Championship
Ferrari
Williams-BMW
McLaren-Mercedes

2004

Drivers' Championship
Michael Schumacher
Rubens Barrichello
Jenson Button

Constructors' Championship
Ferrari
BAR-Honda
Renault

2005

Drivers' Championship
Fernando Alonso
Kimi Raikkonen
Michael Schumacher

Constructors' Championship
Renault
McLaren-Mercedes
Ferrari

2006

Drivers' Championship
Fernando Alonso
Michael Schumacher
Felipe Massa

Constructors' Championship
Renault
Ferrari
McLaren-Mercedes

2007

Drivers' Championship
Kimi Raikkonen
Lewis Hamilton
Fernando Alonso

Constructors' Championship
Ferrari
BMW Sauber
Renault

2008

Drivers' Championship   **Constructors' Championship**
Lewis Hamilton   Ferrari
Felipe Massa   McLaren-Mercedes
Kimi Raikkonen   BMW Sauber

2009

Drivers' Championship   **Constructors' Championship**
Jenson Button   Brawn-Mercedes
Sebastian Vettel   Red Bull-Renault
Rubens Barrichello   McLaren-Mercedes

Appendix II

TOP TWENTY-SIX GRAND PRIX DRIVERS BY RACES WON

1)	Michael Schumacher	91
2)	Alain Prost	51
3)	Ayrton Senna	41
4)	Nigel Mansell	31
5)	Jackie Stewart	27
6=)	Jim Clark	25
6=)	Niki Lauda	25
8)	Juan Manuel Fangio	24
9)	Nelson Piquet	23
10)	Damon Hill	22
11)	Fernando Alonso	21
12)	Mika Hakkinen	20
13)	Kimi Raikkonen	18
14)	Stirling Moss	16
15=)	Jack Brabham	14
15=)	Graham Hill	14
15=)	Emerson Fittipaldi	14
18=)	Alberto Ascari	13
18=)	David Coulthard	13
20=)	Mario Andretti	12
20=)	Carlos Reutemann	12
20=)	Alan Jones	12
23=)	Jacques Villeneuve	11
23=)	Rubens Barrichello	11
23=)	Felipe Massa	11
23=)	Lewis Hamilton	11

BIBLIOGRAPHY

Allsop, Derick, *Formula One Uncovered*, Headline, London 1998.

Botsford, Keith, *The Champions of Formula One*, Stanley Paul, London 1988.

Collings, Timothy, with Sykes, Stuart, *Jackie Stewart: A Restless Life*, Virgin Books, London 2003.

Dodson, Mike, *Nelson Piquet*, Hazleton Publishing, Richmond, Surrey 1991.

Donaldson, Gerald, *Fangio: The Life Behind the Legend*, Virgin Books, London 2003.

Donaldson, Gerald, *Gilles Villeneuve: The Life of the Legendary Racing Driver*, Virgin Books, London 2003.

Donaldson, Gerald, *James Hunt*, CollinsWillow, London 1994.

Donaldson, Gerald, *Teamwork*, CollinsWillow, London 1998.

Dymock, Eric, *Jim Clark: Racing Legend*, Motorbooks, St Paul 2003.

Edwards, Robert, *Stirling Moss: The Authorised Biography*, Orion, London 2005.

Fangio, Juan Manuel, with Carozzo, Roberto, *Fangio – My Racing Life*, Patrick Stephens, Wellingborough, Northants 1986.

Hamilton, Duncan, with Scott, Lionel, *Touch Wood!*, Barrie and Rockliff, London 1960.

Hamilton, Maurice, *Frank Williams*, MacMillan, London 1998.

Henry, Alan, *Jochen Rindt*, Hazleton Publishing, Richmond, Surrey 1990.

Henry, Alan, *The Power Brokers*, Motorbooks International, St Paul, MN 2003.

Hill, Bette, with Ewart, Neil, *The Other Side of the Hill*, Hutchinson, London 1978.

Hill, Graham, *Life at the Limit*, Patrick Stephens, Yeovil 1993.

Hilton, Christopher, *Alain Prost*, Partridge Press, London 1992.

Hilton, Christopher, *Ayrton Senna: The Whole Story*, Haynes Publishing, Yeovil, Somerset 2004.

Hilton, Christopher, *Michael Schumacher: The Greatest of All?*, Haynes Publishing, Yeovil, Somerset 2002.

Hilton, Christopher, *Nigel Mansell: The Lion at Bay*, Patrick Stephens, Yeovil, Somerset 1995.

Ireland, Innes, *All Arms and Elbows*, Pelham Books, London 1967.

Lauda, Nike, with Völker, Herbert, *To Hell and Back*, Stanley Paul, London 1986.

Lawrence, Mike, *Colin Chapman: Wayward Genius*, Breedon Books, Derby 2002.

Lovell, Terry, *Bernie's Game*, Metro Publishing, London 2003.

Ludwigsen, Karl, *Emerson Fittipaldi*, Haynes, Yeovil, Somerset 2002.

Monkhouse, George C., *Mercedes-Benz Grand Prix Racing 1934–1945*, White Mouse, London 1984.

Moss, Stirling, with Purdey, Ken, *All but My Life*, William Kimber, London 1963.

Neubauer, Alfred, *Speed Was My Life*, Barrie and Rockliff, London 1960.

Nye, Doug, *Jim Clark*, Hazleton Publishing, London 1991.

Nye, Doug, *Racers: The Inside Story of Williams Grand Prix Engineering*, Arthur Barker, London 1982.

Nixon, Chris, *Mon Ami Mate*, Transport Bookman Publications, London 1991.

Prost, Alain, with Moncet, Jean-Louis, *Life in the Fast Lane*, Stanley Paul, London 1989.

Roebuck, Nigel, *Grand Prix Greats*, Patrick Stephens, Wellingborough, Northants 1981.

Rendl, Ivan, *The Chequered Flag*, Weidenfeld, London 1993.

Stewart, Jackie, with Dymock, Eric, *World Champion*, Pelham Books, London 1970.

Tipler, John, *Graham Hill: Master of Motor Sport*, Breedon Books, Derby 2002.

Watkins, Professor Sid, *Life at the Limit*, Macmillan, London 1996.

Williams, Richard, *Enzo Ferrari: A Life*, Yellow Jersey Press, London 2001.

Williams, Richard, *Racers*, Penguin, London 1998.

Williams, Richard, *The Death of Ayrton Senna*, Bloomsbury, London 1999.

INDEX

Abu Dhabi Grand Prix 284, 300–1
Adelaide 230, 232, 241, 262
AGS 222, 225
AIACR (Association Internationale des Automobile Clubs Reconnus) 7
Ain Diab 91, 92
Aintree 31, 51, 59
Aix-les-Bains 91
Albers, Christijan 270
Albi 14, 91, 92
Alboreto, Michele 201
Alesi, Jean 262
Alfa Romeo 5, 6, 8, 10–11, 13, 14–15, 16, 18, 39, 154, 247
  and Enzo Ferrari 33
  and Fangio 24, 25
All American Racing (AAR) 163–4
Alonso, Fernando 268, 287, 291, 293, 297
  and Ferrari 298
  and McLaren 288–9
  and Renault 288, 292
  wins Championship 2005 287, 288
  wins Championship 2006 270, 287
Alpine Rally 56, 69
Amon, Chris 104, 113, 143–4
Andretti, Marco 256
Andretti, Mario 146, 161–2, 164, 166, 231, 256
Andretti, Michael 162, 256
Anglo-American Racing 129, 164
Argentine Grand Prix
  1955 30
  1956 36–7
  1958 61–2
Argetsinger, Cameron 166
Arnoux, René 151, 154, 178, 194, 195, 201, 228

Arrows 162, 223, 224, 225, 226, 279, 283
Arsenal 272
Ascari, Alberto 13, 15, 34, 35–6, 37, 95, 247–8
Ascari, Antonio 247–8
Aston Martin 30
Atteberg, Orjan 93
Australian Grand Prix 212, 215, 230, 232, 241, 253, 259, 262
Austrian Grand Prix 118, 267
Auto Union 6, 8, 9, 10, 11–12, 60, 285
Avus 8, 59, 95

Bahrain Grand Prix 168, 284, 285
Balestre, Jean-Marie 155–6, 174, 275
Bandini, Lorenzo 110, 118
BAR 226, 255, 279, 282
Bari 14, 91
Barnard, John 154, 177, 178, 206, 207, 262
Barrichello, Rubens 127, 167, 242, 267, 268, 270, 279, 282, 297
BBC Sports Personality of the Year 229
Beaufort, Carel de 110
Belgian Grand Prix 14, 80, 164, 175, 213, 292
  1925 247
  1947 13
  1966 109–10
  1982 202–3
  1991 261
  1992 239, 261
  2004 266
Beltoise, Jean-Pierre 104, 126
Benetton 215, 226, 242, 251, 261, 262, 263, 269, 295
Benson & Hedges 225
Bentley 6

Benz, Karl 3
Berger, Gerhard 208, 213, 219, 262
Berthon, Peter 15
Birkin, Tim 163
Blash, Herbie 117
BMW 282
Boavista 91
Bondurant, Bob 109
Boutsen, Thierry 223, 233
Brabham 62, 75, 79, 101, 115, 129, 163, 205, 221, 249, 274, 288
  FanCar 152–3
  and Piquet 175, 185
  record 183
  and turbo technology 154
Brabham, David 256
Brabham, Gary 256
Brabham, Geoff 256
Brabham, Jack 59, 62, 65, 100, 256
  appearance 124
  on Clark and Stewart 108
  as engineer 75, 79
  record 75, 271
  taciturnity 76
  wins Chamionship 1966 101
Brabham, Matthew 256
Bradshaw, Ann 188
Brands Hatch 91, 96, 103, 117, 122, 141, 158
Brauchitsch, Manfred von 10–11, 21, 163
Brawn, Ross 263, 283, 295
Brawn-Mercedes 283, 295–7, 301
Brazilian Grand Prix
  1972 127
  1981 154, 172
  1990 219
  2006 270–1
  2009 296

Bremgarten 91, 92–3
Brenton, Howard 228
Briatore, Flavio 269, 298, 299
Bristow, Chris 110
British American Racing 222
British Empire Trophy 14
British Grand Prix 14, 37, 56, 117
   1949 13
   1950 17
   1951 18, 34
   1955 31, 51
   1976 138, 141–2
   1986 176
   1999 265
   2009 296
BRM (British Racing Motors) 15,
   16–18, 19, 21, 24–5, 52, 62,
   72–3, 129, 207
   and Hill 72–4, 108
   sponsorship 123, 124
   unreliability 110
Brooke Bond Oxo 123
Brooklands, Surrey 5, 95
Brooks, Tony 38, 43, 49, 50, 51,
   56, 59, 65, 92
Brown, David 231
Brundle, Martin 249, 262, 264,
   266
Brunner, Gustav 263
Buenos Aires 36, 91
Bugatti 5, 6, 7
Burton, Richard 145, 146
Button, Jenson 255, 270
   and Brawn-Mercedes 295–7
   and Honda 282
   wins Championship 2009
   295–7
Byrne, Rory 263

Cabianca, Giulio 110
CAD technology 154, 155
Caldwell, Alastair 139
Camel Cigarettes 175, 221
Campari, Giuseppe 9
Campbell, Donald 49
Can-Am series 100, 150
Canadian Grand Prix 167, 242,
   262
Canon 176
Carracciola, Rudolph 8–9, 10, 21,
   163
Carrera Panamericana 30
cars
   active suspension 157–8
   constructors 129–30
   ground-effect 152–4, 180
   safety 97, 122, 216–17, 244–5
   technology 149–55, 157–9
   turbos 150–1, 154
   twin-chassis 153–4
Castellotti, Eugenio 36, 37, 51, 53
Castro, Fidel 28
Catalunya circuit 251
Cevert, François 125, 132–3
Champion Spark Plugs 165

Chapman, Colin 42, 60, 79, 80,
   81, 84–8, 122, 125, 127, 153,
   188
   and Clark 84–8, 100–1, 103,
   108, 184, 186
   death 158
   and Rindt 115–16, 117–18, 119
   and sponsorship 102–3
Charade 117
Cheever, Eddie 162
Chinese Grand Prix 284, 285,
   290, 292
Chiron, Louis 9, 13, 17, 23
Clark, Jim 76, 79–89, 95, 96, 97,
   149, 163, 216
   appearance 124
   background and character
   82–4, 107, 135
   and Chapman 84, 87, 88, 108,
   184, 186
   death 99, 100, 101–2, 107, 121
   indecisiveness 81–2
   and Lotus 73, 74, 75, 79–89,
   101
   record 100
   technical ability 80–1
Collins, Peter 36, 53, 56, 71, 72
   character 139
   death 38, 57
   and Fangio 26–7, 37, 273
   and Ferrari 38–9, 42, 44, 50–1
Coloni 222
computer technology 154–5, 158
Concorde Agreement 156
Connaught 29, 50, 60, 283
Constructors' Championship 15,
   30, 113
Cooper 55, 56, 59–62, 75, 79, 85,
   115, 129, 205
   models 59–62, 73
Cooper, Charles 59
Cooper, Henry 49
Cooper, John 59, 60–1, 80, 85
Cordier, Louise 39, 57
Costin, Frank 60, 80
Cosworth Racing 281
Coulthard, David 251, 252, 279
Courage, Piers 116, 118, 183–4
Cranfield College of Aeronautics
   158
Crombac, Jabby 84
Crystal Palace 91, 136
Cunningham, Iain 188, 242

Daily Express International
   Trophy 17–18
Daimler, Gottlieb 3
Dallas 167, 227–8
Davis, Cliff 70
Davis, Joe 49
de Angelis, Elio 154, 180, 198,
   206
de Cesaris, Andrea 206
De Dion 4
De Lorean 158

Delage 7, 13
Delaunay, Arnaud 54
Delauney, Jaqueline 54
Dennis, Ron 115, 180, 205–7,
   212, 225, 277, 292
Depailler, Patrick 136
Detroit 167
Digital Equipment Corporation
   154
Dijon 131, 194
Domenicali, Stefano 293
Donington Park 11–12, 213, 285
Driver of the Century 161
drivers
   appearance 124–5
   culture of deference 216
   income 124, 175–6, 258
   interchangeability of 157
   sons of 247–56
   strike 156–7, 201
Drivers' Championship 15, 31, 39
drug abuse 27, 87, 158
Ducarouge, Gérard 210
Duckworth, Keith 86
Duetsche Post 225
Dundrod 91, 93
Dutch Grand Prix 72, 73, 85, 94
   1967 101
   1968 111
   1970 117, 184
   1973 133
   1975 137
   1979 193, 194

Eagle 129, 164
Ecclestone, Bernie 155–6, 157,
   175, 185, 221, 223, 267,
   273, 274–8, 283, 297, 299
Edwards, Guy 142
Eläintarhanajot 91, 93
ELF petroleum 123, 201
engines
   and minor teams 223–4
   power of 159
Ensign Racing 130
ERA (English Racing
   Automobiles) 12, 13, 15,
   16
Ertl, Harald 142
Espinosa, 'Beba' 28
Esso 165
Estoril 284
Étancelin, Philippe 9, 17
EuroBrun 222
European Grand Prix 158, 230,
   259

Fagioli, Luigi 21
FanCar 152–3
Fangio, Juan Manuel 15, 17, 55,
   69, 76, 96, 127, 214, 273
   and Alfa Romeo 24–5
   cars driven by 96–7
   character and background
   23–4, 27–8

and Ferrari 26–7, 31, 33, 36–7,
39
German Grand Prix 1957
42–4
and Maserati 25, 26, 42–4, 50
and Mercedes 23, 26, 28–31,
248
record 271
retirement 45, 50
universal admiration 114
Farina, Nino 15, 17, 18, 23, 24,
55
Farina, Pinin 38
fatalities 35, 37, 38, 41, 49, 57,
58, 93, 95, 99, 100, 110,
114, 118, 119–20, 121, 122,
132–3, 184, 188, 203, 242–4,
247
Ferguson, Andrew 103
Ferrari 15, 18, 62, 87, 104, 108,
118, 130, 154, 276, 283, 287
and Alonso 298
and Ascari 34, 35–6, 247–8
and Collins 38–9
deaths 35, 37, 38
and Fangio 26–7, 31, 33, 36–7,
39
and Lauda 139–40
lean years 35, 196–7, 203, 262,
297
loyalty to 188
models 16, 29, 34, 35, 36, 38,
42, 66, 196, 197
and Moss 35, 67–8
and Pironi 201, 202
and Prost 218, 219
and Raikkonen 291
record 183, 196
relations with McLaren 142
reorganisation 262–3
rise of 33–4
road cars 38
and Schumacher 253, 255,
260–1, 262, 263–71, 279
sponsorship 123
and turbo technology 151–2,
154, 197, 198
and Villeneuve 193, 195–7,
200–3
Ferrari, Dino 38
Ferrari, Enzo 9, 27, 33–9, 57,
67–8, 87, 139, 152, 187–8,
196, 197, 199, 203
FIA (Federation Internationale de
l'Automobile) 7, 8, 14, 18,
153, 215, 219, 268, 275,
276, 277, 299, 300
Fiat 5, 6, 151, 193, 196, 262
Finland 290–1
Firestone 165
FISA (Fédération Internationale
du Sport Automobiloe) 151,
155–7, 166, 216, 219
Fish, Calvin 209
Fisichella, Giancarlo 270

Fittipaldi, Christian 256
Fittipaldi, Emerson 121, 132, 138,
256
character and appearance 122,
125–6
wins 1972 Championship
126–7, 131
Fittipaldi, Maria Helena 126
Fittipaldi Automotive 130, 138
FOCA (Formula One Constructors
Association) 151, 155–7,
201, 274–5
football 257
Force India 283
Ford 165, 280, 281
Forghieri, Mauro 140, 196–7, 198
Formula Ford 121
Formula One
audience for 258, 266–7,
273–4
as big business 273
bureaucracy and finance
274–8, 299–300
changed centre of gravity
158–9
ethics 271, 298–9
FISA-FOCA wars 155–7, 276
geography 91
length of season 45, 100
newspaper interest 181
origins 14
rules changed 18, 236, 258,
277, 283, 295
sponsorship and costs 123–4,
176–7
television coverage 169, 176–7,
266–7, 273–4
see also tracks
Formula Three 121, 261
Formula Two 14, 18, 99, 100, 206
Formule Libre 7
Forte, Charles 49, 51
Francis, Alf 67
Frank Williams Racing Cars 130
French Grand Prix 14, 117, 163
1976 141
1979 151, 194, 201
Frentzen, Heinz-Harald 255
fuel 159
Fuji Speedway 145
Fukui, Takeo 282

Gabor, Zsa Zsa 38
Gavea 91, 92
George VI, King 17
German Grand Prix 15, 37, 65,
73, 110, 175, 296
1954 29
1957 42–4
1976 142–4
1982 172
1991 218–19
1994 262
1996 253
Gethin, Peter 210

Giambertone, Marcello 37
Ginther, Richie 67, 162, 163
girls 39, 71–2, 82, 125, 137, 138
Gonzales, Jose Friolán 27, 29–30,
34, 127
Goodwood 14, 62, 68, 118
Goodyear 165
Gotu, Osamu 263
Grace, Princess 70
Graffenried, 'Toulo' de 13
Graham, George 272
Gran Premio de Penya Rhin 14
Grand Prix
circuits see tracks
number of 45, 100
origins of 6–7, 14
prize money 165–6
Grand Prix Drivers' Association
(GPDA) 112, 122, 243, 244
Grand Prix Manufacturers'
Association 276
Grand Prix de Paris 14
Grand Prix de Pau 6
Grandes Épreuves 7, 45, 91
ground-effect 152–4, 180, 199
Gurney, Dan 73, 163–4

Haas Lola 162
Hagman, Larry 228
Hakkinen, Mika 167, 221, 266,
291
Hamilton, Duncan 52–3, 57
Hamilton, Lewis 167, 289–90,
291, 292–3, 296
wins Championship 2008 293,
297
Hamilton, Maurice 134
Hart, Brian 177
Hawthorn, Leslie 53
Hawthorn, Mike
appearance 49–50
character 134, 139
and Collins 57
death 49, 58
and Ferrari 29–30, 42, 43, 44,
50
Le Mans crash 1955 54
National Service scandal 53–4
partying 51–3, 71, 72
private life 54
record 51
relationship with Moss 55,
56–7, 273
wins Championship 1958 49,
51, 59, 65, 181, 297
Hayes, Walter 75
Head, Patrick 171, 184
Herbert, Johnny 221, 249, 280
Hesketh, Thomas Alexander
Femour, Lord 136
Hesketh Racing 129, 136–8, 139
Heuer chronometer company
123
Hickman, Ron 87
Hill, Bette 71–2

Hill, Damon 223, 225, 244,
    248–56, 259, 261, 262
  on Frank Williams 188
  Spanish Grand Prix 1994
    250–1
  and Williams 241, 242, 249,
    250–2, 253, 254
  wins 1996 Championship 186,
    247
Hill, Graham 69–75, 79, 86, 100,
    117, 248
  accident at Watkins Glen 121
  appearance 124
  and BRM 72–3, 108
  character 135
  crash at Spanish Grand Prix
    (1969) 113
  death 249
  engineering skills 73–4
  failure to win 69–70, 75, 88, 89
  later career 133–4
  and Lotus 101, 121–2
  and media 76–7
  partying 70–2
  record 74
  rescues Stewart at Spa 109
  Spanish Grand Prix, 1968 103,
    104–5, 121–2, 250–1
  victories at Monaco 70, 74, 252
  wins Championship 1968 297
Hill, Phil 65, 68, 74, 79, 162–3,
    169
Hitler, Adolf 11
Hockenheim 99, 117, 168, 175,
    218–19, 284, 285
Hocking, Gary 110
Holden, William 38
Honda 130, 163, 176, 226, 282,
    287, 295
Hopkins, 'Tex' 94, 122
Horsley, 'Bubbles' 136, 137
Hulme, Denny 74, 76, 101, 104,
    126, 254
Hungarian Grand Prix 234,
    287–8, 296
Hunnlein, Adolf 11
Hunt, James 127, 134–46, 155,
    179
  appearance 134, 137, 138, 139,
    146
  background 134–5
  British Grand Prix 1976 141–2
  character 134, 135–6, 139
  excesses 138, 140–1, 145
  German Grand Prix 1976 144
  and Hesketh Racing 136–8, 139
  and McLaren 138–46
  on Mansell 230, 232
  retirement 149, 171
  wins Championship 1976 138,
    145–6, 206, 229, 297
Hunt, Suzy 145, 146

Ickx, Jacky 118, 119, 121, 132,
    209–10

Imola 188, 213, 242–4
Imperial Tobacco 126
India 284
Indianapolis Speedway 5, 6, 150,
    167, 268
Brickyard 400 82–3
Indianapolis 500 74, 75, 100,
    161, 163
Indy Car 229, 252
International Glover Trophy Race
    68
Ireland, Innes 66, 86
Irvine, Eddie 187, 241, 263–4,
    265–6, 280
Istanbul 285
Italian Grand Prix 14, 60, 73,
    131, 214
  1924 247
  1952 26
  1953 27
  1958 56
  1970 118–19
  1972 127

Jabouille, Jean-Pierre 151
Jaguar 30, 54, 226, 279–81, 283,
    296
Japanese Grand Prix
  1976 145–6
  1988 212
  1989 214–15
  1990 217, 269
  1993 241
  1996 254
Jarama 104, 110, 117, 197–9, 250
Jardine, Douglas 272
Jenkinson, Denis 83, 116, 118,
    125, 191, 195
Jerez 255, 264
Jersey 14
John Player & Sons 102, 103,
    126, 221
Jones, Alan 156, 171–3, 174–5,
    181, 192, 198, 267
  and Williams 184, 186,
    195
Jones, Bernie 184
Jones, Parnelli 82
Jordan, Eddie 224–5, 226
Jordan Grand Prix 224–6, 255,
    261, 279

Kent, Duke of 146
Kenward, Moi 52
King, Hugh Locke 5
Klein, Christian 281
Kling, Karl 30
Komatsu 221

Laffite, Jacques 141, 172, 180,
    195, 198
Lampredi, Aurelio 35
Lancia 36, 42, 80, 196, 248
Lang, Hermann 8
Las Vegas Grand Prix 167, 173

Lauda, Nicki 132, 153, 157, 180,
    199, 254
  accident at Nürburgring 142–4,
    145
  British Grand Prix 1976 141–2
  character 140
  and Ferrari 138, 139–40, 141,
    149, 196
  on Hunt 136
  and Jaguar 280–1
  Japanese Grand Prix 1976
    145–6
  and McLaren 206, 207
  on Piquet 173, 174
  on Prost 178
  record 271
  on Rosberg 185, 186
  on Schumacher 265
Le Mans 5, 34, 85
  24 Hours 74, 164
  1955 accident at 30, 54
  Grand Prix d'Endurance 6
Levegh, Pierre 30
Lewis-Evans, Stuart 92, 93
Leyton House 222
Life 222, 225
Ligier 154, 226
Lola Racing Cars 130
Long Beach 136, 166
Lotus 15, 34, 60, 62, 288
  active suspension 157–8
  and Andretti 161–2
  and Chapman 84–8, 102, 108
  and Clark 73, 74, 79, 81, 82,
    84–9, 108, 216
  Constructors' title 1973 131
  failure rates 86
  financial problems 81, 86, 88
  and Hill 101, 121–2
  models 79–80, 101, 102, 131–2
  and Moss 66–7, 68
  and Piquet 176
  record 183
  and Rindt 115–16, 117
  and Senna 210
  Spanish Grand Prix 1968
    104–5
  sponsorship 102–3, 123, 126,
    221
  twin-chassis 153–4
Lunger, Brett 142

McEnroe, John 272
Macklin, Lance 30, 54
McLaren 15, 62, 129, 205–7, 276,
    279, 283
  1988 season 208, 266
  and Alonso 288–9, 291
  carbon-fibre chassis 154, 206
  efficiency 215
  and Hunt 138–46
  and Lauda 206, 207
  and Lewis Hamilton 289–90,
    292–3
  models 104, 132, 138, 154

and Prost 179–80, 206, 207–8, 212, 216, 217
public image 205
record 183, 206
relations with Ferrari 142
and Senna 210, 212, 216
sponsorship 123, 138, 206
McLaren, Bruce 59, 65, 73, 104, 118
McNab, Neil 52
Malaysian Grand Prix 168, 284–5
Manchester United 157
Mansell, Greg 256
Mansell, Leo 256
Mansell, Nigel 174, 228–36, 295–6
British Grand Prix 1986 176
on Button 296
character 181, 228, 229, 230, 231–2
and Ferrari 218, 232
on Hamilton 290
income 233, 234, 251
Indy Car champion 229
and Lotus 154, 158, 221, 228
and Piquet 230–1, 289
and Prost 232, 234–5
record 232–3
and Williams 185, 207, 230, 232, 233–6, 249, 251
wins Championship 1992 229, 233
March Engineering 118, 123, 125, 129, 137, 138, 157, 222, 275, 288
Marimón, Onofre 41, 127
Marlboro 138, 206
Martinelli, Paolo 264
Maserati 13, 15, 18, 34, 39, 248, 283
and Fangio 25, 26, 37, 42, 43, 44, 50
models 7, 16, 26, 37, 42
and Moss 31
Mass, Jochen 157, 203
Massa, Felipe 127, 270, 271, 291, 292, 293, 297
Matra 104, 110, 113, 130
Mayer, Teddy 117, 139, 146, 157, 206
Mays, Raymond 15–16, 17, 18–19, 21, 52, 72, 73
media invasiveness 71, 181
Melbourne 253
Mercedes 5, 8, 11–12, 21–3, 30–1, 35, 36, 187, 283, 289
and Fangio 26, 28, 248
models 7, 8, 10, 22–3, 26, 30, 31, 34
and Moss 28–9, 50, 51, 68
sports cars 30, 34
Mercedes-Benz 35
Merzario, Arturo 142
Mexican Grand Prix 163
Michelin 167

Miles, John 119
Mille Miglia 30, 34, 37, 56, 69
Minardi 226, 279, 282–3, 287
Mobil 165
Monaco Grand Prix 14, 59, 62, 85, 91, 110, 131, 168, 173, 268, 284
1956 52
1961 65–7
1984 209–10
1988 211
2006 268–70
Hill's victories at 70, 74, 252
street circuit 5, 13, 93, 96
monocoque construction 80
Monteverdi, Peter 222
Montezemola, Luca di 262–3, 300
Monza 5, 25, 26, 56, 60, 73, 91, 118–19, 127, 131, 168, 214, 247, 248, 284
layout and fatalities 95–6
Morgan, Dave 135
Mosley, Max 219, 273, 274, 275–8, 292, 295, 299–301
Mosley, Sir Oswald 275
Moss, Stirling 93, 177, 181
accident at Goodwood 1962 68–9, 73, 86
Argentine Grand Prix 1958 61–2
awarded OBE 57
British Grand Prix 1955 55
and Cooper 59
and Fangio 24, 26, 27, 29, 39, 55, 69
and Ferrari 35, 39, 67–8
on Graham Hill 71, 75
on Hamilton 290
and Hawthorn 55, 56–7, 273
and Lotus 85
and Maserati 37
and Mercedes 28–9, 30, 50, 51, 58
Monaco Grand Prix 1961 65–7
record 69
rise of 55–6, 65
on Schumacher 265, 270
and Vanwall 42, 43, 44, 50, 60
Motor Racing Developments see Brabham
Murray, Gordon 174, 198–9
Musso, Luigi 36, 37, 42, 53

Nannini, Alessandro 215
National Maritime Institute 154
Nazi regime 8, 13
Neubauer, Alfred 16, 21–2, 23, 29, 30, 187
Newman/Haas team 231
newspaper coverage 181
non-Championship events 14, 91, 96
Nürburgring 5, 10–11, 30, 37,

41–2, 65, 73, 91, 93, 96, 110, 168, 284
1,000 km 56, 69
Collins killed at 38, 57
Fangio's win at (1957) 42–5, 96
Lauda's accident 1976 142–4
new 253, 280
Stewart's win at (1968) 111
Nuvolari, Tazio 9–11, 12, 15, 34, 43, 56, 199

Oliver, Jackie 134
Onyx 222, 226
Orriss, Viv 184–5
Oscar Gálvez track 91
Oscar (James Hunt's dog) 137
Osella/Fondmetal 154, 222, 226
Österreichring 285
Owen, Sir Alfred 18, 52, 72

Pace, Carlos 127, 139
Paletti, Riccardo 242
Palmer, Jonathan 231–2
Panasonic 282
Panhard et Levassor 4
Parent, Gaston 196–7
Paris–Madrid (1903) 4–5
Paris–Rouen Trial (1894) 4
Parnell, Reg 15, 50
Parnelli Team 161
Patrese, Riccardo 223, 233, 269
Pau 6, 91, 92
Pedralbes 91
Perón, Evita 28
Pescara 14, 60, 91, 93
Peterson, Ronnie 125, 131–2, 133, 137, 138, 162, 192
Peugeot 4
Phillippe, Maurice 116
Phoenix 167
Piccinini, Marco 196–7
Piquet, Nelson 127, 157, 173–6, 180, 181, 207
and Brabham 153, 154, 221
character and behaviour 173–5, 211
earnings 175–6, 177
on Fittipaldi 122
on Lauda 140
and Lotus 221
and Mansell 230–1, 289
record 175, 271
and Senna 211
wins Championship 1981 153
wins Championship 1983 154, 174–5, 178–9
wins Championship 1987 208
Piquet, Nelson Junior 256, 298–9
Pironi, Didier 197, 199, 200–3, 212, 214
Porsche 73, 150, 163
Porsche, Ferdinand 9–10
Portago, Fon de 37, 53
Portuguese Grand Prix

1958 56–7
1996 253–4
Postlethwaite, 'Doc' Harvey 136
Project Four Racing 206
Prost, Alain 157, 174, 177–81,
  199, 227
  1988 season 208
  character 177–8, 179
  and Ferrari 203, 218, 219
  on Jones 172
  on Lauda 140, 177–8
  and McLaren 179–80, 206,
    207–8, 212, 216, 217
  and Mansell 232, 234–5
  record 271
  and Renault 178–9
  retirement 241–2
  rivalry with Senna 208–10,
    211–13, 214–15, 217–19,
    266
  sabatical year 219, 234
  and Williams 234–6
  wins Championship 1985 207
  wins Championship 1986 207,
    254
  wins Championship 1993 239,
    241
Prost, Nicolas 256
Prost (team) 226
Purley, David 133, 134

Race of Champions 104
Racer magazine 161
Raikkonen, Kimi 266, 270, 290–1,
  292, 297
Rainier, Prince 70
RAM 222
Ratzenberger, Roland 243
rear engines 59–60, 61–2, 79
Red Bull 283, 296, 301
Regazzoni, Clay 118, 119, 132,
  138, 140, 141
Reims 13, 59, 94–5
Renault 3, 162, 279, 283, 287,
  298
  and Alonso 288, 292
  models 150–1
  and Piquet Junior 298–9
  and Prost 178–9, 180
  and turbo technology 150–2,
    153
Renault, Marcel 5
Repco 76, 101
Reutemann, Carlos 127, 132, 139,
  172, 173, 192, 198, 200
Revson, Peter 164
Rindt, Jochen 113, 114–20, 205
  appearance 124
  death 119–20, 121
  posthumous Championship
    119, 120, 121
Rindt, Nina 114, 120
risk-taking 93
Riverside (California) 165
R.J.Reynolds 175

Rodriguez, Pedro 104, 122
Rodriguez, Ricardo 110
Rolls-Royce 16
Rosberg, Keke 157, 185–6, 228,
  230, 256, 268–9, 291
Rosberg, Nico 256
Rosemeyer, Bernd 9, 10
Rossellini, Roberto 38
Rudd, Tony 24, 72, 75

Salazar, Eliseo 175
Salo, Mika 291
Salvadori, Roy 50, 51
San Marino Grand Prix
  1982 201–2
  1989 213
  1994 242–4
São Paulo 270
Sato, Takuma 270
Sauber 226, 279, 283
Scheckter, Jody 132, 133, 138,
  144, 193, 194, 195, 196,
  197, 200, 203, 256
Scheckter, Tomas 256
Schell, Harry 110
Schlesser, Jean-Louis 256
Schlesser, Jo 118, 256
Schumacher, Corinna 265
Schumacher, Michael 241, 256,
  259–72
  Belgian Grand Prix 1992 239
  and Benetton 242, 251,
    261–2
  Brazilian Grand Prix 2006
    270–1
  cars of 263
  character 259–60, 265, 272
  disqualifications 255, 259–60,
    261, 264–5
  earnings 258, 260
  and Ferrari 183, 203, 253, 255,
    260–1, 262, 263–71, 279
  and Jordan 224
  Monaco Grand Prix 2006
    268–70
  record 259, 271, 272, 279
  retirement 270, 271, 287
  San Marino Grand Prix 1994
    243
  US Grand Prix 2000 167
  wins Championship 1994 245,
    259, 261
  wins Championship 1995
    262
  wins Championships 2000-4
    266
Schumacher, Mick 256
Schumacher, Ralf 256, 261, 279,
  282
Scuderia Ferrari *see* Ferrari
Sebring track 165
  12 Hours 69
Second World War 13
  airfields 62–3
Segrave, Henry 6

Senna, Ayrton 127, 180, 208–19,
  229, 233, 236, 239–45
  background 208
  character 208–9, 211, 218, 271
  charity work 244
  death 188, 242–4, 250
  driving mystique 211
  Japanese Grand Prix 1989
    214–15
  legend of 244
  and Lotus 221
  and McLaren 210
  powers of recall 210
  record 271
  rivalry with Prost 179, 208–10,
    211–13, 214–15, 217–19,
    266, 269
  spirituality 240–1, 271
  suspension 215, 216
  and Williams 234–5, 239–40,
    242
  wins Championship 1988 208,
    212
  wins Championship 1991
    218
Sepang Circuit 284–5
Shadow Racing Team 129, 223
Shanghai 168, 285, 292, 296
side-skirts 152, 153, 180
Siffert, Jo 122
Silva Ramos, Hernando da 126
Silverstone 13, 17, 37, 56, 62, 91,
  168, 169, 265, 285
Singapore Grand Prix 284, 292
  2009 298
Snetterton 62
Sommer, Raymond 13, 18
South African Grand Prix 73, 102,
  110, 230
  1982 156
South Korea 284
Spa-Francorchamps 13, 80, 91,
  93–4, 109–10, 213, 239, 247,
  266, 284
Spanish Grand Prix
  1968 99–105, 121–2, 250
  1969 113
  1970 116–17
  1975 132
  1976 141
  1980 156
  1981 197–9
  1986 213
  1991 229
  1994 250
  1997 255, 264
Sparshott, Bob 101, 105
Speed, Scott 162, 270
Spence, Mike 216
sponsorship 88, 102–3, 123, 124,
  126, 138, 158, 176, 206,
  225, 274, 277
sports cars 30, 34, 100, 261
sportsmanship 272, 273
Stacey, Alan 110

steam cars 4
Stepney, Nigel 210
Stewart, Helen 114, 125
Stewart, Jackie 76, 96, 100,
    107–20, 177
  1972 season 126–7
  appearance 125
  background and character
    107–8, 111, 114
  and BRM 74
  on Clark 81–2
  crash at Spa 109–10
  and death of Cevert 132–3
  on Hamilton 290
  income 124
  and Jochen Rindt 114, 115,
    116, 117, 119–20
  and Lotus 86
  record 133, 271
  retirement 133
  on Schumacher 263, 269
  and Senna 211, 218
  starts team 280
  track safety campaign 112–13
  and Tyrrell 103–4, 186
  wins at Zandvoort and
    Nürburgring 111
  wins Championship 1969 113,
    297
  wins Championship 1973 131
Stewart Grand Prix Team 280,
    296
Stokes, Sally 81, 82
Sunbeam 5, 6
Surtees, John 74, 88–9, 108, 110,
    124
Surtees Racing 123, 129
Suzuka 208, 212, 214, 217,
    233, 241, 254, 269, 270,
    284
Swedish Grand Prix, 1978 153
Swiss Grand Prix 14
Symonds, Pat 299
Syracuse (Sicily) 91–2

Talbot 7, 13, 15
Tambay, Patrick 154, 174, 177
Tamiya 221
Targa Florio 30, 247
Taruffi, Piero 35
Tasman Series 100
Tauranac, Ron 115
Tavoni, Romolo 57
Taylor, John 110, 118
teams
  cost of running 124, 258
  hierarchy 216
  minor 222–6, 279–83
  see also by name
technology 149–55, 157–9
television coverage 169, 176–7,
    276
  audience figures 258, 266–7,
    273–4

Terry, Len 164
Texaco 138, 165
Thruxton 62
Tilke, Hermann 284–5, 292
TNT (trinitrotoluene) 159
tobacco industry 102, 103, 126,
    138, 175, 206, 221, 225, 277
Todt, Jean 260–1, 263, 267, 300
Toleman 201, 209–10, 222
toluene 159
Toro Rosso 162, 283
Toyota 226, 279, 281–2
tracks 91–6
  Asian 284
  design and spectators
    enjoyment 168–9, 285–6
  number of 283
  safety 112–13, 122, 143–4,
    244–5, 285
  stadium 168–9
traction control 262
Trintignant, Maurice 15, 62
Trips, Wolfgang 'Taffy' von 65,
    95, 110
Triumph 66
Truro, Bishop of 240
turbocharged engines 150–1, 154
Turkey 284, 285
Tyrrell, Ken 103, 110, 113, 186,
    222
Tyrrell Racing 129, 131, 132–3,
    221–2, 288

Ugolini, Nello 44, 60
Uhlenhaut, Rudi 23, 30
United States, Formula One in
    161–9
United States Grand Prix 73, 105,
    116, 121, 127, 132, 165,
    227–8, 268
  1979 194–5
United States Grand Prix West
    136, 154, 166, 223
USF&G Financial Services Group
    223

Vadim, Roger 38
Vandervell, Tony 60
Vanwall 38, 42, 43, 44, 60, 61,
    68, 283
Varzi, Achille 9
Vettel, Sebastian 296
Victorian era 3
Villeneuve, Gilles 191–203, 252,
    255, 256
  character 191–4, 199–200,
    211
  death 203, 248
  and Ferrari 151, 193, 195–7,
    200–3
  rivalry with Pironi 200–3, 212,
    214
  Spanish Grand Prix 1981
    197–9

win at Watkins Glen 1979
    194–5
Villeneuve, Jacques 248, 252–6,
    259, 264
  German Grand Prix 1996 253
  relationship with father 200,
    252
  wins 1997 Championship 186,
    247, 255
Villeneuve, Joann 200
Villoresi, Luigi 35

Walker, Murray 230
Walker, Rob 49, 58, 66, 68, 74–5,
    88
Walkerley, Roger 43, 44
Warr, Peter 81, 135
Watkins, Professor Sid 95, 174,
    240, 243
Watkins Glen 73, 94, 105, 116,
    121, 127, 132, 165–6, 194–5,
    284
Watson, John 180, 198, 206,
    210
Webber, Max 296
Weslake Engineering 164
Weston, Sally 27
Whitehead, Peter 50
Williams 15, 130, 154, 183–9,
    208, 276, 279, 283, 288
  and Damon Hill 249, 250–2,
    253, 254
  and Jacques Villeneuve 255
  and Jones 184, 186
  and Mansell 185, 231, 232,
    233–6, 251
  models 235–6, 242
  and Piquet 175, 176, 185, 186,
    231
  and Prost 234–6
  record 183, 185
  and Senna 234–5, 239–40,
    242
Williams, Frank 171–2, 183–9,
    231, 232, 233, 235, 240,
    242, 250, 251, 254
Williamson, Roger 133, 142
Wimille, Jean-Pierre 9, 13
Windsor, Peter 187, 193, 235
Winkelhock, Manfred 256
Winkelhock, Marcus 256
Wissell, Reine 121
Wolf Racing 135
Woods, Aubrey 164
World Sportscar Championships
    34
Wright, Peter 158

Yardley cosmetics 123, 124

Zakspeed 222, 225
Zandvoort 73, 91, 94, 111, 117,
    133, 193, 194, 284
Zolder 203

PICTURE CREDITS

1. Hitler with Nuvolari, 1939 (Popperfoto/Getty Images)
2. Kling, Fangio, Neubauer and Moss, 1955 (Popperfoto/Getty Images)
3. Fangio, Monaco, 1957 (Klemantaski Collection/Getty Images)
4. Moss and Fangio, Monza, 1957 (Keystone/Getty Images)
5. Collins with Ferrari, 1957 (Klemantaski Collection/Getty Images)
6. Moss, Monaco, 1961 (Central Press/Hulton Archive/Getty Images)
7. Hawthorn, Monaco, 1957 (J. Hardman/Fox Photos/Getty Images)
8. The Nürburgring, 1960s (Phipps/Sutton Motorsport/TopFoto)
9. Graham Hill, 1965 (Victor Blackman/Express/Hulton Archive/Getty Images)
10. Graham Hill as 'Miss Earth' (Victor Blackman/Express/Getty Images)
11. Clark, 1975 (Victor Blackman/Express/Getty Images)
12. Clark and Chapman, 1963 (Bentley Archive/Popperfoto/Getty Images)
13. Hulme and Brabham, 1967 (Mike McLaren/Central Press/Hulton Archive/Getty Images)
14. Stewart, 1968 (Central Press/Getty Images)
15. Jochen and Nina Rindt, 1970 (Bentley Archive/Popperfoto/Getty Images)
16. Rindt's crash, 1970 (Popperfoto/Getty Images)
17. Fittipaldi, Brands Hatch, 1972 (Roger Jackson/Central Press/Hulton Archive/Getty Images)
18. Fittipaldi, Stewart and Peterson (Popperfoto/Getty Images)
19. Fittipaldi, Silverstone, 1973 (Bob Thomas/Getty Images)
20. Hunt, 1976 (Alvis Upitis/Getty Images)
21. Lauda, 1976 (Central Press/Getty Images)
22. Gilles Villeneuve, 1980 (Steve Powell/Allsport/Getty Images)
23. Piquet, South Africa, 1982 (Klemantaski Collection/Getty Images)
24. Senna, Prost, Mansell, Piquet, Estoril, 1986 (Dominique Faget/AFP/Getty Images)
25. Prost and Senna, Suzuka, 1989 (Toshifumi Kitamura/AFP/Getty Images)
26. Prost and Senna, Monaco, 1989 (AFP/Getty Images)
27. Prost, Senna and Damon Hill (Allsport UK/Allsport/Getty Images)
28. Senna, San Marino, 1994 (Jean-Loup Gautreau/AFP/Getty Images)
29. Schumacher, Briatore, Damon Hill, 1994 (Mike Hewitt/Getty Images)
30. Schumacher, Interlagos, 2006 (Marcus Brandt/AFP/Getty Images)
31. Hamilton and Dennis, Interlagos, 2008 (Antonio Scorza/AFP/Getty Images)
32. Button, Brawn and Barrichello, 2009 (Clive Mason/Getty Images)